Dad's Divorce Guide

The practical and essential guide for men getting
divorced and successfully co-parenting

Chris Batcheller

CheckSix Creative Studio, LLC

Dedication and Acknowledgement

This book is dedicated to everyone struggling as they open a new chapter in their life. I hope your next chapters are filled with happiness, satisfaction and fond memories!

I'd like to thank those who helped me write this book without knowing it. First is my kids, who are growing up to be amazing human beings! To my friends, who encouraged me even when I thought I would never finish. And as unlikely as this may seem, my exes, who taught me something from each relationship. To my therapist, thanks for being a place where I can vent and figure out how to process my life and the actions of others.

Finally, I'd like to thank those that helped me directly in some way with this book. To my amazing editor, without you, this book would not have happened. To the professionals that I've asked questions to, your answers helped make this book happen. Finally, to the advocates for social change, thank you for advocating for others because change is a long and hard journey.

Contents

Introduction

I'm writing this book, so you'll have the guide that I didn't. Many times during my divorce, I wished I had some sort of instruction manual. I felt lost and unsure about the process or the next step. What was happening? What's the next step? What's the best way to do something? Why am I feeling this way? What's the right strategy?

I often felt confused and without answers. I found that digging on the Internet took forever. How did I know I was getting the right answer? I found a lot of the information was biased toward moms and women. I found books on divorce, but many were general. Not many were specific for men or fathers. I could ask my lawyer, but that was an expensive way to get answers. I wanted a quick reference guide for my circumstances as a father and a man going through a divorce. That didn't exist for me then, so I wrote this book.

I wanted to give you a resource to navigate the process of divorce. Your divorce will determine so much of your future. It's important that you don't make your situation worse, which is easy to do. I don't want you to lose time with your kids. I don't want you to feel like you're going to go broke. I don't want you to feel more pain than you have to.

Why not just write the "Divorce Guide"? Why did I write the "Dad's Divorce Guide"? While the process for both men and women (or husbands and wives) is similar, it's a highly opposing experience. The way men and women are perceived in and out of court is frustrating because it has been clear for years that men have to act differently. We are held to different standards and have a steeper hill to climb to prove that we are fit, willing, and able parents. Because of this, there are many things a man must do differently from a woman.

In divorce, friends will become enemies, routines are changed, and life as you know it is permanently altered. Your world will be turned upside down. This book will help you get through those changes.

Divorce is devastating, but it doesn't have to be utter total destruction. There are some key things you can do during the process to make sure that you protect yourself emotionally, physically, and financially as much as possible. This book will help you with the key things you can do to protect yourself.

When I was going through my divorce, I often had questions about what the next step was. No one told me. I would read court papers not knowing what was supposed to happen next. Sometimes the legal jargon was hard to understand. One thing was clear, I didn't know what was going on or what lay ahead.

If you are one that remembers Saturday morning cartoons, then you know from G.I. Joe that "Knowing is half the battle." After reading this book that you will have some knowledge of the divorce process and relevant topics around divorce, parenting, and the legal system. This book will not tell you everything you need to know! It's designed to simply give you an introduction. You will need to dig deeper into many subjects.

A long divorce battle can impact everyone involved. Parents can give less of their time and money to their children. Careers can and have been destroyed. Friends are lost. Children become confused. Lots of changes occur in the family during a divorce resulting in the need for therapy that doesn't guarantee to heal the original wounds.

In contrast to the people going through the divorce process, everyone in the divorce industry benefits. Lawyers make their money. The states get a cut of child support and they also get federal money through the Title IV-D program. Guardian Ad Litems, therapists and psychologists all get paid. It's amazing to think of the number of people that bank on your marital demise.

Like any war, your best strategy is to get in and get out as quickly as possible. Read that again! Get in and get out! Long-term wars drain economies and cause massive amounts of destruction. The same thing will happen with your life! My goal is for this book to help you through this process quickly with the least amount of damage to your physical health, mental health, your children, and your finances.

Maintaining your sanity and rebuilding your life becomes the most difficult challenges of your post-divorce life. Many have done it before you and you can do it, too. Much of the damage done during divorce is emotional. A good portion of this book will talk about emotions and how to control them during the process and recover emotionally afterward.

I cannot state enough how much you influence the divorce process. How you act, what you do and what you say have major impacts on the process. What you post (or have posted in the past) on social media will be used against you. Even small things will be taken out of context and turned against you. You can either be a positive or negative influence on the process. My goal is to give you tools to help you manage your emotions and to allow you to positively influence the process.

Having emotional control during this time is difficult but achievable. Not having emotional control will set you up for a very long and costly divorce. One of the most difficult things during the divorce process is to not get caught in the emotional weeds of divorce. Remember, the process of divorce is not there to emotionally heal you or give you any sort of validation. The process of divorce (strictly legally speaking) is so you can separate property and determine matters of custody and child support. That is it.

All your healing needs to happen after the divorce. It's perfectly fine to remember that things will be crazy during the process. The trick is to maintain enough sanity while going through the process so that you can make good, sound decisions.

While that sounds like a pretty easy thing to do, under the stress of a divorce, it can be nearly impossible. You probably make sound decisions hundreds of times a day, but when it comes to divorce, it's very easy to make an emotionally-based decision (rather than one that is fact-based). It takes a very strong person to be able to emotionally step back from the situation and make decisions that are based on facts during the divorce process. This is one of the reasons why you want a lawyer on your side because he or she will make decisions that are legally based and not emotional. Listen to the advice that they give you. Remember, your perspective is an emotional one and the attorney is usually offering a rational solution.

I'm hoping that one of the things that I can teach you is that divorce really is a transactional process. It cannot and will not offer validation. It cannot tell you that you should feel the way you are feeling. It is devoid of emotion, even though it is a very emotional process.

The transaction of divorce will answer some important questions. What is the new life going to look like? Who will have the kids? Who will get what property? Who will pay what expenses? And who will pay child support?

During your divorce, you will likely have to dig into some battle wounds. In some places (jurisdictions) the past history is not very relevant. In other jurisdictions, that information is precisely key to what determines the future.

I want this book to be here for you as a guide. It is not intended to give you a deep dive into any subject. Some subjects are discussed at length and others are just touched upon. I offer suggestions where further reading is helpful. On any topic, you can easily search for information. Part of preparing for battle is researching the topic at hand.

The topic of divorce can be as narrow as the actual legal process or as wide as the true effects it causes in the new family unit. This book will cover some of the neighboring topics such as mental and physical health, co-parenting, grief, and trauma recovery. Each of these topics on their own could be several books, so if you are particularly interested in one of them, be prepared to do some additional research and reading.

This book will help you prepare for how you should act during your divorce. It will educate you on the general legal process and will inform you on what to expect to experience physically and emotionally. This book isn't about how to be a lawyer or how to defend yourself. <u>This book is in no way, shape or form legal advice of any kind and shall not be construed as such under any circumstances!</u> For legal matters, consult a licensed attorney in your state.

It is not uncommon for divorces to drag on for years. In that case, you need to buckle down and realize that you will be in this for the long haul. It's a marathon, not a sprint. Don't worry, we'll talk about some techniques that you can use when dealing with long-term conflict.

It is not uncommon for men to experience trauma symptoms similar to PTSD (Post Traumatic Stress Disorder) which is what some war veterans have. In a lot of ways, a divorce is like combat. While it may not be bullets flying through the air, the battles are fought with words, emails and court filings. It's important that if you start having symptoms, to get professional therapeutic help right away.

We also have to talk about bias in the family court system. Unfortunately, there still is a bias in many court systems. For years, the mother has been seen as the de facto nurturer and childcare provider for the children. For years, the mother has been seen as "the better parent". Modern research shows that simply isn't true. The children need both parents in their lives. Unfortunately, it is taking the courts a while to catch up. For the latest in shared parenting research visit the National Parents Organization (https://www.sha redparenting.org/).

The studies show that fathers being involved in a child's life is exponentially better than the father being absent. On the flip side, studies show when a father is not involved in his child's life, there are severe consequences to the child's development and behavioral patterns. Being involved in your child's life is significantly important to their development. Put simply, dads have a lot to offer their children and it's way more than just having a fun time playing with them.

It's important to note that the needle has moved. Some courts now are using 50-50 shared custody as the starting point. As of the time of this writing a few states have passed full shared parenting laws (Kentucky, Arkansas, and West Virginia). Many more have advocates that are trying to pass shared parenting in their state.

Often the father becomes a target by the mother in the court process because getting more time means more child support (money). There's very little in the way of consequences (usually none) for a parent who wants to manipulate the system for financial gain.

While things may seem dark now, be assured that the future is bright. Thousands and thousands of men have passed through the divorce process successfully. They have rebuilt their lives. Many have a better life than they had before. Change is inevitable in your life. How you handle that change is up to you.

While we're on the topic of feeling overwhelmed about your divorce, you must also know that research has shown that male suicides as a result of divorce are much higher than the average rate. You are at greater risk for suicide. Because of this, it's important that you recognize the need for support if you feel this way. It's important that you find a support system now. That support system may not be the usual family and friends which you've come to rely upon. I would strongly recommend finding a good therapist that you feel comfortable with and can talk to.

The great news is that with every challenge comes an opportunity. If you look at your divorce through the lens of a challenge, you will learn new skills which will help you in your life both personally and professionally. The ability to make an emotional decision based on fact is a very useful life skill. You'll be surprised at the number of people and businesses that fail simply because people make irrational decisions based on emotions while ignoring facts.

I hope you find this book to be the comforting guide that I did not have. While I was getting divorced, a leader at my company told me "The sun rose today and it will rise tomorrow". Reading a bit deeper, you'll see that it doesn't really matter what's going on in your divorce, life goes on. Think of the divorce as the first step in a new journey and several years from now, many of the details just won't matter.

Legal Suff

I'm not a lawyer and I am not a mental health professional. I cannot give you legal advice. I cannot give you medical advice. I am not responsible for any loss or damage that may occur as a result of your reading or acting on the knowledge in this book.

This book is my opinion unless otherwise expressly stated herein. Not all advice works in all situations. The advice in this book may not work in your situation. The legal processes described in this book may be different in your particular location and situation. I advise you to seek professional help or counsel from either attorneys or mental health professionals for your situation.

<u>Safety First - Mental Awareness:</u>

If you are depressed or having suicidal thoughts it is important that you seek professional help. You can get free professional help in the United States 24 hours a day by calling:

1-800-273-8255 or call and/or text 988 from any U.S. phone

To chat online visit https://suicidepreventionlifeline.org

"National Suicide Prevention Lifeline. We can all help prevent suicide. The Lifeline provides 24/7, free and confidential support for people in distress, prevention and crisis resources for you or your loved ones, and best practices for professionals."

Going through a divorce is hard but you do not have to take this journey alone. If you are considering suicide, please remember that no matter how bad this feels for you right now, try to imagine how bad it will feel for your children to grow up without you. Remember that divorce does not mean your life is over. Things will get better. Your children deserve a life with their father.

Besides the national suicide prevention lifeline, you can always speak to a mental health professional (therapist or social worker). If you cannot do this alone please ask a friend or family member for help. If you don't have friends or family as support, visit your local police or fire station.

Safety First - Gun Ownership:

If you are a gun owner, I would strongly encourage you to think about removing any guns from your home. I write this as a proud American who strongly believes that responsible gun ownership is an essential part of our great country.

That said, you need to take a careful look at what responsible ownership looks like during a divorce. If your divorce turns nasty, the threat of a gun can cause a judge to order a restraining order or a protection from abuse order against you.

You should consider if you need to have a friend keep your firearms for a while or if you need someone to keep the key to them. I would advise asking your attorney what the best thing to do is.

You also need to look at your soon-to-be ex-spouse and his or her access to firearms. You may have a gut feeling that this will be a problem. You should tell your attorney and ask what protections you need if there is a potential issue.

It's important that your lawyer knows if you've removed firearms. That will help them defend you if you need it.

The key here is responsible gun ownership. Take a few minutes to think about the situation. Have a friend help you if you need it. It's your responsibility as a man, a father, and a responsible gun owner.

PART 1 - TAKE COVER

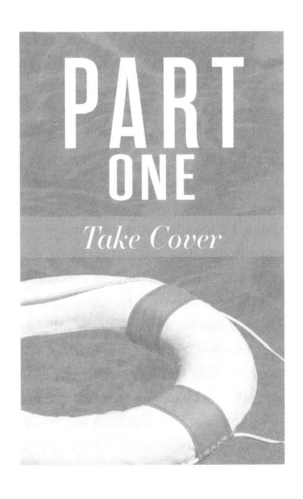

Chapter One

Incoming! Take Cover

T he first days of your divorce will feel like you are under siege. Even if *you* filed for divorce, the first days will be tense, surreal, and unlike anything you have experienced (even if this is not your first divorce). You will feel like things are exploding around you. You may feel like you have no idea where some of the explosions are coming from. That's why I named this section "Take Cover."

Your divorce will happen in stages, and your emotions will pass through stages as well. Remember that the divorce process and your emotions may be in different stages altogether. The divorce process and your emotional process are not likely to proceed at the same rate. This is where you can become overwhelmed and feel like you're on a roller coaster ride. Take comfort that you can and will get through your divorce. The emotional roller coaster is only temporary. Once you are divorced, it's critical that you chart a new course and make a new life. Moving on after your divorce is critical, and it's something that I'll talk about later in this book.

Once you are served or start the divorce process, the next steps are critical to your future. First, it's important that you take steps to protect yourself. Expect nearly every aspect of your life to change or be affected. You need to ensure that your immediate actions do not harm your legal case, which will directly affect your custody and financial matters.

Friends are different. In-laws disappear. People take sides. Your job may change. You will likely have to live somewhere new. You will take on new responsibilities. Once you move through this initial shock, it's important that you look to the future. It's important that you do not lose hope through the process.

As the chaos is exploding around you, be aware that things are going to be crazy for a while. You will be living day-to-day and sometimes moment-to-moment for a while. Don't expect to be a superstar at work. Expect that you will miss some details. It may feel like things are falling apart, and you may question if you can keep up. Just remember that this stage is temporary. Things will calm down, and you will be able to take those first steps on your divorce journey.

<u>You're Not Alone:</u>

The day you find out you're getting divorced will probably start off like all others. Chances are you'll wake up, get dressed for the day and go about your business. At some point during the day, you'll be surprised with divorce papers. That's because, statistically, women file more often than men. One study found that women initiated divorces approximately 70% of the time (LaBier, 2015). If you're one of the few that is filing for divorce - consider yourself lucky. That study looked at both couples that were married and ones that were not married. They found that in the relationships where the parties were not married, there was no significant difference between the percentage of breakups initiated by men and those initiated by women.

In his "Psychology Today" article, Dr. LaBier notes that these findings are consistent with what he has seen in his practice. He says it's often the women who express more overt conflict and dissatisfaction about the state of the marriage. Dr. LaBier says that men can often identify there are issues and will feel bad about how the wife is feeling but otherwise believe things are okay. In other words, most men are often late to the party in recognizing that there is a problem within the marriage.

Men can feel like there are issues, but we guys are often the problem solvers. If you feel this way, take comfort in knowing you're not the only one. Women are also better at hiding their true feelings. Men are typically less able to hide their true feelings when they're angry or sad. Many women can be experts at holding things in or hiding their true emotions.

Any relationship book you read will tell you that communication is the key to a successful relationship. But, unfortunately, it is often communication that breaks down. After some time, one or both partners will go silent. It's at this point when one or both go silent that a partner (usually us guys) can believe that things are okay or even getting better. In fact, the exact opposite is true. Once you have reached this tipping point, the relationship is in deep trouble.

You may not believe that things were that bad. But the reality is if somebody is willing to go to a divorce attorney and pay money to have divorce papers drawn up - chances are, it's a pretty good bet that the relationship is over. That's not to say that things can't be mended, but do not spend too much time telling yourself that you can fix things. Women will often mentally leave the relationship well before they announce it to their partner.

The "Psychology Today" article states that they believe that the reason more women file for divorce than men is because of "traditional" roles in marriage. Traditional roles have the expectation that one person will do the cooking, childcare, and cleaning while the other person goes to work. While this arrangement certainly works for some couples, it may not work for others, and it will be too late to know when it doesn't unless there is communication. The article states that many women seem unsatisfied with this "traditional" lifestyle.

While it's nice to think that this is the only reason women file for divorce 70% of the time, it is hard to ignore the custodial and financial incentives that family courts offer. Certainly, not all women will seek child support, spousal support, or the majority of custody with the children as an incentive. However, the fact still remains that there are those women who do see these things as an incentive. While divorce courts are becoming more equal, you cannot ignore the fact that many men have got the short end of the stick when it comes to custody or financial arrangements post-divorce.

What's interesting about the "Psychology Today" article is the evidence stating that there was no real statistical difference in who started the split in non-marriage relationships. These couples often live together and are otherwise married, except they don't have to break up in divorce court. So it's easy to conclude that financial and custody incentives influence around 20% of cases.

It's these "incentives" that are destroying American marriages. Don't like your marriage? Get a reward for leaving it! Better yet, get that reward until your children are 18 or older! In many courts, it doesn't really matter what happened during the marriage. It doesn't matter if she cheated on you or you cheated on her. It also doesn't matter that she wants to leave for no reason at all. It certainly doesn't matter if you want her to stay.

Men have many incentives to stay in a marriage. Many times there is financial risk-both the short term and long term. Men will lose time with their kids, their retirement, pensions and possessions. All these things the woman stands to gain. This plays into the incentive for women to leave a marriage.

It's a known fact that being in a marriage is healthy for a man (Wilcox & Wolfinger, 2017). Some research has suggested that married men live almost ten years longer than their unmarried peers. Marriage also seems to increase men's earning power between 10 and 24%. Statistically, men who are married have more sex than their single counterparts. In addition, when men receive love, their immune systems work better. This means that they can fight off diseases better than their single counterparts. It's also no secret that married men are more likely to see a doctor when something is wrong (usually at the urging of their spouse).

Now, that's not to say that women don't benefit from marriage. The fact is that many of the benefits that men see are also seen by women. Additionally, women may enjoy the added benefits of feeling secure and protected by their men.

So if we look at the statistics where women file for divorce 70% of the time, we can see there are a few reasons for it. First, they often checked out of the relationship long before their husband did and are more "settled" with the decision. Next, we see that women can feel they have an incentive to be divorced and that they don't feel like they need marriage as much as the man. The grass is always greener on the other side, right?

If you're part of the 70% that was served divorce papers-your big takeaway here is to know that you're in good company. Sometimes it's comforting just to know that these things happen to other people, too. If you are one of the 30% who filed for divorce, making that decision had to be one of the most difficult decisions of your life.

Chapter Two

Do This Now!

If you just found out that you're getting divorced, there are some things you need to do immediately. Below is a list of items you should take care of as soon as possible. Don't put these things off or think that they are not important. Trust me; you want to get this done. So do it right now. Do it today!

1. Passwords - Change the passwords on all your accounts. This includes your financial accounts, email accounts, social media accounts (do the email accounts and social media accounts first), insurance accounts (health, home, auto, etc.), and any other online account you can think of. For those accounts that you share with your soon-to-be-ex (like bank accounts), come up with a plan to separate them and create new accounts that the other person does not have access to. Defer to your lawyer on splitting financial or monetary valuable assets.

2. Lock your credit report - Locking your credit report with the credit report agencies will prevent someone (like your soon-to-be-ex) from starting new credit accounts in your name. The three major credit reporting agencies (Equifax, Experian, and TransUnion) will allow you to lock your credit report for free. You can also use a paid service if you want a more convenient way of doing it. No matter how you do it, locking your credit will prevent someone from

opening new credit in your name, potentially saving you headaches later on.

3. Financial Records - Get copies of all your financial records. This includes bank records, loan records, mortgage records, credit card statements, titles and deeds, or copies of any legal paperwork you have, such as trusts or durable power of attorneys. Really any other official record that you can think of. If you can't take the originals, make copies and take the copies. Don't forget digital files as well as the paper copies. You will need to get these for as far back as you can, as some states require three or more years of financial records. It is much easier and less expensive to take these records now than to try and get copies of them later. Bring the paper copies somewhere secure (your parent's house, a friend's house, or your work). They need to be somewhere outside your home.

4. Photos - If you have photo albums of you playing with the kids or doing other activities, obtain those images. The images may be on your phone or on a computer. Get copies of any pictures showing you are involved in your children's lives.

5. Don't Move If You Don't Have To- Don't move out of the house if you don't have to. If you don't have to move out of the house, I would highly recommend standing your ground. Sleep in separate bedrooms or sleep on the couch if you have to. If you are forced to move out of your house, you should fight it. When it comes to getting custody of your children, willingly leaving the house will only make custody more of an uphill battle. If you own your house, leaving your house will make this prime for the court to give your ex the house and make you pay for it. The exception here is if you are in danger, in which case, you MUST leave the home. Once you do, sit down and document all the events that occurred to make you feel unsafe in your home. This documentation will be helpful in establishing your concerns for your safety and that of your children.

6. Social Media - Audit your social media accounts. Be ready to suspend some of those accounts and delete others. Remember, any information posted on social media can be used against you. That picture of you holding a beer at a party? The opposing attorney will make you out to be a drunk - even if that was the only beer you had all year. Your political rants? You will be branded as an extremist with an anger problem. Today's divorce cases have caught up with social media even if the law has not.

7. Spouse's Social Media - Audit your spouse's social media accounts. Save screenshots or PDF files of their social media history. Some platforms allow you to download things. Use Google if you don't know how. Your attorney may be able to use this later. Do it soon because chances are you will be blocked from their account if you are not already blocked.

8. Inform the HR Department and Your Boss At Work- Notify your employer's HR department that you are getting divorced. You will need time off work, and it is good for them to know you are going through this in case your emotions get the best of you or your performance starts to drop. Ask if there are any resources for you that they know about, such as EAP (Employee Assistance Programs), that offer free counseling. You may not be able to make any changes to your health insurance or other benefits right away, but it is good to let them know.

9. Take Some Time Off Work - If you have the option of taking a couple of days off of work, it may be more beneficial than you think. Use the time to center yourself and to make some decisions about what you're going to do. It's important to know that the things you're going to do in the early stages of your divorce will have long-lasting effects. Remember, things will be okay. Use the day to take deep breaths and get your emotions out if you can. It may help

to talk to a friend or to see a therapist if you know one. The goal is to get yourself calmed down and centered so you can function.

10. Firearms - Let your attorney know if you have any firearms where you are living or where the other party is living. If you are cohabiting (still living with your soon-to-be ex), you may want to remove any firearms that you have in your house. If you can, get a friend to keep them. The chances of something terrible happening outweigh the positive reasons to have a firearm at home (personal protection from an intruder or shooting for sport). You don't want to get shot with your own guns, and you don't need an attorney saying you are "dangerous" simply because you are a gun owner! If your ex has any firearms, talk to your attorney about having them removed as well.

11. Inventory - Use a video camera or cell phone and slowly walk around your home and property to document the condition of things and record what property you have. This will be useful in court when you are dividing property. Walk around and talk about the things that you see—open cabinets and drawers. Make sure for high-dollar items that you get images or video of them from all sides (like a car). Get pictures of serial numbers and models of high-dollar items. Talk about the ages of things, their condition, and when you got them.

12. Long-Term Decisions - Don't make any long-term decisions on the first day. It's important to wrap your head around your emotions. When you go to make decisions, you want them to be based on facts with a mind balanced in logic and emotion. Making decisions based on emotions rarely leads to outcomes that don't require regret.

13. Acknowledge Your Emotions - It is important that you recognize your emotions. Doing this will allow you to know when you are making an emotional decision. Once you get your emotions wrangled, then you can take another day to start planning and strate-

gizing for the future. If you can separate your emotions from your decision-making, you will come out much further ahead in the long run. You will save a lot of money and time in several areas, with the biggest probably being legal fees. Making these decisions separate from emotions essentially becomes like making a business decision. When you get divorced, really, the things you're fighting about are time and money. These can both be very emotional issues; however, there are logical solutions if you know where to start. By using good business sense, you can save yourself some of the time and hassle (and, of course, heartache) that it takes to get through your divorce. It's important to separate these things into two different boxes. Put your emotions in one box and your business sense and logical decision-making in another. Now, this is easier said than done, but this is where this book and a good support network can really help out. Your support network can be your friends, family, therapist, or an actual support group.

Chapter Three

Your Influence on Conflict

N ow that you've taken some immediate precautions, it's important to consider your influence on the <u>conflict</u> in this divorce
process. In the grand scheme of things, there are only a few possible
paths in the divorce process.

Possible outcomes:

A. The process has its bumps and potholes, but, for the most part,
the divorce is relatively easy, painless, and doesn't require having to
go to court at all. (IDEAL!)

B. The process has some conflict in the beginning, but the parties
work things out in the end without having to go to court much.
(DOABLE.)

C. There is conflict, and as a result, the parties end up in court
some of the time. (TYPICAL)

D. There is a lot of conflict; as a result, the parties end up in court
a lot of the time over most or all of the issues. The parties rarely resolve anything between themselves and instead pay lawyers thousands to settle the disputes. (NOT IDEAL)

If you think the first option (A) sounds like the one that will leave
you in the best possible position post-divorce, you are correct. Ideally, this option will leave you with the most time with your children
and the most money left from your paycheck.

As described, the fourth scenario (D) has the most conflict and attorneys thrive on conflict. Conflict is very expensive. You can spend thousands of dollars fighting over things that are literally worth pennies. When it comes to fighting for time with your children, no one can put a price on that. Sadly, in most states, whatever the mother *believes* you should have for custody can often influence how much you will need to fight for custody.

While it is sad that one person can have so much influence on the case, it is even sadder that that person's opinion of you (which can be naturally negative since you are going through a divorce) has any bearing at all on how much time you will spend with your children post-divorce. It's a total recipe for disaster. I hope that in the future, both men and women will be on equal footing in the divorce courts, but until that time happens, you should be prepared to develop a strategy for parenting time with your children as you enter into the process of divorce.

You should not assume that the laws will protect you or that you will be considered an "equal" with the ex in divorce court. You can assume from this point on that if you need to fight for custody, it may be a long, expensive, uphill battle. At present (with the current laws and the current belief system in the court), it does not matter if you are the most exemplary father in the world or you are the worst father in the world.

It begs the question: do you have any influence on whether or not your divorce will be IDEAL or NOT IDEAL? And that answer is YES! You have a huge influence on how much conflict there is in your divorce. How much conflict you're willing to engage in is directly correlated to your emotional decision-making. If you are able to make decisions based on facts and reality, you are much less likely to have a high-conflict divorce.

Now, that's not to say you have total control over the situation. Remember, you can only control one half of the equation - *your* half. You cannot control the other side, and trying to do so will encourage conflict. You have to realize that the other side is responsible for their own actions, even when the courts do not appear or are unwilling to hold the other parties accountable. The *reality* of the situation is that the courts are not likely to hold the other party responsible or accountable for their actions. There will most likely be lots of things that the courts let slide that will irritate you. The trick is to identify these actions for what they are. Usually, this behavior by the other party is done in a manner that is intended to upset you. They will try and get a reaction from you in order to gain leverage in court. Remember, when you react, the other party wins. If they can get you to yell at them, it gives the other party an advantage over you.

Part of what I hope you get from reading this book is the knowledge of the people who have gone before you. Of course, if you make all the mistakes yourself, you will be no further ahead than the person who made the same mistakes before you. However, if you learn from the knowledge of those that have gone before you, then you will not make them, and you will be able to get much further ahead!

Please heed the advice of those who have gone before you. When this book tells you to put boundaries in place, it is for a good reason and for your protection. Don't be ignorant and think, "I don't need those because that won't happen to me." If you can learn from the words in this book and put into practice some of the things this book talks about, you will be able to ensure that your divorce is much more IDEAL than NOT IDEAL.

The choice is yours. You can save thousands of dollars and ensure a much shorter divorce process, or you can skip the advice and have a divorce fraught with conflict that will put you in bankruptcy and may give you nightmares for the rest of your life. Which one will you choose?

Ask any divorce attorney and they will all tell you that no two divorces are the same. Some are easy, and some are really difficult. A lot of what makes a divorce easy or difficult is the amount of conflict present in the process. For the process to be low conflict, it takes a few things. The biggest is that the two getting divorced need to communicate effectively and set aside their emotions. If they both are able to do this, then the divorce will be low-conflict. But what happens when one or both parties are not able to put their emotions aside or if they are not able to communicate effectively? The result is conflict.

This conflict can be short-lived, or it can last the entire process (and extend into well after the divorce papers are signed). Conflict can come and go. This conflict can be an angry email, a verbal shouting match, or even the other person going silent and not answering communications. In some cases, this conflict can turn physical and can be dangerous. The conflict can even extend into false allegations causing irreparable harm to the other party and the kids involved. When writing this book, it's hard to give you exact advice for your situation because the amount of conflict you're facing could be a little, or it could be a huge amount. If you're in a low-conflict situation, there is some of this book that you don't need. If you're in a high-conflict situation then you need the whole book! You'll have to evaluate what your situation is at the moment and see what fits. If you are in a low-conflict situation, be careful not to create conflict. You have to be intentional though, and think before you do something. You have to ask, "Will this create conflict?" and "How will this be perceived by the other person?". Look before you leap; you want to maintain the low-conflict status if you can. If you're in a high-conflict situation, the same applies too! Make sure the things you're doing and saying are not adding to the conflict. Wherever you can, do things that will reduce conflict! As the process moves on, the conflict may get less and you want to do things that will get you to that low conflict state as quickly as possible.

Chapter Four

Step 1 - Plan the Short Term Game

In the following chapters, I'll walk you through seven steps to getting you headed in the right direction on this divorce journey. I'll cover planning your short-term game, finding an attorney and therapist, finances, setting goals, physical health, and self-care. At the end of this part, you'll be ready to tackle the next sections of the book, where we cover a lot of knowledge about the divorce process, parenting, and how to be successful after your divorce.

Taking the first step is the most important thing you can do to begin your divorce journey. Once you've taken the immediate actions in the previous "Do This Now!" section, the next thing you need to do is plan the short-term game.

Get a pad of paper out and a pencil or pen. Right at the top of your paper, write the word "Today" in big letters. Don't write anything else on this paper yet...

Part of getting through a divorce is taking things day by day. You need to go analog here. Avoid the temptation just to put some notes in your smartphone. This way, you can take some time to really focus on what you are writing.

It's OK to really be aware. What is the texture of the paper like? How does the pen feel in your hand? How does the ink flow from the pen? Slow down and pay attention to some of these details. Again, slowing down and focusing on your environment will help you deal with the pain and anxiety. It's OK to slow down.

The next sheet I want you to label "Things I like doing." Right on this piece of paper in a list format, list activities that you enjoy doing. Try to keep them to things you can actually go out and do, which are things you have the time and resources for. We will make a bucket list later on, so save those things that may be a little bit out of reach financially or that you don't have time for just yet, for the bucket list.

The next sheet should be labeled "Things I need to accomplish." These can be fairly large goals like "Finishing my divorce" or "Moving into a new residence." This page should mainly contain things that you *have* to do, not necessarily things that you enjoy doing, but projects that you need to accomplish to get through the divorce process.

On the next sheet, I want you to label it "Goals." On this sheet, you should list the things that you want to accomplish in life, such as going back to college or learning a new skill. Your goal sheet should contain items that will make you a better person. It can also include things that will build your resume. For now, I want you to forget about the timeline of these goals; simply put down the goals you would like to accomplish.

On the next sheet of paper, I want you to label it "Important Dates." On this sheet of paper, you need to write important dates such as your children's birthdays, your birthday, when your driver's license expires, and when any professional licenses that you have expire. If you have anything important in your life that is "due," make sure you write the dates on this piece of paper. I recommend writing this paper twice. First, jot the dates of everything on the paper in random order. Then make a second page where you put the dates in chronological order starting from the date you make your list.

Now that we've identified things that you like to do and the things that you need to accomplish, you can write your to-do list for today. So, what should you do today? This is where you need to prioritize things that need to happen. Make sure you put things on there that have to absolutely be done today. Avoid putting anything on the list that you don't intend to accomplish.

Check your "Things I need to accomplish" page and your "Due Dates" page. This list should be fairly detailed. If you need to go grocery shopping, then write that. If you need to mail a letter, note that too. On this page, you can write things that are both personally related and work-related.

You may need to find a divorce lawyer; that would be a good to-do item! There are probably a million things that you need to do, but take it one step at a time.

It's important that you put on your list things that you *need* to accomplish, but you might also want to make sure that you have some things on there that you actually enjoy doing. For example, if you have a very active day and accomplish many things but don't do a single thing you enjoy doing, at the end of the day, you're going to feel tired and stressed out.

Be sure, as you keep up this daily routine, that you slowly add recreational activities. One good rule of thumb is to follow the 80/20 rule. The 80/20 rule means you should have about 20% of your list filled with things that you enjoy doing. Don't feel guilty about putting them down. We'll talk more about self-care in a later chapter, but this is a start to doing things that make you feel good. I suggest you check your "Things I like doing" page and make sure you include about two of these items for every eight regular items.

You should continue this routine daily. In the morning or the evening before, write your "Today" list. You can use a journal instead of a piece of paper if you find that helpful. Once you have this process down on paper, you can transfer it to an electronic means if that makes you feel more comfortable. There certainly are a plethora of applications for smartphones to help you with task management and organizing projects.

It's important that you plan your next steps because it's easy to get off track. Wandering through the divorce process is probably one of the worst things that you can do. It will take you longer to get through it, and it will also be more expensive. It's important that you are intentional with everything that you do, from being conscious of how you spend your money to how you act in public and around your children. You have to be mindful of how you communicate with your soon-to-be ex and others. You have to be aware of your presence on the Internet, especially on social media, and you have to be aware of who your friends are and who you *thought* your friends were.

If it sounds complicated, that's because it is! It's important that you sit down and plan things to help you organize all this. Things will be a lot easier once you make a written plan and stick to it. It's important to remember that the short-term is just that, and it will eventually pass. The sooner that you can get through your divorce, the sooner you can move on with life.

While everyone should have a customized short-term game plan, there are some common elements that you can use to get started. It starts with making sure that your basic needs are met.

<u>What are your basic needs?</u>

Your basic needs start with the really basic. We're talking about food and shelter. Where are you going to live? What are you going to eat? It may be really silly, but these are things that you need to think about.

1) Where to Live - Are you going to have to move out and get an apartment or a house? Are you going to have to move out and move

in with friends or family? It's important that you are realistic about where you are going to live for a few reasons. The first, obviously, is what you can afford. So, to start, let's assume that you're not going to be able to afford the same level of lifestyle that you afforded during your marriage.

It's important that you look for something that fulfills your and your children's needs while still being financially affordable. It's also important that where you live is convenient for being involved in your children's lives and where you work. There are a lot of factors to consider (and they are all important!). If you pick a place to live that is too far from your children, chances are you will have less ability to be involved in their life. If you pick a place that is too far from your work, you will spend more money on gas and car expenses, and you will create extra stress on yourself on a daily basis. There's a lot to think about, and where you choose to live will have a HUGE impact on your everyday life.

As you are looking for places to live, I would recommend getting a map out. You can use either a digital one or a physical paper map. Mark each place that you are considering as a place to live. Also, mark out where your kids' schools are and where you work. You will also want to mark out where your ex will be living if you need to go to her house to exchange the kids. Visually seeing all these items together should help you decide which is the right place.

Some factors to consider are:

A) What is the cost of rent?

B) What is the cost of utilities? Are any utilities included in the rent? What utilities will you need to pay for on your own?

C) Is there any maintenance or upkeep required? Do you have to change the furnace filters? Do you have to cut the grass?

D) What is the neighborhood like? Is the neighborhood mostly younger or older people? Is the neighborhood friendly for children?

E) Is the location in your kids' school district? You may not have to live in the same district, but it can be helpful if you are making an argument for custody.

F) Does it have enough space? Does it have any storage space?

G) What are the down payment or deposit requirements?

H) Do they offer an option to pay on credit cards, or do they require a check? Do they allow you to pay online?

I) Is the location convenient for exchanging the kids and going to the kids' school?

J) Is the location convenient for your work?

K) Are there any traffic issues going to either exchange location, your kids' school, or your work?

L) What is the condition of the place? Do the landlords keep it maintained? Does it need a lot of maintenance or restoration?

M) Do you feel comfortable living there? Would you feel comfortable bringing a date there? Would you feel comfortable telling your peers at work that you live there?

N) Does the place have enough bedrooms for you and the children? If not, is there an option for a shorter lease so that you can start working towards giving the kids their own space in your new home?

2) What to Eat - It's easy to fill up on junk food and always eat out at fast food restaurants. But trust me, if you do this, you will gain a ton of weight and you'll just have to work harder to lose that weight at some point.

Some basic nutritional advice is in order. Some people stress eat, taking in loads of carbohydrates in order to deal with the stress. I can tell you from experience that it does nothing but make your belly big and cause regret in your closet! Even if you've never had any issues in the past, you need to be aware that going through trauma and stress may trigger you to have issues you haven't had before. On the other hand, some men are so stressed out that they hardly eat at all. That knot in your stomach and the lump in your throat could cause you to forget that you are hungry and need to eat. The thought of food may make you feel nauseous. Either way, here are some quick tips to ensure that you get the proper nutrition through this process:

A) If you tend to eat your feelings, skip the carbohydrates whenever you can. For example: Going out to a restaurant and ordering a burger? Skip the fries. Instead, order broccoli or some other vegetable. You can still have the bun full of carbohydrates, but skipping the fried potatoes will cut out a lot of unnecessary calories. Packing your lunch? Pack less bread, crackers, and chips, and instead pack more protein.

B) Be cautious of sugar - if you are still loading your coffee up with sugar or putting gobs of sugar on your cereal, this is the time to start cutting back. I would recommend using packets of sugar instead of spooning sugar from a jar. Better yet, use a sugar substitute in small quantities. Instead of putting a couple of scoops of sugar in your coffee - use one pack of sugar substitute. It's amazing how much sugar we consume in the typical American diet. Sugar has a number of negative consequences on our bodies. When we consume sugar, our glucose spikes and then suddenly falls. These rises and falls of glucose get us addicted to sugar. Ideally, our glucose level would have gradual changes throughout the day. When you eat something that has a lot of carbohydrates, this causes those spikes. It's easy to become addicted to carbohydrates because of glucose spikes. In fact, some have argued that sugar addiction is just as hard to break as some hard-core drugs, such as cocaine.

C) Be aware of mindless eating - it's easy to eat mindlessly in today's society. Food is everywhere. You may have a snack machine at work which is giving you hundreds of calories a day that you did not realize! Try this - anytime you're eating that's not for a regular meal, write it down on a piece of paper. Do this for a week and you can identify some of your mindless eating habits. I highly recommend reading "Mindless Eating: Why We Eat More Than We Think" by Brian Wansink (2007). In his book, he details how you eat hundreds to thousands of calories without realizing it! The trick to not gaining weight is to be proactive and not gain it in the first place. By educating yourself, you can ensure that you don't have to go on a massive diet later.

D) Eat protein whenever you can - protein, unlike carbohydrates, does not give you that massive glucose spike. In fact, the body cannot store protein so it is forced to burn it. Think about that: If you take in protein, it cannot be stored as fat. Carbohydrates, on the other hand, are easily converted to fat. This means if you take in too much food, it will burn the protein and store the carbohydrates. So limiting your carbohydrates and eating more protein ensures your body cannot store the excess calories and is forced to burn them. I like to think of carbohydrates as little bastards since they so easily turn into fat cells.

E) Plan your eating - A surefire way to gain weight is not to plan any of your meals. Meandering through mealtimes is a sure way to take in too many calories. Instead, decide what you're going to have for breakfast, lunch and dinner ahead of time. That's not to say that you can't be spontaneous every once in a while, but if you are spontaneous all day, every day, you probably will overconsume calories. The 80/20 rule can be applied here too. Eat right 80% of the time, and indulge the other 20% of the time.

There are a number of calorie-tracking applications which can help you determine how many calories you need for your body size and type. It will also help you determine how many calories to eat at each meal. Some days you will eat three balanced meals. On other days you'll be given a choice to eat a large meal at more than one mealtime. It's important that you choose not to overeat at two or more meals. Planning your eating will also help you maintain a routine. It's a fact that routines and habits are easier to maintain than having to make multiple decisions every day. For me, deciding to have a protein shake in the morning is much easier when I make it a habit.

F) Don't eat out too much - try limiting the number of times you eat food from a restaurant to just a few or fewer per week. Eating out for lunch every day is bound to add to your waistline unless you are very careful. Even if you are eating a salad, you would be surprised at the number of calories in some restaurant salads - especially if they have any sort of dressing on them. It's certainly easier to go to a fast food restaurant, order a burger and fries and consume enough calories for the entire day in just one meal. When you move into your new place, try and establish grocery shopping and cooking habits as quickly as possible.

G) If you can't eat - If the thought of food makes you feel sick or that knot in your stomach has simply turned off your hunger cues, then it is very important that you consume some nutrients. Just as I suggested tracking your food in section E if weight gain is a problem, this strategy can also work if you find yourself unable to eat. It's important that you eat something every day in order to keep your blood sugar levels balanced and maintain strength and focus during this hard time. It could be small, nutrient-dense portions like protein bars or fortified cereals with milk. You could make or buy protein shakes or weight gainer shakes if drinking your calories is easier. The goal is to get back to your normal (or healthier than normal) eating habits.

Moving up the hierarchy of needs, the next important need is:

3) The need to ensure that you have an income - Chances are, you already have a job. It's important to ensure that you are able

to perform at that job and, therefore, able to keep it. Don't plan on getting any big raises or promotions while you're going through this process and for a while after. It's natural for your performance to suffer at work, so your plan here should be just to <u>maintain</u> your performance as best as you can.

It's during this process that you may need to rely on friends at work to help you through the tough times. I'm not talking about crying on their shoulder either; I'm talking about the slack they will be picking up for you. It's important to sit down here and write down how you will maintain your performance *without* your peers having to pick up the slack.

It's also a good idea to talk to your manager and HR department and let them know what's going on so they are not surprised if they see a change in your performance. It's better that you let them know ahead of time rather than having them confront you and only finding out once they notice a change in your performance. It's also a good idea to be able to talk openly to them when you are over-whelmed or need some relief.

You may be surprised at how accommodating employers are when you're going through this process. It's in both your interest and your employer's interest to get you through this as best as possible. If you don't have a supportive employer, then you may want to start thinking about a new job anyhow.

If your soon-to-be ex is high-conflict, don't be surprised if she shows up at your work unannounced or forges complaints against you to try to hurt your career or get you fired. Sadly, you should probably expect this (especially after court proceedings) if she didn't get what she felt she was entitled to in terms of child custody, child support, your retirement plan, etc. It's better that your boss knows about the separation before something like this happens. Also, have anyone who witnessed her being at your work or took a "complaint" from her write a statement for you about what they saw and heard. Even if you don't use the statement in court right away, you may want it for a future date.

Once you have housing, food and your job settled-the next thing to focus on is your relationship with your children and your ex-to-be (X2B).

Make some conscious decisions about things that you will not do during this process:

A) Dating.

B) Yell at your ex or be violent in any way.

C) Vent too much to friends.

D) Spend money unnecessarily.

E) Fight over the small stuff.

F) Be petty or try to get revenge.

Let's go over each of those in some detail:

Dating - Dating is out until you finish this process for a few reasons. Number one is because you need time to heal emotionally after this divorce. The amount of time that everybody needs will be different. You need to be able to fully emotionally commit to your new partner. Starting a relationship when you are not ready will not only sabotage that new relationship, but it's also not very fair to the other person.

Think about it like showing up for a game of baseball or soccer, and you don't bring your workout clothes or the gear to play the game. If you are dating during your divorce process, it is very possible that your new relationship could be dragged into the court proceedings. This is something you definitely do not want to have happen! Remember where very early in the first chapter I talked about having a low-conflict divorce? Having a new relationship before you're divorced is a surefire way to have a high-conflict divorce. Remember, your X2B is probably still emotionally trying to get over you OR wants to emotionally attack you. Either way, having a relationship while divorcing is never a good idea.

Verbal conflict with your X2B - this includes yelling or screaming at your ex or even having a conversation with a raised voice. It is much better to have a difficult conversation in writing where you can take your time to reply when you have calmed down. Face-to-face conversations about potentially volatile subjects are almost never a good idea. Something can be said that isn't true or is taken out of context. This will surely not make you feel well, and it will probably make you feel mad. You will naturally want to lash that anger right back at the person who made you angry; however, doing so can jeopardize how the court views you and cost you thousands to defend. It is simply not worth it.

Whenever possible, try to have minimal conversation. When discussing anything that is potentially volatile, make sure you do that on a tracked written communication system like email or a system like Our Family Wizard (OFW). Remember, it only takes one incident to label you as abusive. One protective order can ruin your life and your career. In many states, your X2B can request a protection order from a judge with NO evidence and without you there. You'll end up in court trying to defend why you are not dangerous. It's the "silver bullet" of divorce. Set good boundaries around communication in the beginning and make sure they are in writing.

Venting too much - This is another potential pitfall. It has a couple of downsides. The first is that you will burn your friends out. They will simply be tired of hearing you complain about your X2B. It's better that you find a good therapist and work through your anger and frustration with that person. Remember, your friends genuinely care about you, but there is a limit to how much they can handle. This also includes family members and other persons that may be close to you.

Spending money unnecessarily - While spending some extra cash on you or your kids may feel good at the time being, be very careful about what you spend. Going through a divorce is certainly the time when you want to conserve money whenever you can.

Remember, the more money you can save now, the more you can ensure that you will not end up in bankruptcy court. During this time of divorce, you will have expenses that you didn't normally have before. You most certainly will be paying for legal fees, and you may be paying for a second household. Chances are you will also be paying spousal and child support. None of this comes cheap. Judges would rather put you in bankruptcy so that you can pay spousal and child support than let you pay your bills.

Fight over the small stuff - It is so easy to get caught up and just fight over the small stuff. For example, does your ex want something goofy in the order that you know she won't follow? That's a 'small stuff' thing. You can fight it, but it will cost you thousands of dollars.

It's important that you evaluate everything that you're going to fight for and ask yourself: Is it really worth it, and what is it really going to cost me? Part of the trap that the divorce industry will get you stuck in is to get you to fight over things that are not worth it. Chances are, your lawyer won't tell you that it's not worth fighting for it because they have the incentive to keep the conflict going. If you have an exceptional lawyer, they will tell you that it's not worth it. Unfortunately, exceptional lawyers are few and far between.

Be petty or try to get revenge - It's going to be really tempting, but rarely is it worth it. The courts just don't work that way. True justice served in family court is very few and very far between. You should not expect justice in your case. Instead, expect that both sides will lose something.

Courts will likely not hold the other person accountable. Do the best you can to be the best person you can be, and don't worry about the other person. Let them fall on their own sword. You will look back later in life and wonder why you cared so much about the small things or getting petty revenge. At this point, you need to be tactical. Get in and get out!

Chapter Five

Step 2 - Finding an Attorney

One of the decisions you will make that will have the biggest impact during the divorce process is picking an attorney. Whether you're picking an attorney to get ready to file for divorce or you need to find an attorney because you were just served divorce papers - the decision process is relatively the same. There are some key things you should consider when looking for an attorney.

1. Find an attorney with experience with your "special case."

While you may think of your divorce as just a divorce, your divorce will have several important aspects that need to be addressed. You may have a great amount of property or businesses that must be divided in the divorce. You could also be dealing with a high-conflict ex. You want an attorney who has experience dealing with your specific needs.

Some areas where you may need some specific help include:

- Large amounts of property or unusual property situations (you own property with somebody who is not your spouse)

- Complex property situations (i.e., you own things that are hard to value, such as collectibles or lots of real estate)

- You are self-employed or own a business

- Your spouse has made allegations against you (sexual abuse or other)

- You have a case that will cross state lines or county borders (i.e., you live in different states or counties)

-Your case is international, involving parties in two different countries

- You have young children (under the age of five)

- You, your spouse or your children have medical problems (severe disabilities, cancer, etc.)

- You, your spouse or your children have mental disabilities or personality disorders

When you look through websites for attorneys, you'll see a few common things. The first is that they all claim to be experts in nearly every category. Very few attorneys have figured out that they should specialize in a certain particular niche of law. You will find that attorneys will classify themselves as "contract attorneys," "family law attorneys," "personal injury attorneys," and the like.

Even within these categories, there are niches. For instance, you want a lawyer who has represented men. This is a specific niche. While many lawyers will tell you they represent both men and women, many will favor one gender over the other. It's fair to ask them in the last two years how many men vs. women they have represented. If they tell you a few men, you will know that they probably favor women's cases.

The typical family law attorney will say that they "specialize" in many different niches within family law. It's not possible to be an expert in everything. Many attorneys now join a law firm that will have many attorneys operating under the same name. While it may be true that different members of their firms specialize in different sections of the law, not every attorney will be an expert at every piece of law. In the case of the larger firms, you will typically be assigned an attorney who will work on most of your case, and they will bring in specialized attorneys as needed. In smaller firms, you'll need to find somebody who is more well-rounded.

Be wary of attorneys who claim to "specialize" in too many areas of law. Attorneys who advertise this way are generally not specialists in anything.

When looking for an attorney, it's important that you identify what your specific needs are. You need to look at your specific needs and decide which ones are the most important to you. You may find an attorney who is very good with custody matters, but then they fall short when it comes to property division.

It will help to write down your top three issues prior to talking with an attorney. Brainstorm all of your issues on a blank piece of paper, then from this list of issues, decide which are your top three. For instance, your number one issue may be to ensure you get as much time with your children as possible. Write these down now.

Issue 1: _____

Issue 2: _____

Issue 3: _____

You will also need to talk to potential attorneys about the problems you will have in your divorce. These are things that may cause problems with the legal proceedings in the divorce. If you have any skeletons in your closet, now is the time to bring them out.

It's important that you are honest with your attorney so they can defend you in the best way possible. If they do not know about a specific problem or issue, it is hard for them to defend your position or come up with a strategy about the issue. You do not want your attorney to be surprised in the courtroom! With potential problems in your case, it's important that you disclose all the issues to your attorney. When in doubt, disclose it.

2. Find an attorney that you are comfortable with.

It's important you find an attorney to whom you are comfortable talking to. Picking somebody who you are not comfortable with will cause issues, as you'll be working closely with this person. It's important that you are able to clearly communicate with your attorney, so make sure you pick one that you find easy to talk to.

If at all possible, I would recommend meeting attorneys in person prior to hiring them. Having a face-to-face meeting in person will allow you to see how they interact with you. You can watch their body language, especially during the times when you talk about the issues in your case. Their body language will tell you how they feel about handling certain issues.

Depending on the issues in your case, you may feel more comfortable with a male or female attorney. It may not matter to you whether you find a male or female attorney. If this is the case then fantastic, otherwise don't force yourself to choose an attorney you are not comfortable with because they are male or female.

3. Find an attorney who practices in the jurisdiction where your case is.

It may surprise you, but even courts within the same state will operate differently from one another. Generally, most family law courts are divided by the county into district courts. If you find an attorney who is based in a different district from yours, they may have a disadvantage with how this court operates. The lawyers generally have a good knowledge of what judges "typically do," and this knowledge can be helpful when deciding many things.

The flip side of this coin is that you may want to choose an attorney who does not operate in the same district that your case is. Attorneys and judges typically run in a very tight social circle. Remember that judges are attorneys before they become judges. There are times when it is an advantage to bring in an attorney from outside the district. If you are finding that your attorney is reluctant to do what you ask (and what you are asking is reasonable), it may be because of political or social pressures that you are not aware of.

It may be to your benefit to switch to an attorney who is not in the district where your case is. The new attorney will not have any social liability with the opposing attorney or the judge. You may also find that sometimes attorneys from outside of your district will fight harder because they do not have to deal with the opposing attorney or judge on a regular basis.

4. Find an attorney who is willing to work with your financial situation.

Because getting divorced is a huge financial burden, chances are you may not be able to afford all of the attorney fees as they are billed. You may have to make a payment arrangement with the attorney. Some attorneys will work with you and take a payment arrangement, while others will essentially stop working on your case soon as you cannot pay. It's important that you work out these details upfront so you're not surprised once the attorney has started to work on your case.

Ask your attorney how much the retainer will be and what the hourly rate is. You can also ask if there are any fees that they collect on a regular basis. While it's hard to tell how attorneys bill before you have hired them, some attorneys will nickel and dime you.

5. Do an Internet search for your attorney's name.

In the age of the Internet, it doesn't take a long time to do some research about an attorney that you want to hire. Simply type their name and city in Google or your preferred search engine and check the results.

You want to look for things that they have been in the news about. Sometimes an attorney's past cases will make news. You want to get a sense of things that they tend to work on a lot. Sometimes attorneys are also politically active, and you can get a sense of their political leanings through an Internet search.

You are looking for an attorney who will be able to represent you well. If you find anything during an Internet search that does not particularly sit well with you, look for a different attorney. Look for their political opinions, any laws that they have helped change, and cases that they have worked on.

6. Look for an attorney who will give you a straight answer.

Sometimes attorneys will just tell you what they think you want to hear in the first interview. Others will be doom and gloom. Some attorneys will not give you much of their opinion one way or the other (this is typical).

What you're looking for here is someone who will listen to the issues in your divorce and give you a straight answer on what is an issue and what is not an issue. You may not always like hearing the answer; however, it is better that you hear an honest opinion from your attorney rather than be surprised in court. Ideally, you will find an attorney who tells you some things will be an issue and others (which you may think are a big deal) are really a non-issue.

7. Interview at least three attorneys.

It'll be tempting to hire the first attorney you talk to. I recommend you talk to at least a few. This will give you a sense of what is out there. You can always go back to that first one.

8. Ask your friends.

If you have any friends that have gotten divorced, ask them for their opinions on the attorneys involved. You may find that people love or hate their attorneys, and the experiences that they have had with these individuals can be important in helping you make the right decision.

Chapter Six

Step 3 - Find a therapist

Whether you like it or not, going through a divorce is an emotional time. You will be experiencing many emotions, but grief is the emotion that you will likely need to start to understand first. Unless you have a specialized degree in grief counseling, chances are you really know very little about grief and are ill-prepared to handle grief alone. Even experienced counselors need other counselors to help them cope with losses and grief. This is really just a fancy way of saying you can't be your own therapist (even if you are one).

Simply put, if you're going through a divorce, one of the first things you should do is go and start seeing a counselor. Find someone who can be consistently there for you during the divorce process. I highly recommend against finding somebody who is a friend or family member to whom you can vent to. This is a job for a professional. Venting to someone you are close to is not the same as receiving good quality counseling or therapy.

There is a type of therapy license called LMFT or a "licensed marriage and family therapist." This branch of therapy specifically focuses on issues within families and divorce. If you can find someone with this license, that will be a good place to start. Look for the letters LMFT after their name. This is the person that you can go to and express anger and all sorts of other feelings in a safe environment.

However, you need to be aware when using any professional (therapist, doctor, etc.) that really anything you tell them could possibly be used against you in the divorce. Remember that lawyers have something special called "attorney-client privilege," but therapists and other medical professionals do not. Therapists have certain confidentiality rules, but they can be called into court or subpoenaed to testify in other ways.

Therapists are also mandatory reporters. They are legally obligated to report abuse. In other words, if a therapist thinks you told him or her you're abusing a child, they have an obligation to report that to the state. Other mandatory reports include (but are not limited to) doctors, dentists, law enforcement, and teachers.

Like your attorney, it's important that you pick somebody whom you're going to be comfortable talking with. This will play into your decision whether you are looking for somebody who's male or female. Once you start therapy, it's ok if you need to change therapists. Try not to change therapists several times, as this can hinder your progress.

When picking a therapist, make sure their office is somewhere you can get to without going too far out of your way. Since therapy can be uncomfortable, chances are if it's too hard to get to their office, you will find ways to cancel the appointment.

There may be a benefit to picking an out-of-the-way therapist if you live in a small town. Picking someone in the next town over may insulate you from having a chance that they run in the same social circles as you.

It's important to note that counselors and therapists are not allowed to have relations with their clients. This is because when you're emotionally in a bad place, you will be vulnerable. It would be easy to develop feelings for someone who helps you through a tough time and to whom you are also attracted to.

No matter which therapist you choose, it's important to make sure you make your mental health a priority. Make sure you make an appointment and stick with it. Especially in the beginning, therapy will seem silly and like you are not marketing any progress. Try and leave each session and reflect on what you talked about and how you're going to apply that to your life moving forward.

Chapter Seven

Step 4 - Finances

When I lived in Florida, we had four hurricanes come through in a single year. The running joke on the news became that you needed to "hunker down." Everyone got sick of hearing that hunker-down joke after a while. But truth be told when a hurricane comes to town, you need to take shelter. The same is true with your finances when going through a divorce. In a lot of ways, there are similarities between a hurricane coming and your finances being in danger. What is very true is that you do need to "hunker down" your finances.

Undoubtedly, this will probably be one part of your life where your finances will be challenged to the extreme. In essence, you need to "hunker down" to protect yourself in the best way possible. You may end up paying for two residences, and you may end up paying a lot more for child and spousal support than you anticipated.

There is a very good chance that you may go bankrupt as a result of the family court system. The family court system doesn't care what your debts are; they only care how much money you make to give to your children and to your ex-wife.

The family court system doesn't care that you can't pay your credit cards. The family court system doesn't care that you can't pay your mortgage. The family court system doesn't care that you can't pay your car loan. If you're like the typical American and have leveraged your credit to the maximum, there is a very good chance that you will go bankrupt... and the family court system could care less. To get on the right track, you will need to make a budget and be realistic about what resources you have and what resources will be taken away.

Step one is to outline your current budget- The very first step is to understand what your current budget is. I'm not talking about what you want to spend; I'm talking about what you are actually spending. If you're using accounting software like QuickBooks, then this process will be much easier. If you're not using accounting software, now would be a great time to start using one or make a spreadsheet.

When you get divorced, you will need excellent tracking of your finances to prove how much you're spending on your children. This will be useful in determining child support and how much each party will pay. I highly recommend using accounting software to track every aspect of your finances.

If you're not using QuickBooks, then you can use a spreadsheet to track how much you're spending. I would make several different categories and list your income and expenses under each category. You should have a category for:

-Income

-Mortgage or rent

-Home expenses (like maintenance and utilities)

- Groceries

-Meals (eating out) and entertainment (including hobbies)

- Medical expenses

- Children's expenses

-Transportation costs (including car loans, registration, and insurance)

- Student loans

- Credit cards

-Other loans

-Miscellaneous category for anything else that doesn't fit within the above categories.

Under each of these categories, list your monthly expenses. If you don't know, go through last month's bank statement and add up each category. You can make columns that go across the top so you can have one for each month. At the beginning of each month, simply insert a new column and add your income and expenses. This very simple tracking spreadsheet can help you determine what you have paid for the month and what you still have left to pay.

It can also be helpful to have a column that shows the due date for the month for each expense. This way, you can take a quick look at the spreadsheet and determine which bills you have paid and what you still need to pay, and when your paychecks are available.

At the bottom of each column, you want to add up your income and then subtract out all of your expenses. If the number that results is positive, you have a positive cash flow (you make more money than you spend). If the number is negative, then you are spending more money than you are making.

Step two is to eliminate any unnecessary expenses- Take a good, hard look at your expenses and see if there are any that you can eliminate. You may be able to eliminate monthly subscriptions for things that you're not using. It may be a little tougher to decide to eliminate the monthly subscriptions for things that you are using. Make no mistake about it; this is the time to conserve money. At this point, I wouldn't make any cancellations just yet. On your spread-sheet, put a note or colorize them so that you know which of these expenses you could potentially eliminate.

Step three is to talk with your attorney about your financial situation. It's very important you talk with your attorney to figure out your financial situation. Your attorney will be able to tell you which expenses you will need to eliminate to conserve money and which ones you may want to keep because they will be used in the calculations for child and spousal support. Since states differ in their laws and regulations for child support and spousal support, it wouldn't make any sense to go into it here. There are many resources on what each individual state does, but the best resource is your attorney because they know the local system.

Step four is to make a post-divorce budget- Take whatever number your attorney is giving you that will be your liability for child support and spousal support and add that to your old budget. You can do this very simply on an Excel spreadsheet by copying your original budget at the bottom where the tabs are. Right-click on the tab and select "duplicate." Rename the new tab to whatever you want it to be, and then you can go in and edit it. With the new edited budget, are you still cash-positive? Or is the number at the bottom now negative? If the number is negative, it's time to see what expenses you will be able to get rid of.

Step five is to consider talking to a bankruptcy attorney. While a lot of people want to put off this step, it is very important that you do it early. A good bankruptcy attorney will be able to tell you if you will be able to file a Chapter 7 or Chapter 13 bankruptcy once your divorce is complete. There are many benefits if you can file a Chapter 7 bankruptcy. The difference between a Chapter 7 and a Chapter 13 bankruptcy is with a Chapter 7 bankruptcy; you get to walk away from most of your debts. With a Chapter 13 bankruptcy, you will be required to pay back your debts typically within a five-year time. That payment will be based on your income and available cash flow, so the payments to a Chapter 13 bankruptcy will likely be less than the payments that you would have made if you were just making credit card minimums and other regular payments. Either way, there may be a benefit to going bankrupt. It really sucks to have your credit hurt, but if you can go bankrupt and save thousands of dollars in payments, you will be better off. It's also good to know that after bankruptcy, your credit will typically recover faster than if you would have just spent the time to make those payments to those credit cards originally. If you go bankrupt, your credit will start to recover in only a couple of years. It's not uncommon for people to be able to get loans or car loans as soon as two or three years after going bankrupt. The trick after going bankrupt is to ensure that you do not miss payments and that you use your credit wisely.

Step six is to gather all of your financial documents. When you go through a divorce, you will need an excessive number of financial documents. Laws vary from state to state, but it is not uncommon to need up to three years of banking statements prior to the divorce to be disclosed to the other party. You should be prepared to provide several years' worth of bank statements, credit card statements, mortgage statements, loan statements for your vehicles, and more. It doesn't make much sense to try and hide these documents, as they will just subpoena them and get them anyway. A sticky situation is when your ex is the only one who has these documents. I would highly recommend if you're going to move out of the house, you either take all of these documents with you or make copies of them and take the copies with you.

Step seven is to make an inventory of the things that you will need to purchase post-separation. Since you will be starting a new household, chances are you will need to buy some things to start up your new household. It's likely that your ex will get to have all of the existing items unless you are able to split the property amicably. I would not get into a fight over property as things are easily replaced, and most times, the fight costs more in legal fees than the items are actually worth.

Make a list of the things that you will need in your new residence. Will you need a new bed and bed sheets? Pillows? Kitchen utensils? How about pots and pans? Don't forget the coffee maker, either. What about a table and chairs to eat breakfast and lunch at? How about a couch and a TV? Make a list of the household items that you will not be able to take from your current residence when you start your new one. Instead of going out and blindly spending money on these things, you can make a budget to determine how much you can afford for each one of these items. If you don't want to buy new, there are several options when buying household items used. Places like Goodwill and Facebook Marketplace are some good options.

At this point in your life, you don't want to buy the best; you just need something basic to get by. Remember that divorce is a transition. And if you end up combining households with someone else later on, then you will have two of everything.

Step eight is to order your credit report. I would highly advise ordering a three-bureau credit report to see what is on there. It's entirely possible that your soon-to-be ex-wife has started some credit accounts that you were not aware of. Obtaining your credit report will allow you to find this out on your own without being surprised. Ordering a three-bureau credit report is simple and free if you go to each credit agency individually and request it.

Another thing you may want to consider in your post-divorce budget is to pay for credit monitoring through one of the credit agencies. This will help you protect your credit to ensure that your ex-wife or someone else is not using and abusing your credit.

You can also "lock" your credit report, which will prevent new accounts from being opened and also prevent someone from checking your credit. This is a great safeguard to have during this transition. There are paid services to do this, or the credit agencies also let you do this for free.

Having credit monitoring after the divorce is also a good idea since court documents are public. You can be vulnerable if a lawyer, court clerk, or legal aid forgets to cross out your Social Security number on any of the documents. Bad actors could use these public documents to create new accounts in your name.

Step nine is to get credit cards to use just for legal fees. If you are going to be putting your lawyer's fees on credit cards, I would highly recommend using separate credit cards solely for this purpose. If your state makes you split the lawyer expenses between both parties, it will make it easier to determine exactly how much was spent on the attorneys. For instance, some states will add up the attorney's fees on both sides and say that each party is responsible for half. If this is the case in your state, then it is imperative to ensure that your lawyer's fees are not commingled with other expenses, especially when on credit cards.

Additionally, if you're going to go bankrupt after your divorce, it will be much easier to walk away from these credit cards than if they were to be used for mixed purposes.

Step ten is to change all of your passwords. If you have any accounts which are joint accounts with your ex, then you need to separate those accounts as quickly as possible. This includes starting new accounts in just your name and transferring funds as appropriate.

Change all of the usernames and passwords that you can on any account that you can. This includes non-financial accounts as well. I'm talking about financial accounts, email accounts, social media accounts, insurance accounts, and anything else you can think of that has an online login. It's imperative that you put up a wall as soon as possible.

Chapter Eight

Step 5 - Dream and set some goals

D ivorce is probably going to be one of the greatest shifts in your life. The transition from being married to divorced is much harder than the transition from being single to married. It's also much more difficult from that transition of not having any kids to that transition of having kids.

Since this is probably one of the most difficult transitions that you will have to face in your life, it's important for you to have some hopes and dreams along the way to help you pull through some of the rougher times. Not having hopes and dreams makes it much more difficult. It's also much easier to set goals when you have a dream.

The size of your hopes and dreams doesn't have to be monumental. They don't have to be "curing world hunger" or "making world peace universal." It's okay to start small and work into something larger. When setting your dreams, they generally fall into a few categories, and those include your short-term goals and dreams and the longer ones.

It's important that you make a distinction between goals and dreams. Goals are the practical things that you want to accomplish in your life, while dreams are the larger ones that drive your goals. For example, I dream of hiking on a volcano and scuba diving in the Cayman Islands. To make that dream happen, I will need goals. For example, if you want to go on an exotic trip - you'll need the time and the money to do that.

A simple way to tell between a dream and a goal is that a dream is something that you never imagined that you would be able to do or something that seemed very unlikely. Goals are simply the way that you achieve your dreams. By setting a number of smaller and shorter-term goals, you can accomplish big things!

It can be helpful to dream big when going through a divorce, or it may not be. You will have to decide what is right for you based on your personality. It's okay to have one big dream and a few smaller ones.

While you should dream big, you should also be realistic and choose dreams that you can accomplish. This practical side of dreaming may not be the most fun thing in the world, but it is important to make sure that you pick dreams that you can actually accomplish. If your dream is so big, it may seem impossible. You may stop working toward your goals to accomplish it.

Remember, your dreams can change. Just because you pick one dream today doesn't mean you can't change your mind tomorrow. So, for now, pick a dream that's a little way out there but is something that you totally want to do. It should be something that you are completely committed to.

It's important that you set your sights on achieving this goal after your divorce is finished. Finishing your divorce is your number one goal in the short run. I hope for you that your divorce process is quick and easy. The reality is sometimes divorce is long and difficult. Having this goal to accomplish once you get divorced will give you sort of a carrot to reach out for after the divorce. When you're feeling down or sad, you can remember that dream and remind yourself that you're going to achieve it.

Now that you have your dream identified and some goals set to accomplish that dream, you need to visualize that dream. Hang something up at your place of work and also something at home to remind you daily of that dream. Then, when things get bad and you start to feel down, I want you to look at this dream. Look at this physical reminder of your dream and tell yourself that the process will not last forever and that someday you will be able to accomplish whatever it is that you dreamed of.

I want you to put this book down and take a minute to go ahead and get some of those visual reminders ready. If it's a place you want to go, simply print out a few pictures of the place. Hang them up on the walls and maybe save a copy of that picture on your screensaver on your phone.

Seeing these visual reminders of your dream will be some of the much-needed boost that you need to keep pressing forward. Getting through the process of divorce is sometimes more about the small little actions that you do to keep yourself going than it is about the big ones.

Dream big and make sure your dreams are things that are somewhat realistic for you to accomplish. It's okay to have a dream that's a little bit out of what you think you can accomplish but be careful about setting dreams which are unrealistic. Setting unrealistic dreams can cause you to get discouraged, and you will just give up and never achieve them. You'll need a big win on the other side of your divorce.

It's common for people who are under stress to not be very creative, or at least not feel very creative. Here's a list of dream ideas to kickstart your thinking:

- Take a trip to the Caribbean.

- Visit the Grand Canyon.

- Take a road trip from one end of the country to the other.

- Visit a family member in a foreign land.

- Take time off work and go somewhere that you've never been before.

- Build something.

- Build a piece of furniture.

- Build a motorcycle or mountain bike.

- Build a gaming computer.

One thing when dreaming is to make sure that you don't pick a dream that is controlled by somebody else. You may dream of being the Vice President of your company someday, but realistically you don't have as much control over that dream as you would like. Getting a position like that is somewhat luck mixed in with being at the right place at the right time, having the right qualifications, and knowing the right people. Not all of those things are factors that you can control. It's important that you pick out dreams which you can control. You want to be able to control the entire dream, from soup to nuts. Good examples of dreams are going on a vacation somewhere, moving somewhere you want to live, learning a new skill or task, or picking up a hobby.

It's very important that you do not pick dreams which may be controlled by your ex. For example, if you're going to share custody with your ex of your children, then having a goal of moving halfway across the country may not be very realistic (at least not without giving up custody of your children). Try and stay away from dreaming about things that you cannot do because of the limitations you have in your new divorce.

Go ahead and write down that big dream now:

My   dream   is

to:_____

You've just taken the first step on your journey! Now to achieve your dream, you'll need to identify some goals. These goals may be, in some ways, a form of smaller dreams but they should be attainable in reasonable amounts of time and effort.

At this point, you should write down three goals to be able to achieve your dream. If you want to take a trip, then your goal should be to save enough money for that trip. Or you may need to save enough time off of work for that trip.

To obtain my goal, I will need to:

One._____
_____

Two._____
_____

Three._____
_____

Your dreams and goals will help you remember that there is life beyond divorce and that you will have things to look forward to in the new chapter of your life.

Chapter Nine

Step 6 - Physical Health

A n important thing to take away from this chapter is that now, more than ever, you need to make a plan and be intentional about how you live. Take some time and think about how you're going to live a bit healthier. You can't make better health choices without deciding to do them first. These things don't just happen.

It's important as you go through this process that you remember to take care of both your mind and body. It's easy to put those aside and let both your mind and body go. But now, more so than ever, you need to take care of both. Put a health plan together. Chances are you won't be able to follow this plan perfectly, but it's better than not having a plan at all.

The benefits of being healthy are numerous and well documented, so I won't cover them in this book other than to say that a healthy body will help you have a healthy mind.

Going through a divorce is very stressful. During this time, you are at risk for stress eating. Let's face it, comfort food tastes good and gives you a temporary reprieve. Like any vice, those tasty snacks will end up on your belly, and as you get older losing weight gets harder. Eating, smoking, drinking, and even sexual additions are all easy enough to fall on. Resist the urge, and you will be rewarded.

Avoid that whole mess by not stress eating and taking care of stress in healthy ways. The initial stress of the divorce makes it easy to lose 20 lbs. I had no appetite from the stress. That tapered off and I began to stress eat, gaining back those twenty and adding 20 more. So if you are reading this thinking some buff-super-healthy dude wrote the "get healthy section," you're wrong!

Going through the challenge of divorce is both physically and mentally stressful. One of the best ways to combat stress is through exercise. Numerous studies prove that there's a direct link between the amount of exercise somebody does and their ability to cope with mental and physical stress.

One of the challenges that you will go through with your divorce will be how to manage your time. The divorce will probably take more of your time than you expect, so it's easy to put off taking care of yourself as new things take up your day. Resist the urge! Make sure you make time to eat right and exercise!

When you're going through a challenging time in your life, this is the time to double down on self-care. Many guys will throw self-care out the window when life gets tough. Don't do it! Your mental health and physical health are important! Since I cover mental health in another chapter, I'll focus mostly on diet and exercise here.

<u>Exercise</u>

Remember, you don't have to work out five times a day and have a goal to look like Arnold Schwarzenegger. You simply want to maintain your fitness or get into a little better shape. This little bit of exercise will release the right chemicals in your brain (endorphins called serotonin and dopamine) to help you cope with stress better.

When I go to the gym, I feel a bit intimidated. It's not that I'm worried about not being as buff as everyone else. It's that I don't know *what* to do. The good news is there are lots of resources. Probably the best resource will be a trainer at your local gym. There are also YouTube videos, online articles, and books. I'm by no means an exercise expert, so I will leave that to the professionals. The following are some tips just to get you started.

If you get plenty of exercise at work, consider yourself one of the lucky ones. My job has me walking some, but I don't get the exercise that I should. It's important that you plan time to exercise. You don't have to get ripped (although you can if that's your goal). You should do enough exercise to ensure that your health doesn't decline.

It's important to note that you should check with your doctor before starting an exercise routine. Your goal should be to maintain or improve your health, and you don't want to do anything that would hurt you.

So how much should you exercise and what should you do? The CDC recommends that "adults need 150 minutes of moderate-intensity physical activity and two days of muscle strengthening activity, according to the current Physical Activity Guidelines for Americans" (CDC, 2022). This could be a jog, power walk or weights. They go on to say that "We know 150 minutes of physical activity each week sounds like a lot, but you don't have to do it all at once. It could be 30 minutes a day, five days a week. You can spread your activity out during the week and break it up into smaller chunks of time".

If you have the time and money, it's best to consult a personal trainer to see what would be the best routine for your body type and schedule. Make sure you pick something that you can stick with. Working out two or three times a month will not get or keep you healthy!

It's important that you stay healthy for your kids. Exercise is a big part of that. As your kids grow up, there will be physical activities that you want to participate in with them. It may be team sports, scouts, hiking, biking, or a myriad of other activities. If you don't maintain your health, you will have to be a bystander. Trust me; you are going to want to be there and be healthy enough to participate with your kids!

Another great reason to exercise is that it is an excellent way to relieve stress. Since going through a divorce will probably be one of the most stressful times of your life, anything you can do to help relieve stress will go a long way.

If you can't afford a gym membership or an appointment with a personal trainer, check out your local YMCA (low-cost) or scope out local parks (free) for outdoor exercise equipment or trails to run on. If you live in a more rural area, or it's the winter and you have 3 feet of snow on the ground, your best option will probably be a DVD or streaming program. If you can afford new running shoes or workout clothes, buy them as a reward to yourself for starting your new fitness journey.

<u>Diet</u>

You can't out-exercise a bad diet. There simply isn't enough time in the day. So watching what you eat and making healthy choices is the first step on this journey. It's ok to slip up now and then. And by "now and then," I mean maybe once or twice a week. If you are eating high-calorie or poor-quality foods once or twice a day, no matter how much gym time you get, your body will pack on the pounds.

If you are like me (and a lot of other people), you love carbohydrates. Bread, pasta, and sweets. The problem is your body loves carbs too, and carbs are like little jerks in the body. Your body will burn proteins first, and any extra energy left from carbs will get stored. You are what you eat!

The diet that is right for me may not be right for you. This is especially true as we age. For decades the debate on what is "right" to eat has raged on. Eggs are good, Eggs are bad, then they are good again. The same debate has raged on with grains.

What is important is that you find out what works for you. Some people will feel better on a high-protein diet while others may feel better on one based more on plants. Some people have a higher tolerance for carbohydrates (bread, pasta, and sugars). You may be sensitive to gluten or lactose. What is important is that you learn what makes you feel good.

When you are eating, pay attention to how you feel - especially an hour or two after the meal. Are you tired, or do you get a headache? Do you feel no different? If it helps, take some notes.

In general, try to cut out the fast food. Resist the urge to eat out every night or to order pizza. You should be cooking your own meals several nights a week. If you are eating out, opt for lower-calorie options: more salads and less high-calorie foods, especially fried foods.

While we are on the topic of things not to consume, we should talk about alcohol. While there is little harm in having a drink now and then, being in a vulnerable time in your life, you are at risk of consuming more alcohol than you should. We all know that being an alcoholic is bad, but you need to be aware that you will be under a microscope in family court and the odds are not in your favor. Do yourself a favor and stay away from alcohol (and drugs, too, even weed). Avoid that trap altogether.

Eat the foods that make you feel good, and your self-care journey during this divorce will be a lot easier. Like all the topics above, you don't want your health to be an issue in the custody case.

Chapter Ten

Step 7 - Self-Care

B efore I got divorced, I hadn't given much thought to "self-care." Don't worry if you're in the same boat!

Have you ever heard that announcement they make on a commercial flight where the flight attendant tells you that in the "unlikely event the cabin loses pressure, oxygen masks will drop from under the overhead bin compartments"? They go on to say, "If you're traveling with small children, be sure to put your oxygen mask on yourself before helping others." That's a pretty good description of self-care. You need to do things to take care of yourself before you can help others. In the case of raising kids, you have to take care of yourself so you'll be able to take care of your kids.

You need to make sure you take care of yourself physically and mentally. It's important that you have a plan for self-care. This is one of the first things that will get thrown out the window as you get thrown into the tornado of divorce. When you are going through a divorce, everything is coming at you fast. It's tempting to put your needs aside. You need the benefits of self-care more than ever when you are going through a divorce, so make the time!

Sometimes the benefits of self-care aren't immediately apparent. Stick with it!

One final note before I get into self-care. Some of the things in this chapter may be obvious to you (like grooming and taking showers).

While this advice may seem condescending to those that already do that, remember that some need to hear this advice. They may not be taking care of the basics because of depression or some other reason. If you already are doing some of the things in this chapter, then great! Keep doing them.

Types of Self-Care

Some self-care things are the same for everyone, while other things will be different for everyone. Make sure to make time for everything in the basic list:

- Grooming - bathing, shaving, brushing teeth, wearing deodorant

- Cleaning - cleaning your living space to your level of comfort (or maybe just a little more)

- Exercise - working out, walking, not sitting for long periods of time

When you hear the word self-care, your first thought may be something like grooming or fitness. While those are basic self-care items that you must do, here are some examples of other kinds of self-care:

- Reading

- Hobbies (something you're passionate about)

- Relaxing - watching a tv series or a movie

- Talking with friends

- Meditating

How much time should you spend on self-care?

The amount of self-care that you need will vary from person to person. The amount of stress that you are under will also change how much self-care you need. You will have to experiment a bit to see how much you need and how much you can make time for. As a rule of thumb, you want to try and get an extra 60 minutes of self-care per day. This time should be split between the basic self-care items (grooming, cleaning, and exercise) and something from the extra list above (reading, hobbies, etc.).

If you can find extra time, then great! If you can't, don't worry about it. It's important that you make time for the basic self-care items. It's easy to let things go if you don't make an effort, but trust me, it will be worth it.

Why the Basics Are Important

As a human, you have certain basic needs. These include food, water, and shelter. You can't do anything else until you have these needs met. That's the basics of life. Beyond the needs of food, water, and shelter - grooming, cleaning, and exercise come next.

Some may argue that an income should be included before cleaning or exercising. I'll argue, though, that while an income is important, it will be hard to keep a job if you're not taking care of yourself. For that reason, I'm leaving it off our self-care list for now because I believe it's lower down on the list.

Grooming

Let's face it, if you stink- most people will not want to be around you. While a certain amount of body odor is acceptable in some cultures, in Western culture, it's generally expected that you're pungent-free.

It's equally important that you keep up your grooming routine so your inner mountain man stays, well, inner. You may think that this will not affect your divorce. However, you may have to show up in court. The opposing lawyer could say that you "can't even take care of yourself," so how will you be able to take care of your kids? It's a fair point, to be honest. If you want to try the mountain man thing out, just make sure the timing is right.

So just to get the basics out of the way, here is what you should do at a minimum on a daily basis:

- Shower daily

- Wash your face daily

- Brush your teeth at least once a day (twice preferred) and use mouthwash at least daily

- Clip your finger and toenails at least once a week

- Get a haircut at least every 4-5 weeks. You may need one more often depending on how fast your hair grows.

- Shave - Shave at least every few days. You may need to shave daily.

- Socks and underwear - Change to clean pairs daily!

Keeping yourself groomed is important to you personally and it is also important for your kids. Not only are you setting an example, but you also don't want your personal care coming up as an issue in your custody case.

Cleaning

It's important that you keep your living space at least somewhat clean. A dirty living environment is unhealthy and will attract unwelcome visitors like germs and bugs. If you are living on your own for the first time or in a very long time, you should establish a cleaning habit. Make it at least once a week. On a weekly basis, you should, at a minimum:

- Vacuum, sweep and mop floors.

- Wash down kitchen counters and other surfaces with a disinfectant kitchen cleaner.

- Wash any dishes, including pots and pans and reusable water bottles.

- Take the trash out.

- Clean the bathrooms, including scrubbing the toilets and cleaning the floors (you would be amazed at how much pee can get on a floor when you have kids!). Be sure to also wipe down the counters and the sinks with a disinfectant cleaner.

- Do laundry.

- Wash bed sheets.

You don't have to be perfect with your cleaning. Just make sure you do a good enough job that all the crumbs and food are picked up and that there is nothing that will get worse with time (i.e., grow).

If you want to spread your cleaning time out, you can do one thing at a time (like the bathrooms), then the next day do something else (like the kitchen). While this is important to you personally, keeping a clean house is also important when going through a custody battle. While hopefully the cleanliness of your house/home doesn't come up, if it does, you want to make sure this is not an issue in your court case.

Here is a tip for cleaning when you are depressed or overwhelmed! Gather all the supplies you need first (rags, spray cleaner, vacuum, etc.). Then, set a timer for, let's say, fifteen minutes. If after the timer goes off, you can't bare to clean anymore: Stop and take a break. Set the timer again. Most people will find that once the fifteen minutes are up, they are in a good groove and will continue cleaning.

<u>Why other types of Self-Care are Important</u>

Unfortunately, mental health in men has been stigmatized in Western culture. Our society has conditioned men to feel "less than" when they confront or show their emotions. As a result, many men convert all their emotions into anger, and this is what <u>you do not want to do</u>. This is an unhealthy way of dealing with your mental health.

I will cover the emotion of anger in more detail in the mental health section of the book. For now, I'm going to take just a moment to talk about it here because anger is common during divorce and expressing it will hurt any sort of legal case you have. If you have anger, make sure you get professional help as soon as you can. Don't take it out on your family, kids, co-workers, or friends. Especially do not take it out on your ex or anyone that has contact with her.

Taking care of your mental health during and after the divorce is important to keep you headed in the right direction. It's much easier to navigate the difficulties and the obstacles of divorce if you have a straight head-on.

Something that we don't think about often is how our mental health affects our daily lives. Everything becomes harder when your mental health is not in a good state. Depression may take hold and you may find it harder to just get out of bed and do the things that you need to do on a daily basis. Working and having fun becomes a greater challenge when your mental health slips.

Planning *and doing* self-care is a great way to keep your head on straight and to keep moving forward. While self-care cannot elimi-nate the possibility that you will get depressed or have some other mental health issue, it will help you get through it if you do have some mental health issues.

Emotional Self-Care

While physical self-care is pretty easy to identify, any sane person will tell you that these things are a must-do. After all, if you don't shower or take a bath, chances are your friends, family, and co-workers will let you know that you NEED to take care of that. Emotional self-care isn't really the same. You can neglect your emotional self-care, and it's much harder for other people to notice.

What's included in emotional self-care?

1)Knowing when to take a break.

Knowing when you are going too fast and when you have too much stress. This can be a tough one as we are all go-go-go. Chances are, if you are feeling overwhelmed and feel like you can't catch a break, it's time to slow down and schedule some time off. You also need to make sure that you don't beat yourself up for taking a break. Schedule the time, relax during that time, and recharge so you can get back to your regularly scheduled life.

2)Knowing when you need to manage the toxic people in your life.

Toxic people bring us down emotionally more than we like to admit. When you have a toxic person in your life, they take a LOT of your energy. This is energy that can't be used for other things. For this reason, it's important that you try to be aware and regulate the contact and amount of toxic people in your life.

The best thing is to cut out toxic people from your life, even though it may not be easy. The benefits outweigh the emotional cost of having them in your life! You may not even know who all the toxic people in your life are yet. One red flag could be you seem to be having a decent day with no drama, the biggest problem you have is do you want tacos or a salad for dinner...? Then BAM! A family member calls you, tells you a story about all this drama going on, and now you're upset with someone else in the family. Sure, you only heard one side of the story, but it was pretty bad. All of a sudden you are upset, not hungry, and don't even want to speak to that other person you heard all about! Hang on a sec; what just happened there? Your caller may be a toxic person to you. There are many books dedicated to this subject, so I won't go into any more detail here, but if you find your mood or energy levels suddenly change when you speak to or around a certain person, they may be toxic to you.

3)Knowing when to set boundaries.

If you have poor boundaries with family, friends, and coworkers, then the first step is to recognize that these poor boundaries are causing you problems. There are books and books written on this, so if you need to do more research - get to reading! You know you have poor boundaries when you are setting schedules or are doing things that you don't want to do - often with little or no benefit to you. If you do have poor boundaries, know that it isn't an overnight change to having good boundaries. This is a process and one that sometimes takes some time.

4)Managing your feelings.

When you are going through a tough time, your feelings can consume you. They can be confusing and overwhelming. This is normal when you're going through something as traumatic as a divorce. You don't want to internalize and never deal with these feelings, either. The trick here is you will have times when you need to put your feelings aside (like at work), and there are times with family, friends, or your therapist when you can let them out—learning to manage the "when" aspect of your feelings is not easy. It takes a lot of emotional energy. If you want to read more about this, look for books or articles about emotional intelligence.

<u>How to plan Self-Care</u>

Enough talking about why you need to do self-care. Let's talk about planning self-care. It's important that you do self-care regularly. Hygiene, grooming, and cleaning should be done daily and for the mental health-related self-care items, a few times a week.

Your planning doesn't need to be complex. First, write out on some paper what you want to do. Once you write it down, then decide how often you want to do it. If you don't do something on the day that you had planned, be sure to make an effort to make up that self-care time later in the week. Try not to skip your self-care, but don't beat yourself up if you do.

You may find it helpful to use a paper or electronic calendar to keep track of when and where you will be doing certain self-care things. You should write down a checklist for your daily items, but for those things that you will do a few times a week, it may be helpful to write those things down on a calendar. Many calendar apps have a "reoccurring" function so you can set things to happen at a specific time every Tuesday or whatever day you need it to remind you.

Remember that you are not going to move mountains in a day. Your goal here should be to build positive habits, one small step at a time. Building the habit of self-care will make sure that you take care of yourself in the future. While it may seem like a pain in the beginning, after some time, your habits will become more automatic. Once that happens, you will start to enjoy the benefits that self-care will bring. Your goals do not need to be big in the beginning. Start with setting aside 15 or 30 minutes for self-care. Add on 15 minutes after a while. Soon you will be able to carve out an hour for self-care time and the whole time you will start seeing the benefits.

It's important that you track your habits as you build on them. This can be in a notebook, on a whiteboard at home or at work, or by using an electronic app on your phone. It doesn't matter how you track it, but you need to track it on a daily basis. Take a few minutes every week to review. How did you make time for self-care? How did you do? What can you adjust in the future? This simple act of tracking will help keep you accountable.

<u>Final Words on Self Care</u>

Self-care may seem silly, especially right now as you are in the middle of or are embarking on the journey of divorce. You may be tempted just to do the "essentials" of self-care including grooming and picking up at home. While this may be tempting, you will be losing out on the mental benefits of other kinds of self-care such as a hobby or relaxation. These types of mental self-care are also essential. Put yourself in the best position to come through the divorce in the best possible manner. Don't neglect your mental health. By engaging in self-care, you are giving your mind and body the best chances of moving forward.

PART 2 - BOOT CAMP

Chapter Eleven

Mental Health Introduction

Why a chapter on mental health?

You're probably thinking, "I thought this book was about divorce; why would there be a chapter about mental health?". In divorce, mental health is one of the most overlooked aspects. We rarely recognize that divorce has a very long-lasting mental health effect on everyone! Parents and kids alike will have challenges with their mental health, especially if it's not recognized and properly addressed.

You may not have studied mental health before. Unless you're a mental health professional, chances are you have very little training or knowledge about mental health. Most lawyers and "professionals" involved with the court system often fail to recognize the damage conflict does to the mental health of the people involved.

Your mental health is important, and divorce will challenge your mental health. Your mental health affects everything that you do and see. It affects how you work, how you play, how you think, and how you feel. It changes how you see the world. Your mental health will also change how you react to various things during the divorce. You will question yourself.

Divorce is a stressful time for everyone, and emotions run high. Even people with extremely high emotional intelligence can have difficulty controlling themselves emotionally during the process of divorce. Being aware of these things and how they affect you can help you control your reactions throughout the process (and save you a lot of money along the way).

If you can keep your mental health relatively good during the divorce, you will have a shorter recovery time after the divorce. On the other hand, if you let your mental health go, you will have a much longer recovery time, and you will be starting from a much more difficult place.

You also may fight with your ex-spouse's mental health. Often in divorce, mental health can be a factor in why people divorce. It may be from you, your ex, or both. Your ex may have a personality disorder that you will need to deal with. Personality disorders in divorces are difficult to deal with because, typically, the lawyers and courts do not recognize them or know how to deal with them.

Lastly, it's important to talk about mental health, as men are at a higher risk for suicide. Many men fall to suicide during or after divorce, and I want to make sure you are not one of them. If you are having suicidal thoughts, get help. Don't wait. Your life is important. Don't let this crummy legal process get the better of you.

If you are depressed or having suicidal thoughts, it's important that you seek professional help. You can get free professional help in the United States 24 hours a day by calling or texting:

National suicide prevention lifeline

- 988 (The Suicide and Crisis Lifeline) or by calling 1-800-273-8255

- To chat online, visit https://suicidepreventionlifeline.org

What are you going to get out of this chapter?

In this chapter, you will get a high-level overview of some common mental health issues seen during the divorce. My goal is to arm you with the information to know when you are dealing with someone who may have a mental health issue. This chapter will also give you some of the basic terminologies that will allow you to research further if you need to.

What you're NOT going to get from this chapter?

First of all, you're not going to get a comprehensive, detailed look at each individual issue, and you certainly will not be getting a degree in mental health! Please understand that the issues discussed in this book are just overviews. This book is also not all-encompassing of mental health disorders, but I have tried to include the most common ones. There are many subsets to these issues within mental health. Mental health is complex because everyone is just a little different, so please understand this is just a surface-level look at these issues.

You may look for the answers to your own mental health struggles. While some things may sound familiar, it is not a good idea to try to self-diagnose. For that, you will need to go see a licensed therapist to help you get through some of these problems. This book is not a replacement for therapy. You will need to seek a professional therapist or counselor for professional help if you want a diagnosis. I highly recommend that after the trauma of divorce, you seek a professional therapist and stick with therapy until you've healed enough to continue the journey on your own. Even if you feel that your mental health is fine, it still is wise to seek therapy during this hard time.

What is Mental Health?

You may shudder when you think of the term "mental health." Many people who are not in the mental health field may have some negative viewpoints about therapy and mental health. Your body is more than just the muscle and bones that make up your physical body. Your mental health is just as important as your physical health. One thing is certain: if you neglect your mental health, your physical health will also decline.

What is mental health? Mental health is simply making sure that your mind is in the proper state for living the life that you want to live. Your thoughts can actually block you from living the life you want to live! Many people are crippled by anxiety or fear, and the thing that is blocking them is simply the thoughts in their heads. You have to get out of your own head sometimes, so you can move *forward*.

How does your mental health change during the divorce?

It's also important to note that your mental health will be in jeopardy during the divorce process. While getting divorced, you are under a tremendous amount of stress and you may also experience trauma. You probably will grieve the loss of your relationship, and you are learning to navigate your new life as things change. All of this combined are substantial changes for your mind to wrap itself around.

It's important that you're aware of your mental health during the divorce process. If you can get ahead of the curve and take care of your mind and get the proper help at the right time, you will be literally years ahead of yourself now as opposed to if you let things go.

Societal views of mental health

In American society, we have done ourselves a great disservice by attaching a stigma to getting help for our minds. Bookshelves are full of self-help books, but there is a certain shame that our society attaches to actually seeing a professional (i.e., a trained therapist or psychologist) for mental health help.

It's crazy to think that someone can actually be shamed for going to a therapist and wanting to get help. There are certain psychological factors that cause us to shame others when we are jealous or too ashamed to do what the other person is doing. In a weird sort of way, the other person who is shaming you is actually envious of you. You can think of this as a backward sort of compliment. That person wishes they had the guts to do what you're doing. They just have a strange way of showing it.

It's important to know that some jobs attach a disproportionately negative statement to mental health. If you are a pilot, you must be extremely careful about the mental health help you receive. Taking some medications for your mental health could limit your ability to hold that job. Make sure you do research before starting treatment. It's important that you understand the consequences and boundaries you need if you have a job that may be jeopardized by receiving mental health help. Check with professional organizations in your field to see what others have done. No matter what value popular culture assigns to getting mental health help, know that there is no shame in getting help when you need it.

I highly recommend you find a good therapist while you're going through the divorce process. As you grow, you may need to find different therapists based on what stage you are in. Some deal specifically with grief and trauma, while others are more apt to help you with growing personally and professionally as a life coach.

What are the different aspects of mental health?

If you were to ask a therapist what the parts of mental health are, they would probably have a much different answer than somebody who is not a licensed professional. The professional will tell you that mental health involves assessing, diagnosing, and treating people for mental health disorders.

You can think of mental health as a long rope. On one end of the rope (spectrum) are mentally healthy people. These are the people who are able to deal with bad situations in their life and it does not interrupt their work, relationships, and other aspects of their life. They are able to cope and move on.

Further down the rope, you have individuals who are able to function normally except when they have a disruption in life. During that disruption, their work, relationships, and other aspects of their life are temporarily interrupted by the disruption. However, once the disruption disappears, they are able to move back to their normal life as if nothing happened.

Quite some way down the rope, you have individuals who have trouble functioning normally and who also have trouble functioning when there is a disruption in their life. Disruptions may cause them to function abnormally for long periods of time. At the very end of the rope, you have individuals who cannot function in normal everyday life.

Don't be surprised if you were in the first or second category before your divorce, and during and after your divorce, you feel like you fit the third or last category. It's completely normal during the divorce process to need some extra help. When the divorce is over and you have healed, you'll likely move back up the rope.

Your feelings also live on a spectrum. Anxiety, fear, and other feelings that may hold you back also are on a spectrum from barely there to crippling you from living life. Remember that during times of heightened trauma, your feelings can be amplified. Where they were on the low end of the spectrum prior to your divorce, the trauma of divorce may amplify them to where they are more of an issue for you.

Keeping your mental health

Mental health is not all about sitting in a therapist's office. Often-times the heavy work is done away from the therapist's office. Think of your therapist as a guide, and that person is simply there to help you navigate your own thoughts (or the journey).

The different aspects can be broken down into a few pieces:

- Self-care

- Knowledge

- Self-reflection

- Self-correction

Self-care

Self-care is the term that people are often unfamiliar with when they first start on their journey to better mental health. Self-care bridges both the physical and the mental worlds. Self-care can be as simple as eating the right foods and making sure you get enough sleep. It can also be activities that you enjoy doing. An example of this would be to have a hobby and to designate a certain amount of time each week to spend on that hobby. The bottom line is if you don't take care of yourself, you will not be successful in your daily life and there's certainly no way that you can take care of your family, either.

Knowledge

Knowledge is a huge factor in having good mental health. Knowl-edge can be comforting, like knowing that others have had the same problem as you in the past. Knowledge can also be a tool to help you move past something that is holding you back. Don't be afraid to research different aspects of mental health if you are unfamiliar. If you need to know what the name of a specific topic is to research, your therapist can be very helpful here in directing you in the right direction.

There are many articles on the Internet, and not all are helpful. Many self-help articles are written by so-called "experts" who have no formal mental health training. While some of these articles are good, some of them are also bad. Be sure when you read an article that you check that the person writing it is reputable or that the site it is published on is reputable. Don't trust any articles that come from tabloid publications!

You also have to know that when researching mental health, there is a disproportionately large amount of articles written on the Internet that are focused on women. The reality of our modern-day society is that many more women than men are interested in mental health topics. The Internet has therefore adjusted to offer more articles that are focused on women than men. While some of these articles may be relevant to both sexes, there are articles on topics that are going to be specific to either males or females. The bottom line is verifying the sources and ensuring the article applies to you and/or your situation.

<u>Self-reflection</u>

A huge part of having healthy mental health is being able to self-reflect. This is something that we are often not comfortable doing when we first start. Our society has taught us never to look back and that we should always move forward. If you never look back and reflect on who you were, what you were trying to do, and how you acted - then you can never make any adjustments to become better. Self-reflecting is simply looking back at situations and thinking about how you felt during that situation, how you acted during that situation, and what you would like to be different in the future.

Self-reflection is helpful because it helps you understand who you are as a person. Understanding who you are and who you want to be are important aspects that you need to grow. Moving through the divorce process, you will certainly need to be a different person than you were before the divorce. Even if you were perfect before the divorce, the process of divorce will introduce grief and trauma, which will change how you think about things and sometimes who you are. Therefore, it's important that after the divorce process is complete, you're able to recenter yourself and build your new life.

Self-reflection is a key ingredient to moving on after divorce. It's also a key ingredient in helping you not repeat the mistakes of the past, allowing you to have a happier future. If you plan on dating after your divorce, understanding what went wrong in the previous relationship will help you have a stronger future relationship.

Self-correction

After self-reflection comes self-correction. Self-correction is understanding how you want to do things in the future. The self-reflection portion will help you understand what you did in the past, while self-correction will help you come up with a plan to ensure that you do things better in the future.

Sometimes self-correction is as simple as giving yourself a set of rules such as "If this happens, then I will do this." Other times, it's not so simple. You may need to dig deeper into how you are feeling and decide how you will act or not act when you have that same feeling in the future. Sometimes the hardest part is recognizing that feeling in the moment.

Self-correction is an important part of making sure that you don't get stuck in the past. Moving on to a better life is possible, but only if you understand what happened in the past and how you should and will act in the future.

Chapter Twelve

Trauma

The American Psychological Association defines trauma as "an emotional response to a terrible event like an accident, rape, or natural disaster. Immediately after the event, shock and denial are typical. Longer-term reactions include unpredictable emotions, flashbacks, strained relationships, and even physical symptoms like headaches or nausea. While these feelings are normal, some people have difficulty moving on with their lives." I think that's a pretty good description of what you go through in a divorce (*Trauma*, 2022). Divorce certainly is a terrible event, and you can bet it will be traumatic to you. The emotional response is how you deal with that trauma.

While the divorce may be traumatic, the thing you have to remember is that even though it may be traumatic, YOU WILL GET THROUGH IT. It may not be easy, and it may not be fast, but you need to persevere. There will be light at the end of the tunnel. On the other side of this divorce you'll be stronger, wiser, and more cautious.

Let's dive a little bit deeper into the different things that go into making an experience traumatic. Trauma can occur from a one-time event, or it can be from an ongoing stressor in your life. Typical one-time events include accidents, getting hurt, being involved in a natural disaster, or being a victim of a violent crime. Trauma can also be caused by ongoing stress, such as living in a high-stress environment or perhaps a crime-infested neighborhood, also from battling a life-threatening illness.

It's important to remember that while there are some very obvious things that will cause you trauma, there are some that are overlooked. This can include having surgery or the sudden death of a friend or loved one. Sometimes even being humiliated or deeply disappointed can cause trauma. Certainly, ending a significant relationship is a traumatic experience.

Divorces can either be amicable, high-conflict or somewhere in the middle. I think it's common in any divorce to have at least some periods during the process which are high-conflict. As the process goes on, respect and mutual feelings towards one another will undoubtedly drive how you treat one another. It's common as the process goes on that sometimes things will be good, and other times things will be much worse. The amount of stress between two parties in the process can ebb and flow, much like the waves of the ocean.

Trauma from divorce is caused by both one-time events and ongoing stress. There certainly is the one-time event of finding out you're getting divorced (if you are not the one who filed), and then there is the stress of having to find a new life - sometimes almost instantaneously. Changing everything about your life, from your friends to your financial situation, is stressful and traumatic. Uncertainty of the future adds yet another layer to your trauma.

Emotionally Painful and Distressing

Getting a divorce is certainly emotionally painful. You thought you were going to spend the rest of your life with the person that you married, and you just found out that this wasn't true. Not only are you breaking up with that person (or that person is breaking up with you), you probably have questions. Why are you not good enough?

Why did things go wrong? Are things really that bad that you had to get a divorce? You will have these questions and a million more.

When talking about car crashes or airplane crashes, it's often joked that it is not the speed that kills you; it's the sudden stop. It's the same way with getting a divorce. If you knew something was coming, then chances are you can prepare yourself mentally. Often in divorce, you will find out suddenly! It was the equivalent of driving straight into a brick wall. It's the sudden stop that got you.

Unless you have had some severely traumatic events in your life, divorce may be one of the most emotionally painful things that you need to endure. Initially, the amount of pain will be proportional to how sudden the stop is. Over the long term, the amount of pain that you endure will be proportional to how invested you were in the relationship, how much your life is changing, and how resistant you are to embrace your new life.

If you have lots of questions that are unanswered and you don't get closure, moving on with your life can be even more difficult. If you are not getting closure, get some professional help in working through the nuances of this pain.

Often in going through a divorce, trauma comes from not just the initial news that you're getting divorced. There are often allegations that you will need to defend (which may be true or false). Going through a high-conflict divorce with false allegations is extremely emotionally painful. Things get said which aren't meant, and sometimes things are said to get the upper hand in the court proceedings or simply to inflict pain on you because the other party is emotionally hurting.

Overwhelming Your Ability To Cope

Divorce can certainly overwhelm your ability to cope quite quickly. For the All-American dad and man who is put together, a divorce will throw your life into a tailspin unlike anything you have experienced in your life. It's common (especially in the beginning stages) not to know what to do or where to turn. Oftentimes, this can lead to a state where you do nothing or don't *feel* you can do anything. At this point in your life, not doing anything is probably the worst thing you can do. While there certainly are a lot of things you can do to hurt your situation, not doing anything is probably the worst thing you can do.

It's important when you start feeling overwhelmed that you ask for help. There are resources out there for you whether it's your family, friends, coworkers, support groups, or social groups. Don't forget; you can also lean on your faith in any sort of religious ties you may have. The important thing here is that you get the help you need when you need it.

If you are overwhelmed, figure out how to get un-overwhelmed. Often that means just taking small steps. You're essentially trying to eat an entire elephant here with this divorce problem. You can't swallow an elephant in a single bite. Remember, you have to eat it in small chunks. Animal rights disclosure - of course, swallowing an elephant is a metaphor. I certainly wouldn't advise eating a real elephant!

Leaving You Powerless

A divorce will take many things from you. One thing it will take from you is your ability to feel you are in control. It can often leave you feeling quite the opposite like you are not in control of anything. This may be the first time in your life where you feel like life is controlling you instead of you being in control of your life. And in some ways giving up that control is part of moving on.

It's important that you ensure that your identity is not tied up in your ability to control your life. Life will throw you curveballs, and it's essential that you are able to be flexible and understand that sometimes life is going to take you places that you didn't intend.

Learning to go with the flow can be an essential part of getting through the divorce in a sane manner.

Even when you *think* you are completely powerless, you are not *really* powerless. If you sit down and think of the things that you actually have control over, you realize you have control over more than you feel you have control over. Write these things down on paper if you need to. You need to worry about the things that you can control. You also need to think about the things which you cannot control. You need to resolve to not worry about these things. It's essential to understand which things you can control and which things you cannot.

Trauma and Divorce

It's important that you don't let the divorce trauma control you. Sometimes, this will be the most difficult thing you have to do. As the old G.I. Joe saying goes, "Knowledge is half the battle." The reason I talk about trauma early in this book is that it's important for you to recognize that you are experiencing trauma. It's that recognition that will help you fight the battle. It's important that you don't let trauma control you. If you succumb to it, it will certainly take over your life, depression will set in, and you won't feel like doing anything.

It's perfectly normal to have short periods where you become overwhelmed and cannot function. It's not normal for these periods to become long in duration. I would say if you're having trouble functioning for more than a week, then you should probably find some professional help.

The problem is: if you can't function during divorce, then the process will be longer, more expensive, and more traumatic (for you and your kids) than it has to be. It's almost important that you learn to "hyper-function" during the divorce. You will be expected to make decisions that will affect you for the rest of your life. How you act when dealing with your ex will certainly influence how much it will cost you and how long the divorce will take.

So, if you feel like you are not functioning at all, then get help. If you're functioning but not very well, then I would also recommend that you get some therapeutic help. A little therapy can go a long way in the beginning. You don't have to go to therapy for the rest of your life.

Don't let trauma define you. You can experience trauma and decide how you react to it. Experience it, deal with it and move on. Your experiences shape who you are, but you also get to decide who you are. Just because you had a traumatic experience doesn't mean it needs to hold you down for the rest of your life.

Chapter Thirteen

Grief

W hy grief? The simple fact is that when you experience unexpected or unwanted change, your mind's natural response is grief. Grief is the natural or normal reaction to loss. Your mind goes through this with both big changes and small changes. Is your favorite coffee shop no longer carrying your favorite coffee? That's a change, and it will cause grief. Getting a divorce? That certainly will cause some grief. No matter what the change is, your brain still goes through the same grief response cycle.

It's important to note when going through a divorce, do not suppress your feelings or be "manly" about them. In order for you to get through the process of divorce and move on from life, it's important that you get *through* these feelings. Understand what went wrong and what part you had in the downfall in order to have successful relationships in the future. It's easy as a man to want to suppress your feelings or to plow through the divorce process. That isn't healthy.

Grief is a confusing emotion. It's actually not just a single emotion but the combination of many emotions. Sometimes those emotions can manifest themselves as other symptoms. You may feel depressed, your appetite may be off, and you may look at things entirely differently than you used to. Once you understand why you're doing the things you're doing or why you're feeling the way you are feeling, you can get some help. Getting help is a big part of getting through a divorce. No one has to walk the journey alone. Find a good therapist and start going to them regularly.

For some men, going through a divorce will be the first time that they really have to confront strong emotional feelings for long periods of time. You may have never cared before how your mind reacts to change. Since you're going to be dealing with a lot of emotions, it's good to talk about grief so you can identify it and know that it's a very natural thing.

So what is grief? A website called The Grief Recovery Method (*The Grief Recovery Method—Home,* 2022) defines grief as "conflicting feelings caused by the end of or change in a familiar pattern of behavior." We can find a simpler definition on Wikipedia (Grief, 2022) that simply states that "grief is a natural response to loss."

It's important for you to realize that grief is natural. While grief normally comes up in the conversation about losing a loved one or friend, it's important that you recognize that divorce really is a loss. It's a substantial change to your life, and in a lot of ways, your significant other "died." While they may not have died physically, there was a loss of the hopes and dreams you had for your future together.

You may have heard that there are five stages of grief. Those are denial, anger, bargaining, depression, and acceptance. It is said that the five stages of grief are universal and experienced by people from all walks of life in many cultures.

Not everybody experiences grief and some people experience grief but do not understand it. There is some psychological research that claims there are no stages of grief. For the purposes of our discussions here, I find the five stages of grief an easy way to categorize some of the feelings you may have while grieving. For that reason, I'll be using these categories to explain some feelings you may have during grief.

It's important to recognize that you may not experience grief the same way that your friend or someone in your family does. In fact, there's a pretty good chance that nobody else experiences grief exactly the way that you do. While we can outline the five stages of grief, it is very hard to say how you will traverse them. You will probably not even experience them in the same order. Some stages may be more intense than others. You may experience a certain stage more than once. You may experience some stages and move on and then regress back and re-experience previous stages. One thing is certain: your experience with grief will be unique.

There are a few factors that will weigh in on how you experience grief. One of those factors is how much loss you have encountered in your life to this point. If this is the first time you're having to grieve, it will be much different from someone who has traveled this road many times before.

One thing that can be helpful is to recognize that you are going through the grief process. Remember, knowledge is half the battle! If you can understand that you're having conflicting emotional feelings because you're going through the grieving process, it will help you through that process. Grief can manifest itself in many forms. While grief is typically an emotional response, it's important to note that your body may physically react to being in the grieving process as well.

Denial

This is a stage where you tell yourself it's not really happening. Many times this is the first stage that people experience. You tell yourself that "This is just a bad dream, and I'm going to wake up soon." We all know somebody that has been in denial about something. We may have even realized that we are in denial about something. It's like when people say that somebody has to "wake up" about something. Denial is a pesky feeling that our brains use to put off facing reality.

Anger

During the anger stage, you can be extremely upset. You may not know where the anger is even coming from, especially if you are someone who is not typically angry. You may have good reason to be angry at your ex and your relationship. Being angry isn't necessarily a bad thing. Sometimes it's good just to get your anger out. Just don't take it out on someone else!

It's important that you are not angry in front of your ex or your children. You must be cognizant not to take your anger out on your friends or family in either verbal or physical ways. It's helpful to find a healthy way to deal with your anger. Everyone will be a little different, so you will need to find what works for you. Beyond getting your anger out physically (like hitting a pillow or yelling in an empty room), therapy can really help here.

Bargaining

This is a stage where you're calling your ex and telling her, "I'll change if you'll just stay," or you go buy gifts for her. You try to negotiate your way back into your old life and out of your grief. The problem with this stage is negotiations almost never work. This stage is futile, and it's best if you can move through this stage fast. I recommend not "involving" your ex in the bargaining. This will only make things more difficult for you and let them know they have the upper hand in negotiations.

Depression

This is a stage where you feel you just can't do anything right. You feel like the world will never be the same again. You feel sad and may be overwhelmed and unable to cope with normal everyday life activities. During the depression stage, going to work can be extremely difficult. Oftentimes, your performance at work will go down significantly. You may not want to hang out with friends, go to activities or be social at all. Depression is something that can overwhelm you easily. This is one of those stages where it's easy to go back and visit several times over. I'll talk more about depression in the next chapter because it's important you know how to deal with it.

<u>Acceptance</u>

This is usually the last stage. You finally have come to terms with the fact that your life differs from what it was before. You come to terms with the fact that you will not go back to how life was. When you reach this stage, you can move on and start living your new life. In this stage, you may feel like a weight is lifted from your shoulders.

No matter what your journey is with grief, make sure that you recognize it and work through it. Suppressing your grief is toxic. I know I keep saying this, but a licensed therapist can really help you on your grief journey.

Chapter Fourteen

Depression

What's bad about depression?

Several things are an indicator that you're depressed. You may treat your loved ones differently. Your energy levels can be decreased. You're not excited to do things with friends or family. Your thoughts are negative. Depression will take away your joy in life. It's a cloudy, gray overcast sky on a blue sunny day. While everybody else can see the sunshine, you can't see past the clouds (even if you're the only one who sees them). Depression can also cause you to drift through life, not really caring about where you go or what you're going to do.

Depression can cause you not to care. You become indifferent. While this sounds like a good thing at first, being indifferent will cause you problems. As a responsible adult, you must care about things! Depression can erode away your ability to be engaged.

Depression can also lead to self-destructive habits and behavior. People who are depressed are more likely to engage in promiscuous sexual behavior, make bad financial decisions, and are also more prone to become addicted to substances such as alcohol and drugs. There are lots of bad things about depression.

What is Depression?

Before we can talk about how depression affects dads, it's important that we talk about what depression is. Depression is categorized into minor, moderate, and major depression. The American Psychiatric Association (APA) (*Depression,* 2022) classifies major depression as a "common and serious medical illness that negatively affects how you feel, and the way you think and how you act." The APA notes that depression can affect anyone, "even a person who appears to live in relatively ideal circumstances." They also say that one in six people, or 16.6% of the population, will experience depression at some point in their life. Depression is a common thing! It is not uncommon to be mildly or moderately depressed.

What are the symptoms of depression? The APA says that symptoms must last for at least two weeks to form a "diagnosis" of depression. Those symptoms can include:

- Feeling sad or having a depressed mood.

- Loss of interest or pleasure in activities that you once enjoyed.

- Changes in appetite and weight loss or weight gain unrelated to dieting.

- Trouble sleeping or sleeping too much.

- Loss of energy or increased fatigue.

- Increased purposeful physical activity (i.e., hand-wringing, pacing, slowed movements), and these are actions that are observable by others.

- Feeling worthless or guilty.

- Difficulty thinking, concentrating or deciding.

- Thoughts of death or suicide (Get immediate help if you have these thoughts).

The APA states that "certain medical conditions can often be confused with symptoms of depression. Things such as brain tumors or vitamin deficiencies can mimic symptoms of depression, so it is important to rule out a general medical cause".

The APA also notes that depression is different from sadness or grief. They say that being sad is not the same thing as being depressed. Both grief and depression may involve intense sadness and withdrawal from usual activities. In grief, painful feelings come and go. With depression, mood and or interests are decreased for more than two weeks. In grief, self-esteem is usually maintained. In depression, feelings of worthlessness and self-loathing are common. When grief and depression coexist, the grief is more severe, and it lasts longer than grief without depression. Despite some overlap between grief and depression, they are different.

Risk Factors

There are four primary risk factors for depression. They are biochemistry, genetics, personality, and environmental factors. In regards to biochemistry, the difference in certain chemicals in the brain may contribute to symptoms of depression. With genetic risk factors, this means depression can run in families. With personality risk factors, depression is typically seen in people who have low self-esteem or are easily overwhelmed by stress. Additionally, individuals who are pessimistic are more likely to experience depression. For environmental risk factors, continuous exposure to violence, neglect, abuse or poverty may make some people depressed.

Depression As A Dad

Of the four primary risk factors for depression, the first three are related to who you are genetically and your chemistry. Those are

biochemistry, genetics, and personality. The last one is environmental factors, and it has the most bearing on you specifically as a
father. While you may be predisposed to depression because of your
biochemistry, genetics or personality (or the combination thereof),
being a dad can expose you to environmental factors which will put
you at risk for depression.

Depression can affect everything that we do. When you're a dad,
you can feel overwhelmed, especially if you are a single dad. It's
amplified even more if you are involved in any legal battle with
your ex-wife! It can cloud our mindset of how we see the world, our
family, and our friends. Depression can be debilitating.

Some environmental factors to watch out for as a dad:

- work stress

- home stress or family life stress

- arguing and conflict with your spouse/ex-spouse

- arguing and conflict with your children or your children arguing with you each other

- financial issues or arguing about financial issues

- the pressure to provide (providing money, a place to live and
  food for your family)

- being involved in a legal fight

- being unsure of what to do as a father

With any of these above factors, you should be on the lookout for
depression. Remember, depression is only diagnosable when you
have the symptoms for over two weeks. It's perfectly reasonable

for people to feel a bit sad about certain life situations for a short period. It's when symptoms exist for prolonged periods of time that it becomes depression. If you're going through one of the above things, don't be afraid to reach out and ask for some help.

Divorce is another aspect of dad life that can often lead to depression. It is no secret that fathers end up getting the short end of the stick (most of the time) in family court. They often are overburdened financially compared to the mother and treated as if they have to prove themselves as a good father rather than coming into court on equal footing with the mother. Just because you're getting divorced doesn't mean you need to stay depressed.

You'll probably go through some periods where you are a little sad or even somewhat depressed, but if you remain depressed, then you will need to ensure that you get help. The suicide rates for divorced fathers are many times that of the average person, so please for your health and because your children need you - take care of depression before it leads to suicide!

When you become a father, there is less time for yourself, as most of your free time is now devoted to your family. That lack of time for yourself can often lead fathers to feel depressed. They can feel like they are doing everything for their family and their family takes up all of their time. It can be very stressful and depressing to know that every second of every day is dedicated to your family with no time for yourself. Make sure you make time for yourself while also making time for the family.

Another challenge that dads face is work pressure. It's hard when you work a stressful full-time job and then come home to deal with additional family pressures. The combination of these two can often be overwhelming.

Relationship pressures can be especially difficult on men. Men generally have less of a support system built up from family and friends. This means that men have fewer people to turn to when things are rough, which may make them feel isolated. Relationship pressures can be your romantic relationships or relationships with your kids or other family members.

It's essential that dads realize what depression is so that we can recognize and correct it. With a bit of help and the right mindset, you can overcome depression. To overcome depression, you have to own it first. Then you can recognize that you're depressed and want to do something about it. Lots of people have fought depression and won. And you can, too!

How do you treat depression?

There are two primary ways professionals will treat depression. They are medication and therapy. The two are not mutually exclusive. However, typically if you are on medication for depression, it will also be combined with a therapy regimen. You can also be in therapy without being on medication. There are also things that you can do to help yourself. These include exercise, practicing gratitude, and practicing re-framing (how you think about a situation).

If you are moderately or severely depressed, you will need to use a licensed therapist to help you through this tough time. A therapist can help you identify the things you can (like maybe *why* you are depressed) and help you come up with solutions where you will no longer be depressed.

A word of note here on therapists: A psychologist is someone who does talk therapy, but they cannot prescribe medications. Most family therapists are psychologists. A psychiatrist can prescribe medications and treats more complex mental health disorders such as schizophrenia, bipolar disorder, and severe depression. You'll generally be good at seeing a psychologist unless your issues are more severe. A psychologist may refer you to a psychiatrist. It's also common practice to see a psychologist, and if you need medicine, your family doctor can prescribe it.

Therapy

People are often reluctant to go to therapy because it signals defeat. As dads and men, we have a strong need to solve problems on our own. When it comes to depression and dealing with high-stress situations, you should not feel that going to a therapist is a loss! You should be open to this help as it will help you recover much quicker than if you are to do things on your own. A good therapist can help you avoid prolonging these issues and help you get back to your regularly scheduled life much faster. Remember, "People in therapy are often in therapy to deal with the people in their lives who won't go to therapy"- *The Empowered Therapist,* The Minds Journal (People In Therapy Are Often In Therapy, 2019).

There are two primary types of therapy used to treat depression. The first is talk therapy, and the second is cognitive behavioral therapy (CBT). Talk therapy is just like what you think it is; you find a therapist and talk about your issues. Talk therapy is commonly done either as an individual, with the family or as couples counseling. The APA says you can usually expect to see improvement in as little as 10 to 15 sessions.

Cognitive Behavioral Therapy (CBT) can happen during talk therapy, and it has been shown to be very effective in treating depression. In CBT, the therapy is focused on the present and problem-solving. The therapist will help the person to recognize the distorted thinking and help change their behaviors and thinking. It's important when you're choosing a therapist to ask what kind of therapies they are experienced with.

Medication

Medication is used for moderate-to-severe depression and is usually combined with therapy. It's important to state that antidepressants are not stimulants and are not uppers. If you take depression medication, you will usually see results within 2 to 3 months. Some patients may see an immediate positive benefit. However, this is often a placebo effect that is not caused by the medicine. You may feel that you are doing better, but the medications have not taken effect yet.

There can be side effects to depression medication. These medications will affect everyone differently. Some will gain or lose their appetite. You may also experience erectile dysfunction. If you do have erectile dysfunction, your doctor can give you Viagra or a generic to counteract this side effect. Be sure to ask your doctor about common side effects before taking a medication.

It's important that you continue to take these medications until the things that cause you to get depressed have subsided. Doctors typically want you to take your depression medications for at least six months after your symptoms are gone. It's important that your life situation be changed and stable before coming off the help of the medication. Do not abruptly stop taking them on your own! Consult your doctor/prescriber about how and when to wean yourself off these medications.

It's important to check with your doctor and do research to see how taking depression medicine may affect you and your job. Depression medications may prevent you from doing certain jobs. For instance, if you're a pilot, then taking some antidepressants may prevent you from flying. Don't take these medicines lightly and make sure you do your research before starting any medication!

Exercise

An excellent way to combat depression is through physical activity and exercise. Not only is exercise good for your health (as it may slim you down a few pounds), but exercise also releases certain chemicals in the brain called endorphins which help you naturally fight depression. "Research has shown that exercise is an effective but often underused treatment for mild to moderate depression. In addition, exercise outside (with the appropriate sun protection) can help boost levels of vitamin D and mood." (Bruce, 2022). So if you don't like taking medicine, exercise is your next best alternative.

<u>Gratitude and Attitude</u>

The next two things are gratitude and attitude. Gratitude is simply being thankful for things. It's important that you practice gratitude and be thankful for what you have right now to overcome depression. The way you practice gratitude is by saying what you are grateful for out loud or by writing it down. You can write it in a notebook or post it on a sticky note on the wall. It can be things as basic as the clothes you own, the meal you just ate, or a roof over your head (even if it is just temporary). If you practice gratitude regularly, it will become much easier. It can seem a little silly at first to verbally and openly be thankful for things, but with practice, it will come naturally.

Your attitude will also affect how depressed you are. If you have the attitude that things will never get better, then they won't. If you have the attitude that you're going to get through this and things will get better, then they likely will. At least with a more positive attitude, you will have a much better chance of getting through things and being happy!

Remember, depression may be caused by either genetics or by your circumstances (environment). Remember, depression does not have to be permanent. You don't have to go at it alone. A professional therapist can help you through it. Dads often get depressed over things that are stressful in their lives and things that they wish that they could do better or things that they don't have control over. Remember that there are several ways to fight depression, including knowledge, therapy, medicine, exercise, practicing gratitude, and having a positive attitude!

Chapter Fifteen

PTSD

You may have heard the term PTSD (or Post-Traumatic Stress Disorder) in the media. It's often associated with veterans returning from war. Divorce can often simulate some of the same stresses that can trigger PTSD. In many ways, divorce is a war. While hopefully there are no bullets flying, divorce puts you under a ton of stress for a prolonged period. PTSD is a complication of trauma.

The National Institute of Mental Health defines PTSD as "a disorder that develops in some people who have experienced a shocking, scary, or a dangerous event" (*Post-Traumatic Stress Disorder,* 2022). The site clarifies that people who have PTSD may feel stressed or frightened even when they are not in danger. Some people who experience trauma will develop ongoing (chronic) or short-term (acute) PTSD.

The difference between experiencing trauma and developing PTSD is your ongoing response to that trauma. If you're able to move on from the trauma and recover, then you have not developed ongoing PTSD or experienced short-term PTSD. If you become stuck, then you may be diagnosed with PTSD.

The US Department of Veterans Affairs explains the symptoms of PTSD as:

1) Reliving the event (also called re-experiencing symptoms). This can include bad memories or nightmares and is sometimes called a flashback.

2) Avoiding situations that remind you of the event - this includes not wanting to talk about the event or avoiding places that remind you of the event. Some of this is completely normal. Your ability to cope with situations that remind you of the event is what differentiates this as a PTSD symptom.

3) Having more negative beliefs and feelings - sometimes trauma can change the way you think about yourself and others. If you are a mostly positive person before the event and become a mostly negative person after the event, this can mean trouble. You may feel that you can't trust anyone. You also may feel that it's hard to be happy.

4) Feeling keyed up (also called hyperarousal) - with this symptom, you are always checking your six (looking behind you). You are constantly on the lookout for danger. You may also have trouble concentrating and sleeping. You may also be angry and irritable or startle easily (jumpy). You could start acting in unhealthy ways to cope (smoking, alcohol, drugs, and even driving recklessly).

One thing to be aware of is that it's easy to misdiagnose yourself with one or more of these conditions. You cannot diagnose yourself! *Only a qualified mental health professional can.* As humans, we are just not good at being subjective enough with our own behaviors. While it's important to be well-informed and to do your own research, it takes the help of a professional to know when you truly have one of these conditions.

If you do have PTSD, then the best thing to do is to seek treatment. With some help, you will live a much better life. You can see a therapist and maybe join a support group. With help, you will learn what triggers you and what to do when you are triggered. You may even find that you have a passion for helping others with the condition. Giving back can be some of the best forms of therapy.

Chapter Sixteen

Personality Disorders

I f you are involved in a high-conflict divorce, then chances are, one or both of the people involved have a personality disorder. Personality-disordered people will throw you for a loop because they can seem normal most of the time. People who are personality disordered also tend to seek people that they can manipulate. If you're a people pleaser, you're at high risk for being in a relationship with someone who has a personality disorder! Catering to their needs will feel good to you (at least in the beginning). When the relationship gets out of hand, you'll ask yourself, what the hell went wrong?

Disclaimer: This chapter is written with no offense towards people who are suffering from a personality disorder. You can get help. You can go to therapy to deal with the issues you have/create in your relationships and the hurt you cause others. This chapter is to help people who are suffering from the wrath that people with personality disorders relinquish upon others when they refuse to acknowledge that they have a problem and refuse to seek mental health therapy (with a certified therapist for the number of continuous years it takes) to help treat or control a personality disorder.

The APA (American Psychological Association) defines a personality disorder in the DSM-5 (Diagnostic and Statistical Manual of the American Psychiatric Association, Fifth Edition or latest) (American

Psychiatric Association, 2022). This book is the standard in diagnosing psychological disorders in the United States. It defines a
personality disorder as "an enduring pattern of inner experience
and behavior that deviates markedly from the expectations of the
individual's culture, is pervasive and inflexible, has an onset in adolescence or early adulthood, is stable over time, and leads to distress
or impairment (DSM-5, P.645)".

While the APA definition is the one that the doctors, psychologists,
psychiatrists, lawyers, and judges use - it may not make much sense
to you. We can pull it apart and make it easier to understand. Simply put, someone's behavior has to become a pattern. A pattern is
something that happens repeatedly. That pattern of behavior has
to be counter to their culture. Prior definitions did not include this
qualifier, and so what is normal in one culture may be abnormal
in another. The next part of "being pervasive and inflexible" is important. If the behavior is pointed out and the person corrects it,
then they are not disordered. People with personality disorders are
inflexible (and that is key!), especially for cluster B types (more on
that later). The final qualifiers are that the behavior has to be stable
over time (otherwise translated to unstable behavior for years on
end), and it must lead to distress or impairment. The definition
notes that the disorder is typically developed in adolescence or
early adulthood. This is a critical time in one's development when
the brain is still developing and determining how it will function.

So there we have it! If someone has a pattern of behavior that
causes havoc to those around them and they are stubborn and inflexible, then they may be personality disordered. It's worth noting
here that people tend to act one way normally and another when
under duress (like when going through a divorce). It's entirely possible for two people without personality disorders to act completely
bonkers toward each other initially when going through a divorce.

For someone to truly be diagnosed as personality disordered, they need to have the behavior prior to the "trauma" as well. To make matters more complicated, some that are disordered (but high functioning) will seem normal most of the time but when they start going through a divorce, they act completely bonkers. The bottom line is it takes someone with the right credentials to truly diagnose someone with a personality disorder!

It is also worth noting that these things exist on a spectrum. Someone can be mildly disordered, mediumly disordered, or highly disordered. Professionals may classify the disorder spectrum differently, but the basic concept is that someone can be disordered a little bit of the time, all the way to highly disordered all of the time, and everywhere in between. Just keep that in mind when trying to understand someone's behavior.

Personality disorders are grouped into three clusters; A, B, and C. Cluster A includes those that are paranoid or those that have eclectic or odd behaviors. Cluster B includes those that are Antisocial, Borderline, Histrionic, or Narcissistic. Cluster C are those with Avoidant, Dependent, or Compulsive disorders.

In the context of divorce, it's the Cluster B personality disorders that will usually cause the most problems and that's what we will look at in this chapter. If you need information on a disorder in Cluster A or C, you will need to do some research on your own. Even in this chapter, I will barely touch the tip of the iceberg on Cluster B disorders, so chances are you will need to dig deeper here, too.

Normal Pathology

It's important to take a moment here to talk about normal pathology. It's human for someone to show emotion. Moments of anger, frustration and other conflicts are part of the human experience. Reacting to things in life is human. That's perfectly normal. It's important to note that it takes a lot of experience to diagnose someone with a personality disorder, so don't read the rest of this chapter and go off trying to diagnose yourself or your friends and family (or your ex!).

<u>Personality Disorder Origins and Notes</u>

Personality disorders often develop in childhood or early adulthood, but the disorders can also be repressed and show up later in life. Oftentimes personality disorders run in families. People with personality disorders typically surround themselves with people that do not question their way of thinking because this would damage their frail ego. While genetics and family life play a role, some people develop these disorders as a product of their environment.

It is important to note that depending on the specific disorder, someone does not need to have ALL the symptoms of a disorder to be diagnosed. People can also exhibit multiple parts of a few or several disorders at the same time. You also have to remember that these things are not black and white rather, they exist on a spectrum as discussed earlier. Even non-disordered people can exhibit traits of a personality disorder, but that doesn't mean they are disordered. Take narcissism as an example. A bit of narcissism is healthy. Having none will mean someone has no confidence at all! Some narcissism is normal and needed to prosper in life. It's the excessive amounts that are unhealthy—everything in moderation.

<u>Beware Cluster B</u>

People with cluster B personality disorders are often at the center of high-conflict divorces. You're much less likely to be in a high-conflict divorce with a cluster A or C individual, which is why those disorders won't be covered in this book. If your divorce seems wildly insane, the fighting has dragged on, things seem to be getting harder instead of easier, and/or you find yourself feeling as if "you're damned if you, and damned if don't," then you are more than likely in a high-conflict divorce, and it's probably with someone in the cluster B group. You may want to do more research on these if you're involved with one. Knowing more about these disorders will most likely help you in dealing with your ex-spouse.

If you want to know what it takes for someone to be diagnosed with one of these personality disorders, you can read these in the American Psychiatric Association's Diagnostic and Statistical Manual of Mental Disorders (DSM-5) (American Psychiatric Association, (2022). This book lists the diagnostic criteria along with the features, prevalence, development, risk, and prognostic factors. It also discusses some differences in culture and gender differences.

You can find a lot of information on the Internet about these disorders. Some of it is helpful, while some are not. The DSM is the one book that all therapists and psychologists are supposed to use when evaluating these disorders. You should also know that as our knowledge of these disorders has increased, the DSM has been updated accordingly. There are significant differences between the DSM-IV and the DSM-5. Be sure that you are looking at the latest information if you're looking at something online.

Here are some helpful definitions:

Antisocial - Someone who is Antisocial disordered will typically be aggressive, irresponsible, impulsive, and have been in trouble with the law. They don't mind stealing, lying and manipulating others. They won't have regard for others' feelings or needs. Men are typically diagnosed with Antisocial Personality Disorder over women at a 3:1 ratio (Compton et al., 2005).

Narcissistic - A classic trait of a narcissist is that they believe they are "special." Their needs and feelings come before yours, and anyone else's for that matter, including sometimes their own children. They know better than everyone else. To top it off, they often see themselves as more important and more successful than they really are! But be careful. Not all narcissists are overt like this. Some are much more subtle, and they are called covert narcissists. Both types will often exaggerate their accomplishments and achievements. They need constant praise and admiration because their egos are inflated like a thin balloon that will burst without it. They can also be jealous anytime something good happens to someone else.

You may think from reading this that the narc (narcissistic person) is secure and has high self-esteem. Not true and in fact, quite the opposite. The narc has low self-esteem and low self-worth. It is this low self-esteem that leads them to overcompensate, thus bringing on narcissistic traits. While studies show that more men (7.7%) than women (4.8%) are formally diagnosed with Narcissistic Personality Disorder (Stinson et al., 2008), I believe the pathology behind this Cluster B disorder prevents most narcissists from ever seeking formal mental health help. It's impossible to know the real percentage because most never seek treatment.

Histrionic - I think the best way to describe someone with a histrionic personality disorder is to think of your fame-seeking YouTube star. These folks want to be in the limelight. They want thousands and millions of followers. They HAVE to be the center of attention and are uncomfortable when they are not. They may seem "dramatic" as they over-exaggerate their expressions. They can be overtly sexual, using their body to bring attention to themselves. Cross a woman going clubbing in a short dress with a YouTube channel, and you get the hint. This type is not exclusive to women, though; that is just an example. It's important to note that these people can be impressionable and easily persuaded. They also can think that relationships are more intimate than they really are - your classic case of moving too fast.

Borderline - While certainly the most talked-about of the personality disorders, Borderline Personality Disorder (BPD) seems to get all the attention on the Internet when someone is talking about a difficult to divorce ex. For someone to be diagnosed as borderline, they need to meet a specific set of criteria. They can be impulsive and like risky behavior such as gambling, unsafe sex, or binge eating. They also have a frail self-image and their relationships can be unstable and often intense. They have an intense fear of being alone and usually have feelings of emptiness. They can have bouts of anger and stress-related paranoia. Last, they sometimes exhibit suicidal behavior or threaten self-injury.

People with Borderline Personality Disorder tend to be highly manipulative, always the victim, poor me's. Because borderlines tend to have a fear of "abandonment," they usually think that other people are either "with them or against them!". This makes them extremely high-conflict exes to deal with because while narcissists may leave you alone for the most part after the divorce is finalized (especially if they got the car, the house, the money), Borderline's will continue to seek out ways to destroy you years or even decades after a divorce, even if the divorce was their idea in the first place! Their weapon of choice is usually the couple's shared children and they tend to go to extremes to destroy the relationship you have with your kid(s). They see "their" children as extensions of themselves and typically cannot tolerate "their" kid(s) thinking highly of someone they hate (especially you, biological father to the kids or not).

Women with Borderline Personality Disorder are most likely to prioritize purposeful Parental Alienation against you and anyone they see to be "on your team." What this means is the mother of your children does things to purposely harm your relationship with your kid(s). For example, you told your kid you couldn't make his/her game that night because of an important work meeting but that you would call them before bed to hear all about it. Your kid was OK with this and totally understood. The Borderline ex will drill into the kid that you didn't prioritize them, and work is more important than them, etc. AND then prevent you from communicating with them. She'll use your phone call that "never came" as further proof that you don't care about your child. Borderlines typically do not care what damage is done to the child as long as it makes you look bad. If you fear you may be experiencing Parental Alienation by your ex, I urge you to seek immediate help from an experienced Licensed Clinical Social Worker or other family therapist that would be willing to participate in custody court as well as an experienced attorney.

If you've read some of the things in the Cluster B description and feel like you can relate these patterns of behavior to someone you know, then chances are you've been dealing with someone who is undiagnosed and hasn't been getting help for their condition. Rarely do these cluster B folks recognize that they have the problem (their behavior is normal to them), and when family or friends ask them to get help, they typically deny that they have an issue. "It's everyone else's fault." Sound familiar?

Dealing with personality disorders is not fun and it can drive you nuts, too. Be careful with thinking that you can change someone, especially when they have no desire to change. If you find yourself in conflict with someone who is personality disordered, then try and have some healthy boundaries to try and maintain your sanity. Oftentimes, we humans get involved with people with personality disorders because we lack healthy boundaries due to our upbringing or because we are naturally empathetic people. Good people often think that they can "kill 'em with kindness". Beware, your kindness will be extorted and manipulated by personality-disordered people and they are simply finding your weaknesses like an animal testing for dead spots in an electric fence. Boundaries is something that can be learned and would be your first step in dealing with a disordered person. It is also very important that you learn boundaries so that you can teach your children to have healthy boundaries if their other parent is disordered.

The second way to help your kids would be to document everything. This is where online communication programs like Our Family Wizard and TalkingParents or FAYR help. It's also a good idea to keep a separate personal log or journal. Keep photos where you can. Document any evidence that you think will show this person's behavior. It's in your best interest to document anything your children tell you, things you hear from other adults that your ex has said or done, that text message that says the parent-teacher conference is at 6 pm when really it was at 5 pm but SHE was there on time and you missed it. If the ex seems overly irritated/aggressive when you go to your child's sports game or doctor's appointment, document that as well (because they are training the kids to not want you there) and if necessary, go for full custody of the kids with the help of a good lawyer.

It's also important to note to be very careful when having a conflict with someone that has a Cluster B personality disorder. These people believe that they are special and that they are superior to you - at least their needs and feelings are superior to your needs and feelings. They are very good at manipulating people and situations. They can easily make you look like YOU are the "crazy" one. There is no doubt that dealing with a Cluster B individual in a divorce can make you ask yourself if you are crazy!

The best advice I can give you when divorcing a cluster B individual is to find yourself a therapist that has experience helping people dealing with personality disorders and be prepared for a long journey of healing and recovery. It takes a lot of therapy after divorcing someone who has a personality disorder for you to feel normal again. Not only do you have to heal the trauma of divorce, but you also have to deal with the additional trauma and conflict that the disordered person is sure to inject.

Chapter Seventeen

Suicide

G oing through a divorce is hard, even if nothing is contested and the split is amicable. With the added stress and uncertainty, going through the process puts you at risk of committing suicide, even if you've never given it a single thought before. Add the stress, depression, and anxiety that divorce causes and you have a deadly recipe. Research has shown that divorce is among the top reasons men commit suicide. Some studies placed divorced or divorcing men as 40 percent more likely to commit suicide than married men.

Simply put - if you are going through a divorce, you need to be mindful that you're at an increased risk of committing suicide. Nothing could be worse for your kids, family, and friends. Suicide causes pain for multiple generations and leaves lasting trauma to the survivors. By being aware that you are at an increased risk of suicide, you can take some steps to help make sure that you don't slip down that path.

Both the male and female suicide rates increased between 2000 and 2016. The male rates increased in all age ranges from 15 years old to 74 years old, with the only decrease being in those ages 75 and older (*CDC*, June 2018).

Suicide is common enough that most people know someone who has committed suicide. It may have been a friend or someone they knew through work. Maybe it was someone down the block. It's real, it's here, and it's also preventable.

People commit suicide when they believe they've reached a wall and there is nowhere to go. It's a way to freedom of sorts. Many reasons could cause someone to feel that way. They could have battled depression. Sometimes it's an incurable disease. It could be a financial barrier. It could also be loneliness. Stress is usually a factor.

Going through divorce puts you in a lot of these risk categories. The best way to ensure that you don't become a casualty of this epidemic is to make sure that you are aware of the risks and that you have the support you need and a plan in case you have suicidal thoughts.

There are some common ways that people commit suicide. The CDC has four categories in its statistics. Those are firearms, poisoning, suffocating, and "other". Firearm deaths account for just over half of those deaths. Suffocation followed with around 30% of the deaths. Poisoning and "other" made up the remainder.

A Special Word on Firearms

With firearm deaths being about half, it's something that must be considered if you own firearms. Owning a firearm means you have a duty to be a responsible firearm owner. Just like you wouldn't leave a loaded gun out with little kids in the house, you need to take special precautions when going through a divorce and owning a firearm.

If you have firearms, I urge you to get them out of your house. You don't have to sell them or give up firearm ownership. Give them to a friend or a close family member for safekeeping. If you don't have any good options with friends or family members, you could ask your lawyer to hold them. Get your firearms in a place where someone else will need to give you access. Simply having them locked up, even at a different location from your house isn't enough. When the divorce is settled and you feel like you're in a good place, you can take them back.

Another important reason for getting firearms out of your house is to remove the possibility that they could be used against you. Having access to a firearm could be used against you in court, claiming you are a threat.

Some states have even enacted "red flag" laws that allow the authorities to come and take your firearms. These new laws are often hastily enacted and they do not have the proper due process. Most of all, they are against your constitutional rights, but they are enforced anyway. In many cases, someone just needs to make a claim and this is enough to allow the police to intervene. This is a handy way to get the upper hand in a divorce. Getting your firearms back once they are seized may be problematic. In addition, having any kind of police contact will be detrimental to your divorce case.

In short - get firearms out of your house until the divorce is over and you've established your new life AND you are not in conflict with your old life. If you are required to have a firearm on a daily basis for your job, it's best to consult your attorney or ask your supervisor what the best course of action is.

While I've been talking specifically about firearms, the same goes for any other kind of weapon. Bow and arrow, crossbow, and knives could all be used against you in the court case. Simply owning and possessing them is enough for the other party to say they are "scared." Treat them the same as firearms and get them out of your possession.

Effect on your children

The suicide or attempted suicide of a parent affects the children by inducing lifelong trauma. The researcher Torjesen (2015) found that "parental suicide attempt conveyed a nearly 5-fold increased odds of suicide attempts in offspring". If you commit suicide or attempt to commit suicide, then your children are five times more likely to do the same. That's a terrible burden to leave your kids. Kids who survive parents that commit suicide may have survivor's guilt and they may also blame themselves for being the cause of the suicide. They also must work through the shame and stigma that suicide brings with it in modern society.

Cain (2006) noted that one unintended consequence of children who have experienced parental suicide is they may decide to not have children of their own. This unintended consequence is an effect on the third generation and is just one way that has been studied how suicide effects are long-lasting into multiple generations. When having suicidal thoughts, refocus your thoughts and think of the effects that you'll be causing for generations to come.

<u>Support</u>

To ensure that you don't feel like you've gotten to the end of the road with no options, make sure you know all the resources that are available to you. Many times men in our society are expected to be the providers. Men have fewer support resources than women and as such, it may seem like you have nowhere to turn when you need help. Help is available. You just have to know who to ask.

Family, friends, medical professionals, and social programs are all available to help you. If you don't know where to start, you can call the suicide prevention hotline.

1) Suicide prevention hotline - available 24 hours a day, seven days a week; you can talk to a professional. I've listed the number at the beginning of this book. But again, you can reach it by calling 988 or 1-800-273-8255.

2) Family and friends - Oftentimes, people don't want to turn to family because they may be embarrassed or worried about a stigma.

I can assure you that your family and friends would rather help you than go to your funeral.

3) Medical Professionals - Many medical professionals can help you. A family physician can help you as well as a therapist. If you need immediate help, you can always go to the emergency room.

Going through a divorce isn't easy, but it doesn't have to be the end. If you are having thoughts of ending your life, please consider the trauma that your kids will have for the rest of their lives. Your divorce situation is only temporary. Don't make a permanent decision for a temporary situation. Please reach out to get the help you need.

Chapter Eighteen

Happiness

Right now, one of the last things on your mind is happiness. But at some point, you will need to find peace. And with peace, happiness can come. Once you are happy, you can truly thrive. It's worth putting happiness on the radar right from the start. So just remember, while your life situation may suck right now, it's not going to suck forever if you are intentional about it. Better days are ahead!

What about happiness?

Some say that happiness is being happy with what you have and not what you want. Others say the way to be happy is to be grateful to other people. Happiness is a term that is just so abstract it's hard to nail down. You have to decide what makes you happy. It's likely this will come after some trial and error, so don't beat yourself up too much if you don't feel happy right off the bat.

For me, I think happiness comes from the process of doing things that I enjoy. For you, it may be different. For some, happiness may be doing nothing. There is no one size fits all answer because everyone is unique.

While everyone is different, there are some things that I can tell you to avoid. They may have the allure of happiness but in the end, it's nothing but an empty mirage and a cruel joke. Many people have chased addictions thinking that their alcohol, drugs, or gambling will bring them happiness. They find once the bottle is empty and the effects of their bad behavior have worn off, they are broke and more miserable than they were when they started. Their attempts to find happiness are only a temporary fix while also destroying friendships, relationships, and their finances. If you have issues with alcohol, drugs, gambling, or any other addiction, you may find that happiness can only be found once you have confronted these problems and moved past them.

Can you buy happiness?

Recent research shows that experiences like traveling can make you happier. That's not to say buying things doesn't make you happy. For me, when I buy something, it does make me happy because I am excited about using that thing. I may find joy again when using that thing that I bought (like riding my bike or hiking in a nice pair of boots), but simply buying is not enough - the happiness comes from use.

You have to be careful about buying things that you may only use sometimes. Ask anyone who has moved and most will tell you - how did I get all this stuff? Purging while moving has become almost an American tradition because we buy so much. Sometimes not buying that thing that will sit in the basement or garage will make you happier in the end because you're not lugging it out to the trash or trying to sell it for much less than you spent on it!

Figure out what makes you happy

Everyone is different - what makes you happy is going to be unique. It's worth reflecting on what makes you happy and then keeping that on your radar so you can make decisions that align with things that make you happy. There likely isn't going to be one thing that makes you happy, and it may change over time. I know that I've reevaluated what makes me happy a few times since divorcing. I've reflected back to earlier points in my life when I felt happy. I asked myself, what made me happy at that moment in time? I urge you to do the same and more importantly, keep asking yourself what makes you happy.

Chapter Nineteen

What's Next?

We talked about the trauma that is driving straight into the brick wall called divorce. We've also talked about grief or how you can and should emotionally handle the trauma. What's next is to create a plan to get through your emotions of trauma and grief. You also need to plan for the practical things, like where to live, what your budget is going to be, and how you're going to make time for yourself. Even though we discussed these things in Part 1, it's important to re-assess these important issues. When you first go through a divorce, things change very fast!

Let's take a moment here to re-evaluate these important aspects of moving forward in happiness. Answer the following questions and take some time to reflect on your answers.

<u>My Current Situation</u>

Where am I going to live right now?

Is my budget working for me? YES or NO

How can I change my budget to better fit my life right now?

How can I make time for myself so I can include self-care (physical and emotional)?

Things I CANNOT change are:

And the things I CAN change are:

Chapter Twenty

Parenting Introduction

B illy Graham said, "A good father is one of the most unsung, unpraised, unnoticed, and yet one of the most valuable assets in our society." Sometimes as dads, we don't realize just how important our roles are in our kids' lives! The truth is our kids are looking up to us. They want to grow up and be just like us! We are their role models and their teachers all in one.

But it's not an easy job. Emma Watson sums it up nicely "I've seen my father's role as a parent being valued less by society. I've seen young men suffering from illness, unable to ask for help for fear it will make them less of a man… I've seen men fragile and insecure by a distorted sense of what constitutes male success. Men don't have the benefits of equality either. We don't often talk about men being imprisoned by gender stereotypes, but I can see that they are." In short, as fathers and men, we have a lot of adversity to overcome!

Research has shown that fathers play an important role in the development of healthy and happy children. Psychology Today (The Importance of Fathers for Child Development | Psychology Today. (2021)) lists several important factors that fathers bring, including:

- Doing better in school

- Higher levels of social competence

- Better peer relationships

Other factors that have been noted (Child Crisis AZ, 2017) include an increase in your child's emotional intelligence and problem-solving capabilities. They also note dads can help boost confidence while providing a different perspective from the mother. Fathers also can be a positive role model for their children giving the kids someone to look up to.

Although the benefits of dad's being in their kids' lives, it's estimated that 33% of kids in America live absent from their biological father (The Extent of Fatherlessness, n.d.). 72% of the population believes that "fatherlessness is the most significant family or social problem facing America." Many vital statistics for child well-being do far worse when fathers are absent, including teen pregnancies, runaways, school performance, suicides and more. It's important that you play a role in your kids' lives!

So far, in this part, we've talked about mental health. This should give you a good foundation to start understanding the complexities of people. In the rest of this part (remember it's titled Boot Camp!), you'll learn some of the parenting basics. I'll cover how to establish good co-parenting with your ex and what to do if they won't co-parent. I'll talk about the important topic of communicating with your ex. We'll talk about some of the basic logistical items like exchanging the kids. We will also cover conflict. These important topics will give you a good foundation for starting to learn how to co-parent and what is expected of you as a parent. These few chapters in no way will be all the knowledge you need to parent, so be prepared to put in some extra time reading books or watching videos to learn more.

While not every parent is going to have the same rules, it's important that you start thinking of the things that are most important to you and the kids' well-being and try to implement them as soon as possible after a separation/break-up/divorce. Remember that this is all new for the kids, too. Every parent makes mistakes along the way. The most important thing is to learn from them and move forward.

When all else fails, don't beat yourself up. Remember that life is a journey, and you'll never have a perfect journey. You can only learn from your experiences and keep moving.

Chapter Twenty-One

Establishing Co-Parenting

It's important that you establish a legal basis for parenting. This will usually be in the form of a formal parenting plan. I'll cover the legal details of these things later in the legal section. For now, I want to talk about the nuts and bolts of working with another person (your ex and others) so that you can successfully co-parent together. It does take two people to co-parent, but you can still co-parent even if the other parent seems to be working against you. Confused? Let me explain. While establishing a new routine is always challenging, it's very important that you try as best you can. It may not happen right away but keep at it. You will find if you keep making the effort, your new routines will get easier and may even become automatic or somewhat automatic. Establishing these new routines and getting the kids used to co-parenting or parallel parenting is going to be key to your success as time goes on.

In an ideal divorced situation, both parents would work together - because that is what is best for the kids! The kids would see two adults working together. They don't have to do everything together or anything together, really. They just have to work like a team when it comes to the kids. We're talking pick up, drop off, picking up meds, and other logistics. It also means being on the same page about discipline, when they can get things, and what they can get. We're also talking about things like what's ok to watch on TV and what isn't. In a perfect world, the kids would know what to expect from each parent, and they wouldn't be able to get something out of one parent that they couldn't get from the other. Think teamwork.

In reality, very few divorced spouses will co-parent perfectly together, and that is OK. What's important is they *try* to co-parent, and hopefully there will be more times that they are aligned than times that they are misaligned. They both work hard to make sure that they do what's really best for the kids in each situation. Adult matters are discussed maturely amongst the adults without the kids around, and the children are allowed to just *be kids.*

In reality, you may have an ex who tries their best NOT to co-parent. This is usually out of spite or simply because the emotions of one or both people are controlling their decisions. In these cases, the reality of each situation has little bearing on the decisions that these people make and the actions that they take.

But just because the other parent refuses to co-parent, it doesn't mean that you give up. **You still be the best parent that you can be.** Sometimes, if the other parent won't work with you and you can't have the same rules at both houses, then you can do something called "parallel parenting." Basically, this is having separate rules and ways at both houses, and each parent is doing their own thing. While this is not ideal, it does seem to be better than the kids being in the middle of continuous conflict. Parallel parenting is often the best parenting plan when you are in a high-conflict divorce.

Keep in mind that this may present new challenges for you as your kids age (think a 15-year-old son allowed to have a girlfriend in his bedroom with the door closed at the ex's house or an 11-year-old daughter wearing clothes and make-up to school that you would deem inappropriate for her age). When having to parallel parent, you will really only have control over what the kids do when they are with you. Remind the kids of your rules, parent with love and boundaries, teach them your morals and values and try to let go of the things they do at the exes that you don't agree with. They will not be children forever.

Regardless if you end up co-parenting or parallel parenting, it's important that once you get separated and the kids' lives change, that you establish some routine and talk to the kids about what the new situation is going to be like and what they can expect. It's best if you can have this chat with them together, but each parent talking with the kids separately works, too (as long as the other parent isn't trashing the parent that's not there).

Chapter Twenty-Two

Nutrition, Feeding and Cooking

If you've been around your kids at all, chances are you have an idea of what they like eating and what they don't. As kids age, their taste buds will mature and they will eat a wider variety of things. Don't fret if your kids will only eat animal cookies, chicken nuggets, and Mac and Cheese. Some kids will try new things regularly. Others will not, and that's ok. However, if there are sudden, seemingly unhealthy changes in your kid's weight (sudden *extreme* weight gain or more worrisome-noticeable weight loss), your kid may be having some hidden anxiety or health problems, and it is important to consult a trusted professional (i.e., pediatrician or counselor).

The bottom line is that kids need to have enough nutrition to sustain themselves. Some parents go nuts with their kids' nutrition. Sometimes, there is a medical need and it's good that the parent is overly conscious of the child's diet. Other times, it comes from the parent being overly controlling or having high anxiety themselves. Keep in mind if you have a picky eater, that a "good enough" size meal for a child is roughly the size of their fist.

Water and Drinks

Whenever the kids are with you, you should carry water. Sometimes kids don't understand or can't communicate to you that they are thirsty. Water should be the majority of what they drink, followed by whole or 2% milk and 100% juice. Of course, an occasional soda or other sugary drink is OK, too. It's all about balance.

Babies/Infants and Young Toddlers

Most babies need a bottle of pumped breast milk, formula or (if older than one year) cow's milk every 2 -3 hours. After age six months, you can also start giving the baby sips of purified water. Real, blended food or baby food can start being introduced at age six months with the exception of honey, smoked and cured meats, nuts, popcorn, and certain cheeses. It is recommended to wait until the baby is older than one year before feeding them honey (including honey-flavored graham crackers and cereals) due to the risk of them developing botulism-a serious type of food poisoning. Ideally, you'll be able to talk to your co-parent about this, but if not, talk to your baby's pediatrician or use online resources or a trusted friend for further and current information. Many young babies do not drink their bottle well with a full diaper. Diaper changes are usually need-ed before or right after a bottle feeding!

What Kids Need to Eat vs. What They Want

The challenging part here is if you let your kids eat whatever they want, they certainly won't get what they need. Given the choice be-tween healthy snacks and sugary garbage, they will let their sweet tooth decide. It's up to you, as the parent, to give them the oppor-tunity to have a good balance of healthy foods/snacks and letting them indulge in unhealthy and sugary foods in moderation.

The key here is balance, moderation and timing. If they want a sugary snack, make sure it's after a meal and don't give them free-range over a whole package!

Breakfast

Kids need to have a good breakfast. It's an essential source of energy. This will give them the energy they need to learn and play throughout the day. Ideally, you'll have some protein for breakfast (sausage, nut butter or eggs) along with some carbs (pancakes, waffles or toast) to get them going. If you don't have time to cook, something like a bowl of cereal is a good start. If you're too short on time for cereal, give them a breakfast bar or protein bar paired with some milk or water.

Lunch

During the school year, the kids will have lunch at school. This can be either a school-bought lunch or one that they bring from home. If your kids are bringing their lunch from home, remember that lunchtime for kids is an important social bonding time with their friends. If they ask to have something fancy or extra for their lunch, it's likely it is to socialize/impress their friends. I recommend you try your best to get them those snacks that they ask for or the bags with their favorite cartoon on them. If your kids are bringing lunch to school, try and make it with them or at least have them help make their lunch. You can turn school lunch-making time into good bonding time and also get them to help you (and help clean up, too!).

During the summertime it's easy to forget about lunch, but don't! Lunch during the summertime is a great opportunity for kids to learn to make their own food (and clean up their own mess). Things like peanut butter and jelly or ham and cheese are great things that kids can make without your help. If your kids are old enough to use a microwave, try to look for easy-to-heat up options like mini pizza snacks or burritos.

Dinner

Dinner time used to be the time that the family would gather and socialize over a meal. Most families that I know don't have everyone together every night for an evening meal. What is important is that they eat something (enough so they are not hungry in an hour). It can greatly help dinner-time stress if you have something the kids are willing to eat. This may be Mac and Cheese every night, but that's OK.

Vegetables are full of vitamins and minerals and are essential to a well-balanced diet. Try to include a vegetable in your dinner. While cooking fresh vegetables may not be in the time or money budget for everyone, remember that frozen and canned vegetables (heated up for them) count as vegetables, too! Some examples of easy-to-make and budget-friendly meals that a lot of kids like are Macaroni and Cheese and hot dogs with canned green beans. Spaghetti sauce (jarred) and rotini/penne pasta with frozen fully-cooked mini meatballs and salad with ranch dressing. Fish sticks, steamed or raw baby carrots and boxed rice. Sloppy Joes on a sesame seed bun with sliced cucumber. Surprisingly, most kids will eat steamed, plain broccoli. Stock up on their favorite dressing or dipping sauce if that helps. You're doing good if most dinners consist of a protein, carbohydrate and vegetable.

Keep in mind that it can help cut the stress (particularly with young kids) to make one thing for adults and another for kids. If you do make something different, then this can be a great time to introduce your kids to new foods. Give them a few bites of what you made for the adults. Just be ok with it if they don't like something. Make sure you give them some encouraging words thanking them for *trying.* That way the next time a new food comes around, they won't have a negative association with trying new food.

Dessert

Not surprisingly, this is probably the easiest thing to try and get your kid to eat! The trick here is moderation. It's ok to have that cookie, pie or ice cream - just not the whole thing!

Snacks

When your children are younger, snacks can make all of the world of a difference in mood and behavior. "Younger kids need to eat three meals and at least two snacks a day. Older kids need to eat three meals and at least one snack a day. They may need two snacks if they're going through a growth spurt or if they are very physically active (When Should My Kids Snack?, 2019). Snacks can be your key to good eating habits in your children as well as regulating their blood sugar levels and moods.

If your kid seems to be having a hard time settling down for bedtime and it's been a couple hours or more since dinner, it is OK to let them have a late-night snack. Just keep it healthy and filling (such as a banana and a glass of milk or a spoonful of peanut butter and a handful of raisins). It is hard for any of us to fall asleep when we are hungry. Their growing bodies are expelling so much energy (especially if you were able to squeeze in some playtime after dinner), and it's possible they need a snack to be able to fall and stay asleep for the night.

Some examples of nutritious snacks for any time of the day would be cheddar-flavored crackers, healthy chips, raw veggies with ranch dressing, fruit, salami, beef/turkey jerky, cheese/cheese sticks, and nuts or popcorn (if the child is old enough to handle without choking). The occasional fruit gummy snack or chocolatey something is OK as a treat snack, but try not to make it a daily habit. Remember, balance is key.

When You and the Co-Parent Don't Agree On Nutrition

In high-conflict situations, you may be accused of not feeding the kids the right foods or even harming your kids through what you are (or aren't) feeding them. While I can't go over what CPS looks for in each state, I can talk about what they are generally looking for. I also need to remind you that I'm not a lawyer and this is not legal advice. For questions about this topic specific to your state, ask your local legal professional. There are also great online resources such as https://www.myplate.gov, https://www.mayoclinic.org, and htt ps://eatingwell.com that have nutrition guidelines for children if you are feeling lost on what to feed them.

If you are making an effort to make sure your kids are fed in a reasonably nutritious manner, then you're probably fine. I had one professional tell me that it didn't matter what the kids ate as long as there was food available. Some co-parents will try to use the legal system against the other parent. It is called "Legal Abuse" or "Administrative Abuse." While this is a sick and sad attempt for one parent to gain power over or "punish" the other parent, you can protect yourself by documenting what your kids are eating.

Now, you don't have to go crazy here. If you think this is going to be an issue with your ex, some minimal documentation can go a *long* way. Saving your grocery receipts can be a simple way of documenting the food you have in your house, but it can be a double-edged sword. If you buy excessive amounts of alcohol, that will likely be used against you.

Another way to document what you are feeding the child(ren) would be to make a food journal. You don't need a list of all the ingredients, just a few words on what was available for each meal. There are several websites and apps like ShopWell and MyFitnessPal that can help make this easy as well. You really can't force your kids to eat at all, but you can at least provide something that shows what you make available to them.

Chapter Twenty-Three

Living Spaces & Bedtimes

When your living situation changes, so will your kids' situation. It's important that you are sensitive to the fact that while change is hard for adults, change is *really* hard for kids. Kids feel secure when there is structure. Kids need to know where they will sleep and where they can keep their stuff. Kids like to know when they are supposed to go to sleep (even if they tell you otherwise). Security and consistency go a long way with kids. It's important that you recognize this and that you at least give it your best shot to provide this for them.

In regards to your new living space: How can you make sure that they have the security and consistency that they want and need? The answer will depend on your situation and resources, but I can tell you that you should be intentional about giving the kids their own space and also making sure that you are consistent with your rules around "their space."

When I mention giving the kids their space, I should clarify that while it's OK for kids to have a common "kid space" like a play area, each kid needs their own *individual* space. Ideally, they will have their own bedroom. If this is not possible, look into your current state laws on children sharing a bedroom with their parents/siblings. It is not uncommon for a judge to deny you equal custody of your child(ren) due to bedroom sharing.

If they must share a bedroom with a sibling, then you need to make sure that everyone has some space to call their own. Keep in mind that Child Protective Services in most states has strict guidelines, such as no more than two children per room and that boys and girls over the age of five should not share a bedroom. Sharing a room with a parent/adult is frowned upon also unless the child is an infant. If room sharing is a must for your home right now, then give each child as much space as you can (of course within reason). This should be a space where they can keep their stuff without the other sibling messing with it. Even in the army, every soldier has his or her own foot locker that is *their* space for personal items.

It's ok for the kids to know that they can have their own personal space that no one will mess with unless you (the parent) have concerns for their health or safety (i.e., teenagers hiding drugs in their room). Sometimes, something as simple as putting masking tape on the floor of a shared bedroom or hanging a curtain in the middle of a room can be enough to make siblings who have to share bedrooms feel secure.

It's also good for the kids to know the rules around both personal spaces and shared spaces. The key here is having the same rules for everyone and making sure that you at least *attempt* to enforce them. If you want to make sure the play area is picked up before they leave the house, then make sure you enforce that rule (within reason). This is something you may need to sit down and think about. Ask yourself: What do I want the rules to be? Don't be afraid to write them down.

Let's say the kids have their own room(s) at your house. Your rule could be that it needs to be cleaned before they go to bed every night, once every Sunday or after homework on Tuesdays. I wouldn't recommend making them clean on "transition days" unless a quick pick-up is a daily thing in your house. Remember dads, it is perfectly OK if you leave the kids' rooms exactly as they left them after they go back to your co-parent's house for the day/week-end/whatever the agreed-upon time is. If it really bothers you, clear out the dirty dishes, trash and dirty laundry, and then just SHUT THE DOOR. Some children, especially teenagers, find it comforting when they come back home to see their room is exactly in the condition they left it in.

It might be wise to put up signs around your home if you want help being consistent. Whatever you decide, the rules are yours now to make.

Remember that the key things are:

1) The kids know what to expect.

2) The kids have some personal space to call their own.

3) The kids respect you and their other siblings' personal and shared space.

<u>Bedtime</u>

It's important for kids of all ages to have a known bedtime. This is the first step in drawing a line in the sand. As a parent, you need them to have a bedtime so *you* can have some time before bed to get things done or wind down. Depending on the age of your kid, it is recommended that they get anywhere between 8 and 16 hours of sleep each day (including naps) (Paruthi et al., 2016).

The bedtime time you choose is up to you. However the younger they are, the earlier it needs to be. For example, in elementary school, you may want to start them off around 8 pm. Try to begin your bedtime routine around the same time every night. For in-stance, start getting ready at 7:00 or 7:30 pm. Try to keep the routine the same. You may start by picking up toys, then give the kid(s) a bath, read them a book or if old enough and able, have them read aloud to you. Lastly, bed. You could add fun to the bedtime routine by letting whoever picks up the most toys pick the book. I mean, we all like incentives, right?

There will be days when your usual routine is not feasible. For instance, when you take a trip or there is something else special going on. In cases like this, it's OK to not follow the same time and routine. For everyday life however, you want to try to follow it. You can make the bedtimes a little later on the weekends, but not by too much. Pushing bedtime later by an hour is fine. However, if you let them go to bed at midnight, they will be tired and cranky come Monday.

As the kids get older, they will become more independent and you may find yourself negotiating bedtime. I would not let them negotiate too far! Most kids *think* they don't need sleep but it's very important to their development and growth. It's up to you, as their parent, to make sure they get the sleep they need.

Chapter Twenty-Four

Screen Time

Sigh….Kids and smartphones/tablets is a topic that drives just about every parent crazy! Unchecked, the kids will become zombies with zero social skills, a stiff neck and bad eyes. Unfortunately, there is no magic sauce here. You will need to decide when your kids can have their own phone and/or tablet and when they can use them. This is a topic that you and your co-parent will definitely want to coordinate on because it's likely the same phone or tablet will travel between houses, particularly when the kids are older. In cases where you and the ex are "parallel parenting"-it is your house, your rules! Remember that toxic exes will sometimes use the children's smartphones/social media apps as a way of interfering with your parenting time and/or as a means to emotionally abuse the kids when they are with you. It's best to set stricter boundaries around electronic devices in these instances.

<u>Rules About Screen Time</u>

The American Academy of Pediatrics has the following recommendations (AACAP, 2020):

- Until 18 months of age limit screen use to video chatting along with an adult (for example, with a parent who is out of town).

- Between 18 and 24 months screen time should be limited to

watching educational programming with a caregiver.

- For children 2-5, limit non-educational screen time to about 1 hour per weekday and 3 hours on weekend days.

- For ages 6 and older, encourage healthy habits and limit activities that include screens.

- Turn off all screens during family meals and outings.

- Learn about and use parental controls.

- Avoid using screens as pacifiers, babysitters, or to stop tantrums.

- Turn off screens and remove them from bedrooms 30-60 minutes before bedtime.

These recommendations may seem like a short amount of time and likely most kids are getting more screen time than this! Keep in mind that "screen time" consists of tablets, phones, computerized games AND TV.

A hard rule in my house is NO screen time before school because the kids are likely to get distracted and forget something important like a sports uniform or breakfast. In the evening, I try to limit their screen time ideally at least an hour before bed, so that their brains have time to disengage. Maybe your rules are "No screens at the dinner table" and "At 7 pm everyone plugs in their devices in the kitchen". Think hard about what you want your rules to be, whether or not these same rules apply to you as well as the kids. Communicate the rules to the kids and implement them with consequences when necessary.

While I try my best to keep screen time to a minimum, I understand that sometimes it is a perfect babysitter to keep your kid(s) content while you get stuff done/think/process whatever is bothering you. Just try your best not to allow them hours on end of screen time for days/weeks/months. This is how kids form "addictions" to screen time.

In this day and age, it's important to have some hard rules regarding screen time. While the amount of time you allot for your kids depending on their age may differ, there are some rules that are simply universal. Examples of "Universal Screen Time Rules" are NO inappropriate videos, movies, apps or games. NO pornography and NO bullying (by them or anyone else!). It is OK for you to remind kids of all ages to never take or send pictures of themselves without you "OK-ing" the picture and recipient first.

Set parental controls on your router and/or devices if you deem it necessary to control content. It might be wise to tell the child(ren) to come *tell* you if they see anything inappropriate or that they know is against your rules. This opens the lines of communication between you and your kid(s).

It is also OK for you to demand that the child(ren) share all their passwords and Usernames with you, as well as that you are made aware of anyone and everyone with whom they might be communicating with via text, gaming, messenger apps and social media. Use your best judgment, be a good example and remember that balance is key.

<u>Entertainment Time, TV, and Playing Outside</u>

I've already covered electronic devices which are a big part of most kids' entertainment these days. Kids (especially teens) are more likely to hide in their rooms and watch something on a streaming service than to sit in the living room and watch something with the family.

To keep my kids from being "cave people," I like to make them come out of their rooms every now and then. This could be to do chores or to go out as a family. I particularly like taking them someplace for entertainment (such as bowling, hiking, going for a walk, whatever!) simply because it gives them a chance to socialize and interact.

Another thing I like to do is "kick them out of the house." I make them go for a walk or ride their bike. We are fortunate that where we live is close to a bike path. Also, my kids are older and have phones, so it's easy to check in with them. If safety is a concern in your town or your kids are younger, you'll probably have to join them if you don't have a fully fenced yard to send them outside to. I've even had them set alarms for a set time (like 30 minutes) and they know when the alarm goes off that it's time to head home. While this may seem harsh to some, I'm a firm believer in the health benefits of sunlight and fresh air. "Sunlight helps children produce adequate levels of vitamin D, and vitamin D sufficiency protects kids from a variety of undesirable health outcomes" (Dewar, 2019).

It's up to you how you let your kids spend their time. I think the important thing to remember is that they are still kids and you are the parent. Kids, especially teenagers, will protest spending time as a family. It's important that you veto their wishes to hide in their room most of the time. You'll find more often than not that they enjoy the time even though they initially protested.

Chapter Twenty-Five

Respect & Discipline

Respect For Other People

One thing that seems to be missing in our modern society is general respect for other human beings. Sadly, this behavior is learned and parents are a huge influence here. If the parents treat people well, then the kids will learn this and do the same. The kids are watching - from how you treat the waitstaff at a restaurant to how you talk about people when those people are not around. If you are rude, your kids will grow up rude.

The moral of the story here is to be a good influence on your children. Be a good person. Use your manners. If you don't know how- do a web search or ask someone who you think has manners for some advice. I'm not talking about knowing which fork to use first at a fancy dinner. I'm talking about saying please and thank you. Holding a door when someone has their hands full. Helping others when they need it. Kids are learning from you all the time. Be the example that you want them to grow up to be.

Doing What You Ask

In my opinion, some moms have a harder time getting the kids to listen to them than most dads do, but it's important that your kids listen to both parents. Now, of course, that would be an ideal co-parenting situation. When you ask your kid to do something, they need to do what you asked. Now, I'm talking about reasonable things here - like picking up their room, turning the TV off, and being quiet when it's bedtime.

I'm not saying your kids should do things that are unreasonable. If you asked them to do something that's way above their skill level or really just an adult thing to do, then that's on you and it's completely reasonable that they not do what you ask. It's important you keep your requests age appropriate and reasonable. It's also important that you ask at an appropriate time. Asking them to do complex homework late at night probably isn't reasonable but an hour or two after they get home from school is.

Assuming your request is reasonable, age-appropriate and time-appropriate, your kids should do what you ask. Let's take a common request like picking up their room. If you ask your kid(s) to pick up their room(s) and they don't with no consequences, then they learn that they can get away with this. They become the alpha over the parent instead of the parent being the alpha of the child.

It's good to know that this dynamic can be reset in case that is your situation right now. If the dynamic is backward, then it's important that you, as the parent, reclaim the alpha status. It must be done intentionally and in a manner that is not harmful. It's also important that you are consistent because nothing will confuse a kid more than if the parent's baseline behavior is erratic.

For example, let's say you ask your kid to clean their room. They don't. Before you go yelling and disciplining them, you need to 'pause' and ask yourself if they were being "anti-authority" or were your instructions not clear. Do your kids understand "Dad's Standard of Clean"? Did they do a quick pick-up when you meant a deep, floor-mopping clean? If they simply ignored you, then it's time for some discipline. You could take away electronics or give them some special *extra* chores to do. Whatever it is, it needs to be appropriate to the level of defiance and age. Don't take away electronics for a year if they didn't clean their room. A day or two or maybe until the room is clean.

It's possible your kid didn't do what you asked because they may not understand your expectations. Oftentimes if kids don't understand, their default position is to just not do anything. So before you go disciplining them for not doing what you ask, make sure the understanding was clear on what was asked of them. Don't be mad or rude; simply ask "Did you not do this because you didn't know what to do?". This gives them an option to still do what you asked. Kids want the approval of their parents, so before you give them a disapproval - give them every opportunity to earn your approval.

If they come back and say they didn't understand, take some time to walk through what you want them to do. It can be helpful to walk through it with them. Tell them the first step, then do it with them. Then give them the next step and let them do that step. This takes time, but it's a good way for your kids to know that you are there for them and they will appreciate that.

With all that said, I believe that most kids will take a mile when you give them an inch - so don't let them be the alpha in this process (i.e., acting like they don't know how so that you do it for them). One way to make sure this doesn't happen is to make them do all the actions while you correctively supervise.

Appropriate Language

When it comes to curse words, I think every family has a different definition of what is acceptable and what isn't. While the F-bomb is universally accepted as a "bad word," there are some families that would consider certain words swears that other families wouldn't. The bottom line with language is that you want your kids to use language that you are comfortable with.

So begs the question, "What language am I comfortable with my kids using?". When it comes to parenting, you are more of a role model than you know. Kids will mimic their parents because, after all, you are the adults that they look up to! When thinking about curse words and your kids, look at the person in the mirror. Now is a good time to evaluate the language you use and how your kids may "pick up" on that.

First, let's start with the easy stuff and then we can move into the words that may straddle the line of being a cuss word. The F-Bomb and sh*t should both be hard no's for your kids to say. The same goes for those derogatory words that describe people.

What about the "almost" cuss words? Words like "suck" and "crap" or "shoot"? You'll have to decide if they are ok for your kids to say or not.

You can't just tell the kids to not use bad words. They have to know what the bad words are, and then you need to give them words to use instead.

<u>Discipline</u>

First, I want to start this section by saying that disciplining kids is hard, it's sometimes exhausting and it may leave you feeling like you're not making any progress. That said, it's one of the more important contributions that a parent can make. It's also one of the areas that a parent can easily traumatize their kids. Remember, discipline means "training that corrects, molds, or perfects the mental faculties or moral character." (*Definition of DISCIPLINE, 2022*)

Be consistent! It's not worth having any discussion on discipline without talking about the thing that makes it work, and that is CONSISTENCY. If you are not consistent in how you discipline your kids, then your kids will not know what to expect. They may also devalue your attempted discipline attempts if you're not consistent with consequences. Moreover, if you fly off the handle over spilled milk one day and laugh it off the next, the kids may start to feel like they have to walk on eggshells around you. Try your best to be consistent with the understanding that while YOU are going through a lot as a divorcing/divorced/single dad, the kids are going through A LOT, too. Consistency with *love* is key. The whole goal here is to raise the kids to be good humans.

It's also worth noting that your strictness and levels of discipline will have to adjust with your kids depending on what is going on in your and their lives. You're not going to have the same discipline and consequences for a toddler as a teenager. You will need to have the appropriate amount of discipline for the age that they are while also keeping in mind what kind of day/week/month you all are having. Are you about to be meeting the ex in court? Did you or the ex just introduce the kids to a new girlfriend or boyfriend? Is it "transition day"? If any of these things could be true, it's probably best to let a teenage eye-roll or other minor crimes in the kids' behavior slide. Maybe they overheard some adult conversation they shouldn't have and are feeling uncomfortable with it? Maybe you've been a little distracted lately and they miss you? Could the new-found attitude in your once sweet and amazing tween or teen just be "normal" puberty stuff? Think about the whole picture.

While the topic of spanking your kids is a hotly contested one in parenting circles, it's generally accepted that spanking your kids is not the most helpful form of discipline. I do not recommend using spankings as a form of discipline. Certainly, if you are going through a divorce, you do not want a spanking to be blown into "he hits the kids," and if you are in a high-conflict divorce, that will happen. It's important that you learn how to discipline your kids *without* spanking them and without losing your temper. If necessary, put YOURSELF in time-out. First, make sure all the kids are safe from anything that could harm them and then take 5-10 minutes to yourself to breathe, calm down and think of a way to discipline the kids without spanking. Call a trusted friend or family member for advice if needed.

Spectrum Of Discipline

When we talk about discipline, the level of cooperation that you expect from your kids is up to you. Both your strictness and the consequences live on a spectrum. On one end, you have the kids not following your rules at all. Imagine yourself just wandering around your house like a squawking parrot that everyone ignores while the kids run amuck half-dressed and squirting chocolate syrup at each other. Absolute chaos. On the other end, you have the kids developing anxiety because you are so strict, "Sir, yes sir!". Certainly, there is a happy medium and you will need to find that balance. I would recommend trying to put the strictness somewhere in the middle.

In the beginning, it may be helpful to *ease* the kids into following the rules. It's especially important if they are coming out of an unstructured environment. You and your co-parent are no longer together for a reason and it's likely that now separate, each of you have two different parenting styles. Put your strictness somewhere to the left of the middle where you are very forgiving and mostly just *gently* reminding them what the *new* rules are and ask them to follow the rules. This will be especially true on "transition" days even if the kids have been in a shared parenting situation for years. It is still normal for them to go through an adjustment phase the first day back home with you.

Kids generally do well with structure. When they know what's coming next (a nap or lunch or maybe bed) they are not left wondering. Be sure that you give them time to adjust to any kind of structural change - like a change in the schedule or going from an unstructured environment to a structured one.

Speaking of structure, now is a good time to talk about how structure and discipline work together. You *cannot* have discipline without structure. It just doesn't work that way. Kids have to know what their daily life looks like in order to feel comfortable in it. Sometimes kids act out because they have no idea what's happening next and acting out is simply a response to the parent(s) lack of structure.

In short, you have to have *some* structure at your house. In the beginning of a separation or divorce and especially with younger kids, you can have looser structure. As the kid(s) get older, you will want to have things defined.

In regards to discipline, here are some things I recommend that you put some thought into: What rules and rituals are most important to you (and the kids) now? It can even be helpful to hang up the rules in their bedroom or some other place where they will see them daily. Remember, kids mostly just want to have fun. You can throw a couple of fun "rules" in there as well to help get younger kids and older teenagers on board.

Timeliness of Discipline

When you are disciplining kids, keep in mind the punishment needs to be timely. In most cases, you can't discipline them for something they did three weeks ago. The discipline needs to happen fairly soon after the behavior (or the discovery of the behavior).

If your kids refuse to pick up their room, then the consequences should happen as soon as possible. I say as soon as possible because it may not work to start their discipline if they are in the middle of a temper tantrum. When you start their discipline they should be in a state that is calm so that you can talk through with them why you are disciplining them.

It's best to keep the discipline as quick and practical as possible and implement it after the behavior. Make sure that they understand why they are being disciplined, and talk through with them what better choices they could have made.

<u>The Consequences of No Discipline</u>

Some parents think they are doing better for their kids by not disciplining them at all. The only thing that you are doing is bringing them up in a false world. Once they grow up to be adults, the *world* will discipline them and it generally will not care if this is their first time learning the consequences of their actions.

For example, a speeding ticket. If your kid grows up without any discipline, they are likely to break the law when they learn to drive. The police officer that they just sped past is going to discipline your kids. He or she will pull them over and give them a ticket. Now let's take the example of a kid who grew up knowing that breaking the law has consequences. When they learn to drive, they will generally obey the speed limits because they have learned to live within the rules of our society.

Society works because we have a common set of rules (including actual laws and societal norms). A child that grows up recognizing the rules and knowing how to obey them will have a much easier time in life than one that doesn't understand why they are constantly in trouble and feel like society is out to get them. Your job as a parent is to ease your kids into living within the rules. That way when they get to the "real world" as an adult, the transition into being a good citizen won't be a culture shock.

It's worth noting here that I am not advocating that you bring your kids up to be robots. They need a certain amount of freedom to think outside the box. It's important to note that a child who grows up with appropriate discipline can learn to think outside the box. It's a lot harder for a child who grows up without discipline to learn how to think *within* the box.

<u>Too Much Discipline</u>

Like having too little discipline, having too much is just as bad. Kids need discipline, but they also need room to explore, make mistakes and learn. Kids learn from mistakes and if they are afraid to make those mistakes, then they will never try. Kids that are too disciplined will feel suffocated and when they become an adult, they will do all those things (and make those mistakes) that you didn't let them. Think sexual exploration, excessive drinking, partying and the like. Most kids who grow up over-disciplined will go wild as soon as mom and dad aren't around to lord over them.

The other downside of too much discipline is that, in excess, it can be considered abuse. If the kids are afraid of the parents, then this is a red flag. So how much discipline is too much? What is the right balance? It's hard to quantify this in a book. It's a broad subject (lots of situations), and it changes with age. You can't expect a 3-year-old to follow the same rules that a 17-year-old does. You do need your kids to respect you, no matter the age. Remember that most importantly regardless of the age of your kids- consistency helps.

Younger kids may need gentle reminders daily on what the rules are. Don't expect them to remember any of the rules. The key here is to be consistent and keep the consequences immediate. It is recommended that an appropriate amount of time for a "time-out" is 1 minute for each year of age. For example, your 4-year-old's "time-outs" should be 4 minutes long. It's ok to restart the timer if they get out early. An hour of time-out for a young child is excessive.

Pre-Teens or Young Teens have a much better understanding of the world. This is the age where they will start to challenge your reasoning and logic (that's a good thing by the way). With this age group, you want the discipline again to be immediate and be sure to ask them about making better choices and what alternate choices they could make. I especially like combining discipline with practical work (chores). Be careful not to make "discipline chores" be part of their normal chores or they will have a negative association with regular chores. Have them do chores that need to be done but aren't the normal 'take the trash out.' As a consequence you could have them clean the garage or storage area, clean up an area outside, paint something, etc. This is a good consequence because you get help with a chore that needs to be done and it gives them time to *think.*

Chapter Twenty-Six

Chores

Despite the protests of children everywhere, chores are great for kids. Not only do they teach important life skills like cleaning and doing laundry, they also teach the kids responsibility and help build their self-esteem. It's important your kids know what to expect with chores, though. You can't be completely relaxed about chores one time and then ask them to do a bunch the next time. Try to be consistent with chores and try to balance their chore time with playtime. Remember that kids have a limited attention span. For the younger ones, pick something that is 5-10 minutes. As they become teenagers, you can give them a few short chores in a row or ask them to do longer chores.

It's also important to note that you shouldn't gender-ize chores. An example would be saying taking the trash out is a "boy" chore while doing the dishes is a "girl" chore. Mix it up and teach them to do all the chores! Not only will you be exposing them to all the life skills that they need, you'll also be teaching them in the best way possible (by example) to not gender stereotype.

If you need help assigning them chores, I've found that a small whiteboard is a great way to communicate expectations of chores to the kids. You can write what they need to do, and they can have fun crossing things off. I've been known to sometimes write a monetary reward to encourage them to do their chores. Our whiteboard hangs on the side of the refrigerator, and I've found it a great way to leave them little notes and to keep track of the chores I've asked them to do.

Remember with chores that balance is key. Make sure you balance their chore time, after-school sports/clubs, and playtime. For example, you don't want to give your high school football player a ton of chores during the busiest part of the football season. It's also very important to make sure that chores are balanced between siblings. This can be a good opportunity for the kids to learn to negotiate and to collaborate. For example, you do X and I'll do Y and the next time we will switch. It could also be that one sibling does a "worse" chore and they get a reward that the others don't. Use your best judgment and work with your kids. In the beginning it will be harder to get them to do things, but once they know what your expectations of chores are, you will get less resistance.

Chapter Twenty-Seven

Communications

When you divorce, communication with your ex-spouse will be different than during your marriage. You are transitioning from a romantic relationship to a formal one that focuses on your children.

It's often hard to communicate with your ex-spouse in the early stages of divorce. Emotions are high and the topics are difficult. Splitting the money, property and kids' time is not easy. Throw in a few attorneys to keep the conflict up, and you have a real mess.

Good communication will benefit everyone, especially the kids. My hope is to give you some tools that will help you effectively communicate with your ex-spouse. These tools should help you keep the emotions out of your conversations and keep you focused on the facts.

What Not To Say

It's easiest to start by talking about what not to say when communicating with your ex-spouse. It may seem obvious, but you shouldn't get into emotionally charged conversations with them. Arguing will get you nowhere. Think of it like a political argument on Facebook. Zero percent of people have had their minds changed by a political rant on Facebook! Everyone just leaves pissed off. Save the emotional stuff for your therapist.

Make sure that all communication with your ex-spouse is clean and professional. Communications should be short and to the point. Good communication starts by not letting your emotions bleed into your communications.

Don't use any foul language. If you are in person, beware of your tone and do not yell under any circumstances. If your buttons are being pushed or you are getting upset - simply remove yourself from the situation. Don't give him or her a "piece of your mind." Stop the conversation and tell them you will have to continue the conversation at a later time. Move the conversation to email if possible.

Just the Facts

In schools across the country, kids are being taught a communication tool called the "5 W's plus H". It's easy to remember and it touches all the bases. This tool will help you from having multiple messages or discussions about the same topic because of a lack of information. And you said you would never use anything you learned in school!

The five W's plus H are:

- WHO are you talking about? Specifically, say which child or person you are discussing. Being specific is key.

- WHAT are you talking about? Be brief and to the point. Try to talk about one topic at a time. If you are using email, write separate emails for different topics.

- WHEN did or will something happen? If the time or date is required, make sure you include those in the communication.

- WHERE did or is something going to happen? If a location is needed, make sure you include it. Be specific about the location. If you say "at the mall," this leaves a lot of questions. Which mall? In the mall or somewhere in the mall parking lot? Where in the mall parking lot? Adding these precise details can save back-and-forth messages.

- WHY can be helpful but not always necessary. Sometimes it's just not necessary and will add unnecessary length to your communication. Make sure you evaluate if you need to explain why you are communicating something or why something happened.

- HOW will things happen? For example, how will you arrive? Will you come by car? Or train? Make sure you explain the important details.

Let's give an example of how you would use the "5 W's plus H". For instance, let's say you need to exchange the kids with your ex-spouse. Your email might look like this:

"For the Labor Day weekend, I would like to exchange Billy and Jenny at the North Mall in Sometown in front of Sears in the parking lot at 2 PM on Wednesday, September 1, 2018. We can exchange them again on Sunday, September 5th at 6 PM at the same location. Please let me know if you can meet me with the children at that place and at those times."

Let's examine this communication for the 5 W's plus H:
- Who - Billy and Jenny

- What - Exchange for the Labor Day weekend

- Where - North Mall in Sometown in front of Sears in the parking lot

- Why - Labor Day weekend

- How - In person (not explicitly stated, but enough details are there to make the point clear)

Notice how this communication was straight to the point and just the facts. It didn't say anything about a hot topic between you two. It only stuck to the facts of explaining the exchange. It also left out the fun plans you had for the kids, which is really none of the ex's business unless you plan on taking them out of the county/state/country.

You can easily see how little details will lead to further communications. Had I not included the amount of detail in the "where", a clarification would be needed - inside the mall or in the parking lot? Be specific to avoid extra messages.

Sometimes it's helpful to write these messages and wait a few hours, then go back and look at what you wrote. Ask yourself, "Am I writing too much detail?" and "Can I say it shorter?". You'll be surprised at how much unnecessary information can be in your communications.

Good communication with an ex-spouse is formal. Keep it that way. Work hard to keep your emotions out of the communications. Pretend that you are writing to someone at work. Ask yourself, "Is this something that I would write to a colleague"?

Good communication can change the dynamics when working with your ex-spouse. Use the 5 W's plus H as a guideline to make sure that you have all the right details. Stick to the facts and stay away from emotions. Remember to be brief and keep things formal. You don't have to respond immediately; however, your response time should be appropriate to the topic at hand.

Communication Methods

You have multiple choices of tools to use to communicate with your ex-spouse. You can have a conversation in person. You can talk on the phone. You can use your attorney. Then there are the mired of written communication tools such as texting, email and social media. Several companies have even developed websites specifically for use in co-parenting. I'll talk about several of these methods and the pros and cons of each.

Note: Do not use social media. Use of public communication tools like this when discussing issues around your divorce or children is NEVER a good idea!

When you receive a communication from your ex-spouse, regardless of the format they sent it to you in, you can choose the method that you respond in. Just because someone sends you a text doesn't mean you have to reply on a text. Just because someone wants to engage in a face-to-face conversation, that doesn't mean you have to have that conversation. You can always say, "I'll respond to you by email". Choosing your response method and sticking to it is an example of having good boundaries. It is not unheard of for personality-disordered high-conflict exes to demand you only communicate with them over email or Co-parenting app, and then they turn around and break their own rule by trying to call, text or speak with you in person. DO NOT ENGAGE. Stick to the agreed-upon method of communication. You'll be glad you did.

In-Person or Phone

In-person or phone conversations with your ex-spouse are typically the least desirable option. If you are dealing with a high-conflict person, be extra careful about having real-time interactive conversations. You must trust the person you are having an in-person or phone conversation with. You will need to use your own judgment. The only exception to this I would say is if there is a true emergency. If someone (the kids especially) is ill or injured and needs to go to urgent care, the hospital, or the emergency room. A phone call is faster. If the ex doesn't answer, leave a message. For your sake, I hope your ex would do the same and it would be wonderful if this is something the two of you could at least agree on in the beginning of a divorce.

With that said, be wary of having non-emergency phone conversations with your ex. Phone conversations aren't recorded automatically, so if you get into a he-said, she-said argument- then it's your word against theirs. One party can always record the conversation, and they may not need to tell you. Some states require both parties to know, others only require one (the party doing the recording). If you get into an argument on the phone and the other party records it, it can be used against you in court.

In-person or phone conversations are also one of the easiest ways to get sidetracked from the topic or subject that you started with. Don't get sidetracked and end up in an emotional conversation where it's easier for your ex to push your buttons. It is harder to think clearly when you are engaged in an emotional conversation. If you are dealing with a manipulative and high-conflict person, this is what they want and you should avoid it, if possible.

With a phone or in-person conversation, you have to respond nearly instantaneously. There is no time to think about what you are going to say in response. With all the other communication methods in this chapter, you can take at least a few minutes to a day or two to think about your response.

While in-person communications have their downsides, sometimes they are the best option. Some things are easier to talk about or explain when the other person can have a dialog and ask questions or tell you their opinion. Use your judgment if the communication that you are having or are going to have needs the back and forth of an in-person conversation. If you have to have an in-person or over-the-phone conversation, be sure to take safeguards such as having another witness with you or recording the event.

Texting

Texting is not a great option, but it is better than the phone or in-person option. Like phone or in-person conversations, text forces you to respond immediately or with minimal delay. Frequent texting can interrupt your day by getting notifications on your phone. It also keeps your ex-spouse in the front of your mind during the time you are texting, which is not emotionally healthy. Text is also a "conversation" type of communication, and like the in-person or phone options, you can be sucked into an emotional dialog or argument by the other party.

However, texting is also a written option that is often used in court. Both what you said (and what the other party said) are tracked. Being used in court can both be to your advantage and disadvantage.

Text can be useful for emergencies or last-minute communications. It has its place, but it's not the one that should be your go-to method. Like the phone or in person, if you are dealing with someone who is high-conflict, they may be upset that you will not have long drawn out text conversations with them. Just ignore their temper tantrums and go about your day.

Email

Email is a good option when communicating with an ex-spouse during and after the divorce process. Used properly (as described in the first part of this series) you will reduce the number of messages that go back and forth. It is a written form of communication, and it eliminates many of the he-said, she-said dilemmas when used as evidence in court. The sending time is also tracked which can be helpful in court.

Many mail programs will allow you to automatically sort your mail using "mail rules" or filters. I would suggest having your mail system move all the emails from your ex to a folder. Keep ALL emails to and from your ex. Some systems also delete mail after 30 days or more, so be sure you mark emails from your ex-spouse to not get deleted.

Attorney

If you're divorced or going through the divorce process, you probably have an attorney. Using an attorney is the most expensive but least risky way to communicate with an ex-spouse. The attorney will act as a buffer to make sure that the communications are professional without emotion. They will also try and ensure that your communications will not get you in trouble in court!

Another good reason for using an attorney is you can learn how they respond. By studying what the attorney wrote against what you would have written, you can see some legally safer ways to communicate. This is worth its weight in gold! I learned from my attorneys that I was including too much detail and that you don't always need to explain yourself.

You can also consult with the attorney before sending it to the other party yourself. You may be surprised at how an attorney responds versus how you would have responded. Depending on your attorney, you may want to go into their office to get their direct attention so you can explain details if there are questions.

You won't be able to use an attorney forever unless you have a very large budget for legal fees. Use their time wisely and try to learn how to communicate better from them.

Family Communication Tools

Another option is to use a website designed for parents to communicate in high-conflict divorces. These sites have advantages over the other methods discussed in this article. One of these sites is Our Family Wizard (OFW) [www.ourfamilywizard.com]. OFW was designed specifically for high-conflict parents to communicate to be effective co-parents. All communications within the system are tracked and can be used in court. Attorneys and judges can even log in and see what the parties have been saying. There is a yearly cost to use the system, so make sure to factor that into your budget.

The OFW site recommends sending a message that you write only as a last resort. OFW has several tools to help reduce the number of written messages that go back and forth between the parties. Experience has shown "free-form communications" often cause the most conflict. The OFW system has several tools including a calendar, expense tools, a database for doctors and school info and some other features to help you reduce the amount of written messages. OFW even has mobile apps to help you communicate on the go.

The part I enjoy the most when using OFW is you can choose when to log in and when to answer your messages. It can be a real lifesaver when you get into a new relationship. Constant communication with an ex-spouse can be a strain on your new relationship.

Many people can get this option required in their divorce decree as the primary means of communication between the parties. You may have to request it, and don't be surprised if you have to explain to your attorney what OFW is. If you can get this established in your divorce decree early on, it may save you a lot of headaches further down the line if you are in a high-conflict situation.

<u>When to respond</u>

You should respond to communications in a reasonable amount of time; however, you don't need to respond immediately. When you respond depends on the subject matter. It could require you to answer in a day or two depending on the subject. Emergency communications are the exception, and you should respond to those as soon as practical.

If your ex-spouse asks you to answer in a particular time frame, try to do so unless their request is unreasonable. Beware of things that are not urgent that your ex-spouse wants you to respond to "immediately." Unless something is a real emergency, be sure to think about what a reasonable response time is.

I like to use a "write and wait" policy if an immediate response is not needed. I will write a message and wait a 1/2 day or a day before sending it. When I revisit the message, I will objectively ask myself if it sounds factual or emotional. Is the right information there? Is anything missing? Is there anything there that is not necessary? Take some time to edit the message if you need to, and then send it. You'll be surprised at how some time can help you take your emotions out of your communications.

<u>Guidelines</u>

What I have written here should be considered a guideline and not hard and fast rules. When you are raising kids, you will need to be flexible and you will need to use your best judgment to communicate with your kids' other parent. It is best to communicate with your ex in a way that keeps your kids free from having to relay any messages as well as free from hearing any adult conversation (i.e., arguments or discussions about money). Sometimes you will need to communicate in person or through a telephone conversation. Some things are just easier to communicate through a conversation; just be cautious about the pitfalls of in-person, phone and text conversations. If you and the ex seem to co-parent well, then a Co-parenting app may not be necessary for your situation right now. However, it could come in handy if down the road your co-parenting relationship becomes not so good. The key is to beware of the strengths and weaknesses of each form of communication when using them.

You have several options available when communicating with an ex-spouse. Not only can you choose what you say to them, you can also choose the way you communicate it with them. You don't always have to use the same communication method that they used to contact you. You have a choice to pick the method that is best for your situation. You will likely need to use a combination of the methods mentioned in this article when communicating with an ex-spouse. Be strategic in using the way that is best for your situation.

Remember, you don't have to reply immediately to communications! However, you should respond in a reasonable amount of time based on the situation. If you are communicating with a high conflict person, it is likely that they will complain that you do not respond fast enough. They may also complain if you change the communication method (i.e. switching from text to email). Just ignore this complaint and do what you think is best.

<u>Sharing Information</u>

It's important that you and your co-parent share information about the kids. Things like information about schools, doctors appointments and extracurricular activities. In many cases, the divorce court order will specify that both parties are entitled to this sort of information.

The best way to share this information is automatic, where you don't have to do something to remember to send the information to the other person. If your kid's school or sports team has an email or text message list - try and put both parents' emails or numbers on it. That way when a message goes out, you or your co-parent won't have to remember to forward this information. Similarly, if you get an email that your co-parent should know about and they are not on the email - forward it to them.

It is best to over-communicate these sorts of things rather than under-communicate. There isn't much harm in getting an extra email, but there may be some issues if the other parent misses a game or music recital because they didn't know it was happening.

Your co-parent may not always give you the same courtesy, but you want to make sure that you give it to them. In short, keep everyone in the loop and work as a team to make sure everyone's informed.

Keep in mind that most schools ask for updated Student, Parent and Emergency Contact information yearly. Sadly, most schools only send one form home and to only the "primary" home address listed for the student. Beware in high-conflict situations, that it is not uncommon for a high-conflict ex to conveniently leave your information off or out of these forms. Also, it is not uncommon for them to list you as a tertiary Emergency Contact. You may have to call or physically go to each of your kids' schools to be sure you are added as a primary or at least secondary contact. You also may have to do this every year. It is important that you be added to all of your kids' school records as this is the way that most schools post grades, absences, missing assignments, Code Red alerts and other communications. Do not allow a high-conflict ex to dictate what information you receive from the kids' schools, regardless of the amount of custody you have right now. Being involved and informed is a big part of being the best dad you can be.

<u>Customer Service</u>

Whenever you are in contact with the other parent, use the concept of providing excellent customer service to them. Pretend that they are your customer. Now, this doesn't mean you let them walk all over you. You need to have a good, strong boundary here, but it does mean that if you treat them like a customer (and not your ex who you have a ton of emotions about), it will be easier to make sure you are doing your best to work with them and communicate with them.

What do I mean when I say treat them like a customer? Think about when you are a customer. You have certain expectations. These expectations are:

- You want to be treated with respect.

- You want something at a fair price.

- You want to have a pleasant shopping experience.

- When it's time to check out, you don't want to get yelled at.

- You want to be able to ask for help and that someone will be there to help you.

Any store or establishment that doesn't have a good customer experience is sure to not last very long in a competitive environment. Think about how YOU want to be treated by your co-parent. Would you want to be treated the same way you are treating them?

Co-parenting with your ex while using some common customer service skills will give you a leg up. While it may be unnatural to use customer service skills when dealing with an ex (particularly one who is high-conflict), pretending like you're a customer service agent may be an easy way for you to help navigate these troubled waters.

If you remember two basic ideas here you'll be off to a great start. As you become more used to co-parenting with your ex you'll gain skills and know exactly how to deal with different situations.

Remember the golden rules? "If you don't have something nice to say, don't say anything at all?". The other is "Treat people how you want to be treated". It's that simple. If you do these two things, you'll be miles ahead.

Emotions

Whenever you co-parent with an ex, there is a chance that emotions will get in the way, especially in the beginning when emotions run high. As time goes on the emotions will subside, but in the beginning, they will get in the way all the time.

The easiest way to make sure that your emotions are not getting in the way of communicating and co-parenting with your ex is to treat it like a business environment. Hopefully you're not sending emotionally fueled emails at work (if you are, stop!). You shouldn't be sending emotional emails to your co-parent. Remember, it's just the facts when communicating with a co-parent.

That's not to say you have to be stoic, stone-faced and unemotional. You can be compassionate and empathetic without being emotionally driven. The best way to do this is to recognize someone else's emotions. You can say things like "I understand that you are upset" without blaming or disrespecting them.

When co-parenting with an ex, you are basically in a business transaction with that person. The kids are the common bond and it's up to the co-parents to make sure their physical, social and emotional needs are met. While it's easy to let emotions consume you, remember to keep it business-like and this will make things easier.

Chapter Twenty-Eight

Logistics

When you are divorced and co-parenting, you become the CEO of a logistics company without even knowing it. Meshing two households and sometimes two blended families together can sometimes feel like a full-time job. Balancing school activities, sports, doctor appointments, etc., can take a lot of time and a good calendar.

It can be daunting at first as things may be new to you if you weren't the "scheduler" in the previous family unit, but as time passes and routines are developed, the logistics will become easier. The kids will settle into the routines and won't take so much prompting. Emotions that kids have going between households will lessen (unless you are in a high-conflict situation) and at some point, things will fall into a rhythm.

There are a few things that will help all this become routine and easier. The first is to have a set schedule. Ideally, this will be clearly spelled out in the custody arrangement that will include specific times, days and a custody exchange place. Arguments or misunderstandings about who picks up who, when and where all add an additional layer of stress. If you don't have a court document, consider asking your co-parent to write something down.

Exchanges

Kid exchanges are the heart and soul of the co-parenting experience. It's hard to be a parent if you never get to be a parent in-person around your kids!

If you are new to exchanges, you may find that kids are very emotional around the time before, during and after the exchange. Commonly referred to as "transition days," a lot of kids will have anxiety and can often act out by either being defiant or by crying. Typically this won't last forever. When kids settle into the routine, they may even start to look forward to exchanges or act indifferent to them. If exchanges are hard and emotional on your kids in the beginning, don't worry as it's probably going to get better. If some time has passed (a year or more) and transitions don't seem to be getting easier on your kids, then it's time to consider whether or not you are in a high-conflict situation. Is there something you can do to make transition day easier for the kids? Is there something going on that you may not be aware of? Could your high-conflict ex be working on emotionally alienating you from the kids? Long-term or newly found frequent anxiety on transition days should be a cause for concern and I would not let it fly under the radar. This is where having a good therapist for yourself (and maybe a separate one for your children) would come in handy.

When you exchange the kids, try and keep it about the exchange. Your co-parent may want to chit-chat or otherwise discuss something. Try and keep the exchange focused on the exchange (here are their clothes, backpacks, etc.). Politely ask your co-parent to address other issues at another time. If you have a narcissistic ex, they may try and trap you into making decisions. Avoid snap-decision making if possible.

This should go without saying, but be respectful of your co-parent's time. If you agree to exchange at a time and place, be there. I like to try and make sure I am there at least 5 minutes early. If you are consistently late, this is likely something that will be used against you in a court battle. If you are running late, let your co-parent know - send them a courtesy text or call them.

At the exchange, try to politely greet your co-parent. This can be hard, especially if you are involved in an active court battle. You don't have to go beyond the hello and goodbye, but try your best to. This can go a long way in diffusing tension between co-parents. If it is not possible for you to watch your tone and facial expressions, having a gray rock (neutral) facial expression is recommended. People with personality disorders (Narcissists and Borderlines especially) have a tendency to misread neutral facial expressions as negative ones. In their minds, your neutral face will be interpreted as "angry" or "seething" or as giving them a "dirty look". From that, one can only imagine what they would interpret an actual scowl to be! If dealing with a high-conflict ex on a sunny day, leaving your sunglasses on during an exchange may even make it feel like you have a little invisibility cloak on. The goal is to have an amicable exchange to ease the tension for the kids. Do what you must to maintain your composure, keep your boundaries and make your kids feel comfortable while you are welcoming them back to you or leaving them for a few days.

Also make sure that you spend some time before the exchange getting things together. Gather clothes, coats, books, bags and other things that need to go to the co-parent's house. If you have younger kids, this will take more time. As the kids grow older, these things become more their responsibility, but it's still up to you as the parent to give them some gentle reminders.

Inevitably, your kids will forget something they need at the other parent's house. When it comes to these "bonus" exchanges, be sure to be polite and not angry that you had to go out of your way to get something. Ideally, the co-parent will meet you halfway to pick something up but if you have to drive all the way there, just do it. Your kids will appreciate the effort even if they don't say thank you. Showing them that you're willing to go the extra mile on their behalf will show them that you're a good parent and that you are there for them. They will remember this later in life when they have issues of any kind. It's important that you care and are someone that they can come to.

One option if you are in a high-conflict situation with your co-parent is to exchange at school or daycare. One parent can drop them off in the AM and the other picks up in the afternoon. This arrangement will have the minimum of in-person time with the other co-parent and works well. Also, neutral locations such as grocery store parking lots can allow the children to leave one car and get into the other. Some parents choose to exchange at a park or playground, but I would beware of choosing a location such as this in a high-conflict situation. The reason I say this is because usually a custody exchange is in the morning or the evening which tends to mean there are not a lot of witnesses around at a playground. Also, it is only natural for a child to want to play and to hopefully have both of their parents standing there watching them do the new trick they learned on the monkey bars, etc. While this is completely innocent of your child, it will more than likely be uncomfortable for you and it will be hard for you to make a quick exit without upsetting your child. Save the park or playground as a separate special place for AFTER the custody exchange.

Holidays

It's likely in your custody schedule that you will have a different schedule for holidays. Typically the holidays can be split by year (mom gets even-numbered years for Christmas Day while dad gets odd-numbered years). Some may choose to have one holiday every year while the other parent has a different holiday every year. No matter the agreement, it's important that you stick to this schedule with your co-parent. Exceptions can be made, but kids like it when they know who and where they are going to spend a holiday with. In high-conflict situations, it is not uncommon for a high-conflict ex to agree to "split" or "alternate" holidays and then go back on their word or make the kids feel so bad about being with you for, say, Christmas or Thanksgiving that you end up giving in and forgoing your holiday plans or worse yet, have the magical time you have planned for the kids be ruined by a high-conflict ex's drama. Beware of these manipulations!

If you are parenting with a high-conflict ex and your court custody order has set days with no mention of holidays, then those are your set days and whatever calendar day you have the kids is yours to keep. I have known a few families in high-conflict situations that celebrate holidays on whatever day they have their children, for example, Christmas on December 22nd or 27th. St. Patrick's Day and Thanksgiving could be celebrated on whatever previous day you have the kids. The exception, of course, would be Halloween and New Year's which would be much harder to adjust, but that doesn't mean you can't visit a pumpkin patch earlier in the month or record the ball drop and have a late weekend night with the kids to celebrate! Confetti poppers and sparkling cider could add to your festivities. The important thing is you celebrate whatever holidays are important to you and the kids together with them, regardless of the day.

As with any other exchange, make sure you are on time for holiday custody exchanges. You may need to give yourself some extra time to prepare for the exchange. If you have extra things going back and forth because of the holiday, you want to make sure that you are prepared for the exchange so that you are respecting everyone's time at the actual exchange.

Special Occasions - Birthdays, Graduations, Weddings, etc.

Birthdays can be fun because it's something the kids really look forward to. Some may choose to have a joint birthday celebration, while others may choose to celebrate them separately. No matter which way your family does it, make sure that you have everything ready and your kids know the "who, when and where".

If you are spending time away from your kids on their birthday, try and call or video chat with them if you can. Be sure that this is planned and coordinated with your co-parent. It's ideal if this is in your custody order. Be respectful of your co-parent's time with the kids. You don't want to try and video chat with them in the middle of something! Be prepared for your kids to not want to talk much either, as they may be wrapped up in the excitement and that's ok.

If you do get invited to a birthday celebration, remember that it's your kids' day. It's not about you or your co-parent. Be friendly, be helpful and remember it's not about you. While you are there, keep from talking about the past relationship or any open issues between you and your co-parent. Make sure you are not negative or disparaging in any way toward your co-parent or their family.

If you are too uncomfortable being around your co-parent for long periods of time, politely decline the invitation. You may tell them that you can't attend this time, but to keep you in mind for future events.

Graduation ceremonies, Bah Mitzvahs, Weddings, Quincerias, etc., are all special, once-in-a-lifetime events in your kids' life and the ideal situation would be for both parents and both sides of the family to be able to attend amicably. If there are members of your side of the family that cannot behave themselves and are still not over the divorce (think snide remarks and uncomfortable glares from an ex-in-law), then it might be best that those extended family members not be invited to the occasion. It may sound harsh, but in reality, this is an example of having good boundaries. Remember, these occasions are for the guest(s) of honor and just like a young child's birthday party, an adult child's special event should still be all about them as well.

<u>School Events</u>

One of the first things you have to often do together with your co-parent is attend school events. Plays, concerts and sports are all things that you will want to and should attend. The great part is that this can be "bonus time" when you get to see and interact with your kids on days or times that are your co-parent's time.

Some co-parents will sit together and some will sit apart when being a spectator at an event. There is also the ever-popular "close but not close enough to chit-chat" option. Which one you choose will be up to you and the amount of conflict between you and your co-parent.

If you are in a high-conflict situation, it's best not to sit together. This can lead to frustration and could possibly lead to an altercation at the kids' school. Choose the option that is close but not too close to talk, or just pick someplace that is far away. Most children are well aware of a high-conflict situation even though they probably don't know what it is called or who is the one causing it. Remember, high-conflict people often shift blame. It is not uncommon for a child in a high-conflict divorce to gravitate towards whichever parent will make them feel *the worst* at such events. Even if it is your custody day, if your ex is high-conflict, she will expect your child to sit with her.

Children of cluster B personality-disordered parents often do something called "emotionally regulating." For example, a border-line mother will see your child sitting with you and having a good time. You two may be laughing together or talking about where you're going out to eat afterward. The borderline mother cannot stand this and sees it as a threat to her relationship with the child. When the child returns to her custody, she drills the child and makes them feel guilty for having a good time with you. The kid eventually learns that it is easier to just go sit with her than to face the consequences afterward. Likewise, narcissists are more concerned about how things look to other people. The child "choosing" to sit with them at an event shows that they are the "superior" parent. Again, if you are in a high-conflict situation, a good therapist will be your key to understanding and preserving your relationship with your kids.

It's great if you are not in a high-conflict situation. Kids will take some comfort in knowing that co-parents can get along well enough to at least *tolerate* each other during a game or some other school event. How wonderful would it be for your child to not have to look at two opposite ends of the stadium to find both of their parents! This would be an ideal situation and is best for the kids all around.

One school event that is worth mentioning on its own is parent-teacher conferences. I would recommend that you attend every single parent-teacher conference possible. Attending these not only keeps you looped into your child's education but it also gives you a voice. Skipping parent-teacher conferences will likely result in your co-parent making decisions without you. It's also best to get the information directly from a teacher and not secondhand from a co-parent.

During the conference, the teacher may want you and your co-parent to make decisions on the spot. That can be ok but don't feel forced to do so. It's perfectly acceptable to ask the teacher if you and your co-parent can discuss the issue offline and get back to the teacher. If you're going to do that, then make sure that there is a clear plan in which you or the co-parent is going to communicate back with the teacher.

Doctors Appointments

Like parent-teacher conferences, I would recommend attending all doctors appointments if you can. It's best to hear things straight from a nurse or doctor rather than relying on the co-parent to relay the information. Like the parent-teacher conference, you can let the doctor know that you will get back to them if there is a decision that you and your co-parent need to make after some discussion.

If you can't attend, then ask your co-parent to let you know how things went and if there were any decisions made at the appointment. If your co-parent doesn't give you the information, you can gently ask them for it in an email, text message or co-parenting communication app. As a last resort, you can always call the doctor and ask the nurse to give you an update.

When it comes to routine visits (and I suggest *after* you've been co-parenting a while), you and your co-parent may decide to split the load of taking the kids to see the doc. This can work well when both parents are busy and there is good communication between the parties. If you take the kids to the doc without your co-parent, be sure to give them a summary of what happened and any decisions you made. Always remember to tell them when the next appointment is. If you do make decisions during the appointment, it's best to let your co-parent know what it was and to let you know if they have any objections.

If you are splitting doc duties, when scheduling the next appointment, it may be easiest to schedule the next time on your co-parent's time. For appointments that are routine and far away (6 months or a year), it's likely you may not know a good time. Be sure to ask your co-parent in advance when a good time of day (morning, lunch, afternoon, etc.) and if they prefer one day of the week over another. The best thing you can do is get them on the phone when scheduling the next appointment so they can pick the date and time.

Beware that high-conflict exes like to be in control of everything. It is not uncommon for them to make the kids so uncomfortable after the appointments that the kids ask you not to attend. You are their parent and you have every right to be there. In high-conflict cases, I would recommend you attend all and any until your kids are 18. For private teenage matters, such as a physical or an ob-gyn appointment, you can step outside the room and be called back in when the doctor sees fit. The last thing you want is your child being put on medication that you don't agree with (for example, acne medication or hormone treatment) without your consent or knowledge, as most medications have a list of side effects that you need to be aware of.

Unexpected Events and Emergencies

It never fails, and especially with kids, unexpected things happen. Emergencies happen. Remember that you and your co-parent are a *team*! You may be a reluctant team, but you're still a team. Kids will throw you for a loop. They will do the unexpected.

When the unexpected happens, do your best to work with your co-parent. If your kid breaks a bone and ends up in the hospital, work together to make it work for both co-parents and the kids. It's easy to fall into the old role of being a provider and taking care of things. Be sure not to overstep your bounds, but you can certainly ask if you can help. If your co-parent declines to accept your help, at least you offered.

In the events of emergencies and unexpected events, do your best to help everyone get through. Your kids may need more emotional support (all while you do, too) during times like these. Be sure to be sensitive to their feelings. They may have questions. Do your best to answer them without providing false or misleading answers. Some-times you just don't know and it's ok to not have all the answers.

School and Daycare

You may be new to navigating the school and daycare landscape. If your co-parent was the one who primarily dealt with the school and daycare, then you may be totally in the dark. Now is the time to get up to speed!

The first thing you're going to want to do is to learn where your kids' school and daycare are. Next, you should introduce yourself when you are there picking up or dropping off your kids. Let them know when to expect you and when to expect your co-parent. Ask them if there have been any issues or things that you should know about. Be sure to familiarize yourself with any special procedures that the school or daycare may have. If there are special times to drop off or pick up, you need to find that out.

You also need to find out about car lines and where you need to drive to get into them. Don't show up to pick up your kids and totally block the flow of traffic! Another thing to consider is that some schools want you to have a sign you can hold up with the child's name. This is helpful for the school to tell your kids to come out of the waiting crowd. If you need something like that, it's better to find out in advance.

Ideally, you will find all this information out from your co-parent, but you may have to go get it from the school or daycare directly. If you have to go get the information directly, I would recommend going there during a non-peak time (not during drop off or pick up) and visiting with the front office staff. You will likely find them very helpful as long as you show up when it's not crazy.

While you're there, make sure that the school or daycare has your contact information including your address, phone number and email. Let them know that you want both parents contacted about things, not just a single parent. You may need to bring court paperwork to show that you have a right to the kids' records and show the custody schedule.

Some schools use an app that you may need to sign up for. My kids' school uses an app called Power School and it tells us their grades, lunch balances and it will even send a notification if they are marked absent. Whatever tools your kids' school uses to communicate, it's important that you engage with them.

I would recommend putting important phone numbers in your phone. If the school or daycare calls you, you need to answer that! You will want the number to come up in your phone so you can answer the call and not let it go to voicemail.

At the beginning of the divorce process, you may want to have parent-teacher conferences with your kids' teachers or school counselor, especially if they are elementary or middle-school aged. Let the teacher know that there are some changes at home and that the student may have some rough days during the transition. You should ideally have these with your co-parent present, but if you have to have them separate, be sure you are not disparaging to your co-parent. Let the teacher know they can contact both of you if there are issues. It's also helpful to ask them to contact you if they notice any significant changes for the worse in the student. Having a little face-to-face time with the teacher goes a long way in letting them know that you're going to be an active participant in your kids' education.

As an active participant, you will want to make sure that you attend the kids' school and sporting events, even on the times when it's not your time with the kids. You can miss an event here and there if you have a good reason, but you should be attending a majority of things.

You will also want to make sure that you attend ALL the regular parent-teacher conferences. This is your chance to hear firsthand how your kids are doing and what challenges they are having. It will also give you a voice to influence the decisions about your kids' education. If you don't show up, you can't complain that you don't have any control. If you can't be there in person, ask to be there on a video call or phone call.

Time with Kids

When you get divorced, the hardest thing can be the reduced time that you will have with your kids. Even if you get equal shared parenting (where each parent has the kids half the time), the amount of time you have with your kids is half of what it was when you were married. If you don't get half and have something less than that, your time is even more limited. It's important that you make the most of the time that you do have with your kids. That means being ready to spend time with your kids.

Preparation for Kid Time

A little preparation before your kids' time can go a long way. You need to prepare yourself mentally as well as make sure that your home is ready for them.

Before your "kid time," you should prepare yourself mentally so you can be emotionally there for your kids. It's easy to get wrapped up in life. Things can drag you down, but it's important that, to the best of your abilities, you don't let these things affect your time with your kids. That time is precious and limited. If you've got something bothering you, then you need to put that aside and make room for your kids. You don't want some stress over money or something at work keeping you from missing the little moments with your kids.

It's also important that you prepare your home for your time with your kids. Ideally, you will do these things before each time you have them. Take some time to do the chores that you don't want to have to do while the kids are there. After all, doing chores while kids are around (especially little ones) can be difficult at best. Take a few minutes to get the laundry going, sweep the floors, and clean the kitchen. It's better you do these things before your kids come over so you are not doing them while they are there.

During Kid Time

During your kid time, you want to be there for your kids! While your kids are there, spend time with them. Do activities together. Ask them things, teach them things. Let them explore, be curious with them. Don't underestimate the bonding that happens with your kids when you watch a movie with them. Interacting and playing with them is also a powerful way to strengthen your bonds. Be curious; ask them about their toys or video games. The simple point is that you want to be there for your kids. Not just physically there. You want to be mentally there.

When It's not your kid's time

Even when it's not your kids' time, you can be there for your kids. If they call or message you, be sure to pick up or message them back. Spend your time apart from them doing the boring things that would be difficult with the kids, such as your therapy appointments, dishes, vacuuming, mopping, and laundry. Some chores can be fun to do with the kids, like going through the car wash or taking them grocery shopping and letting them pick out dessert. Co-parenting takes a bit more planning than before you were divorced, but with a little bit of time invested in planning you can make the best of the limited time you have with your kids. Even with 50/50 custody, you still have limited time with the kids.

Chapter Twenty-Nine

Managing Conflict

W<u>hat is conflict?</u>
Dwyer (2020) states that "Conflict is basically a disagreement through which everybody involved perceives a threat to their needs, interests, values, or goals." This basically sums up conflict pretty well. If two people disagree, and there is nothing at stake, then there isn't much conflict. But if two people disagree and one or both has a lot to lose or gain, then there is conflict. This "a lot to lose or gain" is the threat. It's the threat that creates conflict and tension.

Think about a dramatic action movie. If there is no threat and no conflict, then it's gonna be a boring movie! There is actually a pattern that most stories follow called the hero's journey. It's the classic journey where a character goes through conflict and eventually rises to become successful. While conflict makes for good storytelling, it makes for a lousy co-parenting experience for both parents and kids alike. You want a boring co-parenting relationship. Like Ryan Reynolds said in The Hitman's Bodyguard, "Boring is best."

It's important to remember the ingredients that are needed for conflict. The ingredients are a disagreement with a threat to one or both parties' "needs, interests, values, or goals." This comes up a lot in co-parenting. Common topics to disagree on are discipline, school, parenting time, kids' activities and money.

Money, in this case, is a really easy example. Let's take the example of paying for a pair of sneakers for your child. One party may want a name-brand shoe for the kid(s), while the other thinks the generic (at three times less cost) are just fine. Let's assume that each is paying half for these sneakers. The threat is to one person's budget. This may mean that they will have to go without something else if they are paying more for these sneakers. In this case, the threat is probably to their needs (what they will have to give up in order to pay for these sneakers) and also their values (generic vs. name brands).

In this example, you also have to consider the "needs, interests, values, or goals" of the children. How important are name brands to them in a social setting like school? Having a name brand (as stupid as it sounds) may make them more socially accepted. This would fill their goal of being accepted at school. Is that need greater than the need to conserve the budget? Also, keep in mind quality. Will the name-brand shoes last a little longer or have better arch and heel support for your rapidly growing child? Or is it about to be summertime and your "rather be barefoot" kid will only be wearing these shoes for another three weeks before they end up living under the entry room table for the next two months? Try to keep these factors in mind when making decisions.

If you can step back from each situation and try and think what the other person's motivation is (in other words- their needs, interests, values, or goals), then you may be able to understand where they are coming from. This is a valuable tool when negotiating or ratio-nalizing something with the other party. As your kid(s) get older, it is also wise to keep their individual needs, interests and goals in mind. You could even ask your kid if having the name-brand shoe is important to *them*. Sometimes older kid(s) would be willing to negotiate extra chores or re-use last year's backpack in exchange for the name-brand shoes. Would your co-parent be willing to make up the extra cost difference and not hold it against you later if THEY are the ones that are dead-set on the name brand?

The interesting thing about conflict is that if you remove the threat, there is no conflict. You become indifferent because it doesn't affect you.

Sometimes in divorce, we create our own conflict simply because we want to stand our ground. While standing your ground isn't necessarily a bad idea (depending on the circumstances), you do need to pick and choose your battles. You have to decide what's important to you and your family. Ask yourself, is this really that important? Am I going to remember this in a month, two years, or ten years down the road? Is this thing that I'm fighting about really something that has consequences?

This may lead you to conclude not to fight about anything. While it may seem the way to be conflict-free is to just give in to what the other person wants all the time, this will not lead you to a life of happiness. Giving in to whatever someone else wants is an example of unhealthy boundaries and it will simply allow you to be walked all over by various people in your life, from your co-parent to your boss at work, to your friends. Boundaries are important; they help keep us straight and centered. There is a balance between having boundaries (which may include some conflict) and letting go.

When you go through a divorce, you'll be confronted with lots of conflict. Conflict will be everywhere-from the court proceedings to the communications you have with your co-parent. The thing that is unique about conflict is that it does take two people to tango (be in conflict). If you just go along with everything that your co-parent says, then there is virtually no conflict. The problem is our laws don't protect somebody that acts this way. If you just go along with your co-parent, you'll likely lose all your money and most of your time with the kids. Obviously, this is not a desired outcome. Because we want to have our income and time with our kids (among other things), we have to deal with conflict in divorce. Conflict will be apparent not only during the divorce but also after the divorce while co-parenting. In order to successfully navigate your divorce and become a good co-parent, you'll need to learn how to deal with conflict. Just dealing with conflict isn't good enough. You'll need to learn how to successfully reduce and resolve conflict. It's the minimization and de-escalation that makes the difference between a divorce and a really bad divorce.

<u>Is it worth it?</u>

The first step of conflict reduction is for you to decide if there is actually conflict and/or if it's worth being conflict over. If it's not worth being in conflict over, you can simply move on and stop devoting time and energy to whatever topic is at hand.

If it is worth being in conflict over, the next question you need to ask yourself is how much time and energy are you willing to devote to this conflict? You may decide that some things are worth fighting for, but just a little bit. And then there are those things that are worth fighting *a lot* for. Those are the things you're willing to put a lot of time and energy into. So once you've made the decision (if something is worth being in conflict for), the next thing you need to decide is how much time and energy you are willing to devote to this particular topic of conflict. You will be surprised at how stopping to evaluate this can make you realize how many things you are fighting for that just are not worth it.

Something like the amount of child support you pay may be worth devoting a significant amount of conflict to. It will affect you for a number of years to come and cost you significant money. You wouldn't devote the same amount of conflict to, say, giving five dollars to your child for something they need. This is a minor financial impact compared to the larger financial impact of long-term child support.

Don't get me wrong, there are things that are worth fighting for. You may be reading this thinking that nothing is worth fighting for, but that's simply not true. You also may be in a tough place emotionally. You may be feeling very angry, on edge and ready to fight- or the exact opposite where you are beaten down, tired of fighting, tired of the drama and just emotionally exhausted! All of those feelings are normal.

The main point here is to get you in the mindset of:

1) recognizing when there is conflict.

2) deciding if the conflict is worth it.

3) deciding how much time and energy you are willing to devote to this specific conflict.

The amount of time and energy devoted to the conflict should be proportional to the type of conflict it is and the impact it has on your life.

Setting Boundaries

There are four main types of boundaries that you should be aware of after separation (*4 Types of Boundaries in Relationships After Separation,* 2021). These are:

1) Physical Boundaries – having your own space if living together and not having access to the others' space if you live apart (i.e., she doesn't have a key and comes in whenever she wants to your living space).

2) Communication Boundaries – Having boundaries on the kinds of communications you will have and how and when you will have them.

3) Financial Boundaries – Who pays for what, what costs can be incurred, and how the kids spend or get money.

4) Emotional Boundaries – Not being the emotional support for the other person, speaking negatively about the other person, not sharing details of their dating life.

When a conflict comes up, you should stop and think about your boundaries. What are you willing and NOT willing to accept or do? This can be a good way to help you de-escalate situations easily. If your boundaries are reasonable, then you'll keep conflict to a minimum in order to ensure your sanity. It's very easy when going through a divorce to have unreasonable boundaries, which therefore keeps conflict unreasonable…and alive.

It is important you learn to set your boundaries to a reasonable level! On one end of the scale, you should be accommodating to your co-parent as best as possible without letting them totally control your life. Your boundaries should be firm but fluid enough to accommodate life with children. Kids often will change your plans simply because they are unpredictable. Schools will have schedule changes, kids will get sick, and kids also have wildly unstable emotions at times (especially toddlers and teenagers). The truth is, your co-parent and you need to be flexible when it comes to your kids. I say this with caution because if you are co-parenting with a high-conflict ex, then you will need to have stronger boundaries with your ex, but while having strong boundaries with your ex, you can still be flexible for your kids. Some co-parents will try to take advantage of this in order to control their co-parent. I'm not advocating that you let your co-parent control you, but I am advocating that you have reasonable flexibility in order not to induce conflict with your co-parent.

When setting boundaries, it's important to know where you stand on different topics. This will take some amount of self-reflection, and you may not be able to answer where your boundaries are on all topics all at once. You should develop these over time and your boundaries may even change as your co-parenting relationship changes and your kids' needs change. In other words, it's okay to go through the discovery process to figure out who you really are and where your boundaries really are.

<u>When to ask for help</u>

It's important to know when going through a divorce or co-parenting that you're really not ever totally alone. There's always somebody that you can go to to ask for help. Help may come in several different forms, from asking a friend or mentor what they would do in a certain situation to the other end of the spectrum which should be going to professionals such as psychologists or doctors.

Help can come in all different forms, from talking to people or even educating yourself on a particular subject. The thing to remember is that there IS help; you just need to take the initiative to get it. But when do you ask for help? I would say that answer really depends on the situation, but you should plan on asking for help any time that you are unsure if the conflict is worth it. Another time to ask for help would be if you are unsure of what the right answer is or you are trying to decide between several different options.

Sometimes help doesn't always come the instant that you want it. It's okay to remember that for most topics (when in conflict with the co-parent) it's okay to give them a response in a reasonable amount of time. You don't have to instantly answer them about everything. It's okay to say, "I'll get back to you on that." Just make sure that you do! It's not okay to tell them, "I'll get back to you on that," and then never follow through. That will just cause more conflict. It's also good when your co-parent realizes that you will not always give them an immediate answer to things because it will set a precedent. When you immediately answer somebody *every* time, they come to expect that you should give them an instant answer to everything they ask. Not giving them an instant answer will give you some time to reflect and go seek help if you need to.

<u>What are some good sources of help?</u>

Help is all around you; you just need to know where to look. The first good source of help (of course) is the Internet. Just remember not everything on the Internet is true. You can find both good and bad advice on the Internet, so use your best judgment when deciding if something that you're reading on the Internet is actually helpful or not. Articles can be a great way to get information about a particular subject, and all you have to do to find articles about different topics is to simply type a question into a search engine. Check the source or website name for credibility and try to remember the ones that you feel are helpful to you in this new chapter of your life.

If you can't find your answer on the web, your next best area for help is to go to a friend and ask them what they would do in the same situation. It's important you pick a friend who is someone that you trust and that is not in a lot of conflict themselves. Ask them what they would do in your situation. Don't ask them to tell you what to do, but rather ask them what they would do. You want to give them enough information so that they can give you their advice based on what you know. Remember, just because they give you advice-doesn't mean you need to take it. Oftentimes, we make new friends while going through a divorce. Suddenly, you may have more in common with your divorced co-workers than you did before. They may make great mentors for you having been through it before and maybe they can share their triumphs and failures with you now that they've reached the other side and their kids are grown. Just like with the Internet, consider your source when taking advice.

Sometimes it's best to seek advice from two or three different people and see if there's any consistency among their answers. If they're all telling you to do the same thing, it may be good advice. Just be wary that if you ask three different people that are very similar the same thing, it's likely that you will get the same answers. For instance, the three homeless-looking alcoholics at the local bar may all agree on what you should do, but do you really think they're giving you the best advice? Try to get your advice from people who have different perspectives so you can understand how people would view the situation from different lenses.

Sometimes going to your friends and family just really isn't going to cut it. Sometimes you need actual professional advice. Let's face it- if you've got a serious illness, going to your friends and family is only going to get you so far. At some point, you're going to want to talk with someone who has training in the specific area that you're having an issue with. When getting help and advice, if the other two methods of first educating yourself and second seeking out advice from your friends and family doesn't work, the only thing left to do is escalate things to a professional. Picking out professionals can be a process all on its own. I talk about that in other places in this book. Remember, when going to a professional, they will need all relevant information so they can give you their professional opinion. Not giving them *all* information may give you the answer that you want to hear, but not necessarily the one you need.

Conflict around parenting time

Parenting time is another topic that creates a lot of conflict. Things like when does each person have the children, where do you exchange the kids? What time do you exchange? What can the kids do and not do when they're with each parent? All of these topics will create conflict at one point or another. Just like money, it's often best to get this written down so that it does not create conflict later on. Having these strong written boundaries helps prevent conflict in the future. A good parenting plan will be fairly detailed and ensure that both parties are able to comply. When going through a divorce, you should have written down agreements to where and when you'll change the kids. Having things written down can eliminate the conflict before it even starts.

<u>Conflict around money</u>

Another common source of conflict is money. How much to spend, where to spend it, and who gets what are all topics that cause a great amount of conflict, especially in divorce but also during co-parenting. Money is obviously a limited source because if it were unlimited, we certainly wouldn't have conflict around it. Unfortunately, none of us have unlimited financial resources, so this is something that we need to protect, and it's that protection that causes us conflict. The best way to not have conflict after the divorce is to have some clear written guidelines around money and who pays for what in your divorce papers. While you're going *through* the divorce, you may not have this or you may have been asked to pay something unreasonable. Sadly in a lot of divorces, there are times when people are ordered to pay unreasonable amounts of money or for an unreasonable number of things. Unfortunately, in divorce, it's often men who get financially screwed. It's as simple as that, and it causes a great amount of conflict. Our court systems have been slow to recognize the financial responsibilities of women and often hand out child support that isn't fair and is in excess of anything that is reasonable. Short of getting the laws changed in your state, there is not much that you can do to change the system. That being said, you have to learn to live with the cards that you're dealt. You will need to prioritize what your kids get in divorce financially and what you get to use for yourself financially. Not having your financial resources and not having control of your own financial resources can be infuriating! It is honestly one of the more difficult things to come to terms with in divorce and post-divorce.

There can also be a lot of conflict because not only have you been ordered to pay gross amounts of money, that money does not seem to get used on your children. This is a difficult topic for a lot of men and is honestly one that is not dealt with properly in the majority of situations. As each situation is a little different, I can't really go into all of them here, but an attorney in your local jurisdiction will be able to tell you if you have any legal recourse. A lot of times you won't and you'll just need to deal with the conflict (and the associated anger that comes with that conflict). So what do you do when you're paying money for child support and that person that you are paying the money to is using it on themselves and not spending it on the children? Honestly, this is a really tough one. You have to evaluate what your options are and (more importantly) what your *reasonable* options are. This is a sort of thing that will drive you nuts if you let it. A few words of advice though on this: Remember that conflict is between you and your ex-spouse/co-parent. It is not with your children. Keep conflict between the adults. Also, remember that it is not the children's fault. Oftentimes children will get caught in between conflicting adults and it is very tough on them emotionally. Sometimes it's hard not to want to take out your frustrations. Physical showings of emotions (such as punching a wall, screaming, slamming) are definitely not good in front of your children. If you have to do this, do it somewhere private.

Try your best to remember that your kid(s) won't be kids forever. One day they will grow up and be able to look back and remember that you delivered that check to their other parent every month like clockwork, but they still went without as kids at no fault to you. They'll remember seeing their other parent spend money on expensive hair products, fake nails, or going out with friends while they were denied the nice clothes, shoes, and Paw Patrol string cheese for their school lunches. As hard as it is for you right now, when your kids grow up, they will recognize what happened and will end up respecting you more.

<u>Reducing conflict - an example</u>

Let's get into the meat of the situation here, there is something that your co-parent wants and you disagree and want something different. You've gone through the decision process and decided that it *is* something that you want to discuss with them because it is important enough to you. The question is, "How do you do that"? We really only have two options when it comes to negotiating conflict with your co-parent. The first option is to do it in person. The second option is to do it over some form of written communication.

You may want to choose in person if you're comfortable with your co-parent that the disagreement won't escalate to unreasonable levels (like physical violence) or that your co-parent won't accuse you of something, such as bullying, intimidating, etc. In other words, there has to be a certain level of trust in order to negotiate with them in person. This includes both with and without witnesses. In-person may be a good option if neither of you is high-conflict and you both can reasonably discuss things in an adult manner.

If you don't have that level of trust with your co-parent or the topic is simply too heated, you may need to resort to negotiating over written communication. Written communication can be a double-edged sword because things that you write can be used against you. Don't think for one second that it won't be if it gives an advantage to the other party. Just remember, if you do write something down that gives an advantage to the other person, it is likely to be used against you. Written communication will reduce the exposure you have to the "he said, she said." scenario. It also gives you time to form your thoughts and maybe rewrite things once or twice before actually sending it to them.

Whether you're communicating in person or through a written form like email, the tactics and methods actually used to reduce conflict and negotiate what you want are relatively the same.

One issue men sometimes have in communicating with women is men tend to be logical thinkers, while women tend to be emotionally driven. This stereotype doesn't always hold up for everybody, but it is a stereotype because it does apply a lot of the time. Men want to state facts and opinions, while women make decisions based on their emotions. So in order to successfully negotiate with most women, you need to be cognizant of her emotions and understand that your drive to just tell her the facts probably isn't going to work. You'll want to use leaders like "I feel…." Don't be afraid to visualize the future for the other person. Wouldn't it be great if our children were able to do XYZ?

While "I" statements apply to all levels of co-parenting relationships- the good, bad and ugly- it is relatively useless to try to negotiate with a terrorist (aka high-conflict ex). I recommend you do NOT try to visualize the future for them. For example, trying to convince a high-conflict ex to let you have the kid(s) for an additional two days to take the children on a Hawaii vacation with "Wouldn't it be great if the kids got to experience Hawaii?" will only add fuel to the fire. Sadly because no, she doesn't want the kids to go to Hawaii with YOU. No, she doesn't care if the parental alienation she's been embarking on is working and you desperately need some bonding time with them. And also, she doesn't care if it's for their Grandmother's memorial service. In a high-conflict divorce, state the facts over the agreed-upon parenting app "The kid(s) will be going to Hawaii with me on this day. The service is on this day. Could I please return them to you on this day? If yes, is there a particular day you would like in exchange? Thank you." If she says no, then the way to reduce conflict would be to adjust your plans to the court order or the ex's demands. Maybe you will have to catch a red-eye to have them back at the time she demands. Maybe your younger kids simply will not get to go.

In summary, conflict is a part of divorce whether we like it or not. It's important to remember that YOU can make that conflict greater or reduce it. Hopefully, you'll decide to reduce conflict as much as possible and only worry about those truly important things.

Sometimes you will be smack dab in the middle of conflict when you realize that it just isn't that important. You may ask yourself, "How did I get here?". It's okay to recognize that you may have gotten yourself into a conflict inadvertently, but just because you got yourself into conflict doesn't mean that you have to *stay* in conflict. You can choose to de-escalate at any time, even if it means losing some negotiating power you may have had in the beginning.

It's also okay to completely put the conflict on pause and pick it up at another time. Just tell your co-parent, "We'll need to put this on pause." Sometimes a cooling-off period will help both parties reset and start off in a better place when they resume conversations about the topic.

Chapter Thirty

Parental Alienation

The term Parental Alienation comes up often when talking about the family court system. Simply put, Parental Alienation is an attempt by a parent to cause the child or children to dislike (or worse- hate) the other parent. This is not natural, as even children who have been abused by parents still show love towards their abusive parents. Simply put, children have a biological need for their parents and a natural love for them. So for a child to not want anything to do with a parent is not natural (usually).

I say usually because, as with all things that deal with emotions, it's… well… complicated. When you're dealing with the brain (really several brains because you have at least two parents and one child with often more people involved), there are lots of variables and things are not exactly predictable. The best that we can do is study natural child-parent bonds and relationships. Children naturally love both their parents, regardless if they are together or divorced. So when a child starts to distance themselves emotionally from one of their parents, parental alienation becomes a suspect in the equation.

That's not to say that sometimes children will figure out that one parent or the other may not be healthy to be in their lives. Usually, that realization is something that takes a lot of therapy and is hard to do.

So, now that you know that it's not normal for a child to reject one of their parents, the question is how does the child (or children) get to that point? The simple answer is that it can be one of the parents doing a number of things to disparage the other parent. Sometimes it comes in the form of talking bad about the other parent, or they could be openly criticizing the other parent (either directly to the kids or it could be in earshot of the kids) when talking to another adult.

Parental Alienation would be your child hearing things like "Your father is an idiot" or "Your father doesn't care about you." Another common one includes money in the mix - "If your father loved you, he would pay the child support he owes me" or even "Sorry, you can't have that toy/those shoes/that game because your father doesn't give me enough money." Again this could be directly to the kids or sometimes intentionally to another adult when the kids can hear. It's also common for Alienating Parents to criticize how the other parent does things. This could be from parenting styles, what you choose to feed the kids, to the directions that you take when driving somewhere.

Parental Alienation could also be things that make life difficult for the other parent. It could be doing things like making one parent drive much further than the other parent to exchange the kids, or the parent who is in charge of scheduling things purposely telling the other parent the wrong times for important events such as parent/teacher meetings, the kids' games and/or practices, appointments, etc.

Parents that are actively engaged in Parental Alienation want to make the kids hate or loathe the other parent, so the kids don't want to spend any time with that other parent. This can go as far as making the kids believe that they are in danger and should be afraid of that other parent or also be as subtle as the Alienating Parent getting upset when the kids are going to the "other parent's house." What puts even more burden on the kids is when the Alienating Parent appears hurt or upset or even gives the kids the silent treatment when they come back from their other home and they had a good time. These displays of emotions to the kids are training the kids to see your custody time as bad or hurtful to their other parent.

Other subtle examples of Parental Alienation would be referring to you by your first name instead of Dad when speaking to the kids, changing the children's last names to drop yours, and having a negative tone in their voice when speaking of you. Babies, young children, and teens alike are all very perceptive. They pick up on resentment, negativity, tones, and facial expressions.

It's worth noting here that, as with all things emotional, these things exist on a spectrum. At one end of the spectrum, you have parents doing these things and not being aware that they are harmful (i.e., buying your daughter something the other parent didn't approve of). On the other hand, you have parents that are intentionally doing these things for a purpose (like to get more custody time so they can get more money from child support).

Sadly, this is an incredibly complex subject, and when it comes to family court there is very little accountability for these kinds of behaviors. Judges simply don't hold people accountable when they do find out these things are happening and usually unless there is an in-depth trial, the judge never even finds out these things are happening (aside from an accusation). The bottom line here is don't expect accountability (for anything, especially your ex's bad behavior or ill intentions) in family court.

Remember to follow the golden rule here: "If you don't have something nice to say, don't say anything at all." If you have to vent about your ex, make sure the kids are not with you (trust me, they are listening from the other room), and it's generally best to only do this to a professional therapist because even things that you say to your friends can make their way back to your ex or your kids. From here on out, I suggest you take the high road. Be the bigger person. When the ex is working on alienating you from your kids, they will do things to purposely provoke you and then tell the kids, "See how angry/scary your dad is!". Sadly, you're going to have to hone in on those acting skills and learn to control your temper even in the face of provocations from an alienator. Some advice out there on Parental Alienation will tell you not to react, not to defend yourself, not to say anything to the kids, and just go about your merry way. I suggest a happy medium. While I definitely don't suggest engaging in Parental Alienation against the other parent, I do suggest calmly explaining or defending YOUR actions, words, etc. to the kids in an age-appropriate way.

All in all, Parental Alienation is a terrible thing. It has awful consequences for all involved, particularly the children. When faced with Parental Alienation, the best things that you can do is:

- Make sure you yourself are not alienating the other parent.

- Document the other parents' actions the best you can when you do discover it's happening.

- Get yourself (better yet, you AND the kids) into a family therapist to start working on repairing your relationship with your kids asap.

- Don't engage with her, don't feed the fire. Be the bigger person and take the high road.

PART 3 - BATTLE PLAN

Chapter Thirty-One

Legal System Introduction

L egal disclaimer: I'm not a lawyer or attorney and cannot provide legal advice. The legal information in this book is simply that- informational and should not be construed in any other manner. Legal questions can only be answered by a licensed attorney and you should find one for your case. If you are litigating your case pro se, be sure to spend time finding out as much information as you can.

I find that the more information I know about something, the less apprehension I have about it. In this legal section, I hope to give you just a background or a high-level overview of the legal divorce process. As with many things in this book, these next few chapters are designed to give you an introduction and not a deep dive into any one of these topics. There are many books and articles that have been written on such topics and I would encourage you, if you need to know more about something, to do further research. This is the shorthand version of the divorce process. A generic divorce guide meant to summarize all 50 U.S. states. Every state is slightly unique, and some states have very different and complex laws.

Legal System Introduction

The legal system in the United States may be well-intentioned, but the one thing it does really well is getting litigants to fight. What that means for you in a family divorce court is that both you and your ex-spouse will lose a great deal of time, money and energy in the legal system. The only clear winners here are attorneys. The attorneys know the system very well, and they use that to their full advantage. While your attorney may be on your "side," their best interest is to make as much money from you as possible. Now, that's not to say there aren't attorneys out there that do a great deal of good because there are. Conversely, there are attorneys out there that do a great deal of harm as well (whether it be to your time with your kids or just to your finances). Our society doesn't have attorney jokes for no reason at all!

The system is intended to be fair, but over time it's evolved into something that generally seems far from fair. If you're looking to the family court system for any sort of vindication or validation, you are going to be disappointed. At best, everyone loses (mom, dad, kids), and the only winners are the bank accounts of the attorneys and other professionals.

The family court system is a system where there is no fair fight. Oftentimes one party will file without the other's knowledge. That person finds out they are getting kicked out of the house, most of their paycheck will go to the other party and they will now have very limited (if any at all) time with the kids. In this situation, a man is left homeless, penniless, and isolated from his family. Not exactly a great position to start a legal battle in!

Don't take this opening as me saying the legal system has never done anything good for families. There are cases and instances that it has. The current system is not generally set up to peacefully separate families and set up sustainable new lives. It's set up intentionally in an adversarial manner so that each side fights for their money and time with the kids. In this "winner takes all" approach, it assures there is no winner, only those that have lost less than the others.

The ideal solution is to not fight in court if you can avoid it, and this happens in a lot of cases. While good statistics don't exist for most states, many attorneys will tell you a lot of cases don't end up in court. They are settled through endless emails and maybe some face-to-face meetings with all the parties. Nowadays, many family law courts like the divorcing parties to work everything out outside of the courtroom. One method is through mediation, which can save the judges time.

Some divorcing couples have wised up to this expensive legal dance and decided to go completely different routes. Some pick a process called collaborative divorce where both parties agree to settle everything completely out of court. Others are able to settle all the matters with minimal engagement with the attorneys. I would say you can choose which path you take, but I would probably be giving you false hope. The reality is that sometimes the path is chosen by the other party and there is nothing you can do about it.

The best that I can do is to help you understand the different options so you can maybe try and influence the one that you and your ex pick. If you do get forced down a path you don't want (like going through court), then in these following pages, I'll do my best to try and give you some basic information about the process and what you can expect.

There are hundreds of family courts around the country. They are generally set up in each county. Most courts have several judges that hear cases and family court is generally always a busy place. In the following pages, everything written about family courts is stated as a generality. Nothing is meant to apply to any specific court, and the court that you are in may be different. The ones that know your LOCAL legal system the best are the attorneys that practice there every day. In short, these words are a guide, not an absolute. I'm not giving any guarantee that they apply in your specific court.

Because courts can be so specific, I'll talk mostly about the high-level processes which generally don't change much. It's worth noting that a few states are completely different from the others. One aspect is called community property. If you live in Arizona, California, Idaho, Louisiana, Nevada, New Mexico, Texas, Washington or Wisconsin- then you live in a community property state (as of 2020). Additionally, if you live in Alaska, you may be part of community property. These states separate and account for property and who-owes-who completely differently from the rest of the country.

<u>What's the best way to deal with this legal system when you're getting a divorce?</u>

In short, the best battle plan is to get in and get out! Legal battles can stretch on for years at a time. It is not uncommon for divorces to take anywhere from one year to three years- especially when battling for custody, child support and property division. Getting divorced is all about control and power. Who gets control of the money, control of the children and who has the power to make decisions? There are no winners and losers between spouses in the court system; there are only losers. The secret to losing the least is to get in and get out with the least amount of fighting.

If your ex-spouse is being particularly unreasonable, there's a chance that if you don't challenge her in the court system, you will lose everything. You will lose your time, you will lose your dignity, and you will most certainly lose your money. Unfortunately, attorneys do very little to reduce conflict in family court. You see, attorneys survive and thrive from conflict. Attorneys like to win, they like challenging the other attorney. For them, this is a game. It's a game that's costing you $200 to $500 per hour. So, for you, it's a very expensive game. And even if you go bankrupt (which is highly likely), be assured that the attorneys will be the only ones to show up in your bankruptcy hearing requesting to get paid - even though they were the ones that caused the bills which put you in bankruptcy in the first place! They'll argue it's not their fault, they weren't the ones that had a broken relationship and needed a divorce. While this is all sadly true, keep in mind that very few attorneys will try to reduce your costs in a divorce. And why would they? They have no incentive to do so because your fight is what pays their bills! Besides, clients can be hard to find, and the client who is fighting with their ex-spouse is a good source of income.

I will remind you again; The only way to pay the attorneys the least amount of money possible is to get in and get out! This section will talk a little bit about how to do that. You have to decide which fights are worth having and which ones are not. Much like the Kenny Rogers song "The Gambler," you have to "know when to hold 'em, and know when to fold 'em." The key to knowing when to fight and when to let go can be difficult, especially when you're emotional. The first step to making a rational decision when you're emotional, though, is understanding your emotions. Realizing this fact, and being able to take a step back and look at things rationally, is the easiest way to remove that emotion from your decision.

For example, when you're going through the divorce process, the one thing you have to ask yourself continuously is, "What will this look like once the dust is settled?" Try and imagine yourself in that post-divorce world, and most of the conflict has settled down. Imagine what you want your life to be like once exchanges become routine and the finances have been stable for some time. This is what you're fighting for in your divorce! It is easy to lose sight of this post-divorce life when you're in the heat of a legal battle.

The legal fight you're having now has consequences far into the future. If you have young children, the outcome will last until the next legal battle over the kids or until the children become adults - whatever age that may be in your state. With that said, it's important that you fight for the right things and not waste money on things that don't really matter. Most attorneys will fight over anything. Good attorneys will advise you to let go of specific things, but litigants can be emotional, ignoring the professional legal advice.

It's been said that knowledge is power, and that also holds true in the case of divorce. I find that knowledge is comforting. Going through my divorce, no one sat me down and explained the process to me. I did research on the Internet. But of course, like many things on the Internet, I just found bits and pieces of information. I want this book to be your friend, one that sits you down and explains as much to you as you can absorb. I truly hope that this knowledge gives you the power that you need to get through your divorce.

The first part of this legal section will cover the process of divorce in general terms. Each state has its own distinct process, so I encourage you to research your own state's process. What I cover in this book are things that are generally consistent from state to state. Even within states, the process may be slightly different from court to court. Finding an attorney that knows your local court process will be important.

Power and Control

Divorce is about power and control. Nothing more, nothing less. While divorce can be very emotional, the heart of the matter is that divorce is simply a business transaction. It is a dissolution of a marriage and setting up the terms and conditions for the parties' future interactions. The divorce fight is over power and control. This includes power and control of the property and assets that the parties jointly own and the children that the parties have. While it's easy to see that splitting property and assets is simply a business transaction, emotions make it more difficult to see that the issues with the children are simply a business transaction as well. At the end of the day, all issues related to divorce are summarily "business transactions." The question is: "Who will have power and control?" This can be financial power and control. It could be decision-making power and control. If you can frame this process in those terms and remove the emotional element from getting divorced, the process will progress much more quickly. The reason why many divorces drag on is because people become emotionally attached to specific issues. The legal system is not designed to be quick; it's a slow and arduous process on purpose. It's slow and arduous for a good reason, as the decisions made in court have long-lasting effects, and the judges certainly understand this. Sadly, just because the process is slow, that doesn't mean it's fair or equal.

When you look at divorce through the lens of power and control, many issues become much simpler. In the beginning of a divorce, the process seems extremely complex and can be overwhelming. You may find that if you can try to set emotions aside and break down each issue into simpler terms, you won't be so overwhelmed.

In this section of the book. I hope to give you a high-level overview of the divorce process, legally speaking. My hope is that this information will give you comfort because knowledge is power. As cliché as it sounds, it's true. I am a firm believer that if you know what's happened and what is going to happen, then you can prepare for it. While divorce is in some ways similar from case to case, each case typically has its unique points. Again, you may need to dive deeper into some of these issues if they particularly affect you.

It's also important that you don't leave your legal case to simply let your attorney figure it out. Attorneys are extremely busy and they may need reminding from time to time about the particular details in your case. That said, there's a fine line between being involved in your case and being too involved in your case. Your attorney is a professional who knows the law (hopefully!) in your area. You should let them do their job for the most part. Your job as a client is to give them the truthful information that they need to successfully do their job. You should not withhold information from your attorney as you have an attorney-client privilege. The last thing you want is for your attorney to be surprised in court. If your attorney has all of the truthful information about your case, they can better prepare for getting the results you would like.

Moving forward, just remember that these are the guidelines and overviews, not the deep dive. Also remember, as mentioned previously, that legal processes can vary from county to county and state to state. Some states, like California and Louisiana, have particularly different legal processes, so it's important that you understand what normally happens in your area.

Emotional Control

When you're getting divorced, there are few things that will lose you more than losing your temper. In the American legal system, very often parties are not penalized for agitating the other party and getting them to snap or lose their temper! Let's be very clear, losing your temper is a very bad thing when you're getting a divorce. You may have been married for 20 years and have never lost your temper, but one outburst while you're going through the divorce will be used against you.

The things you stand to lose are time with your kids and money. Two very important things, if not the MOST important things. It's unfortunate that the legal system operates this way and there is no penalty for lying or hyperbole. This is a huge reason why the legal system is unfair and unjust, especially to men. If the courts enforce the current rules they have for perjury and conduct, then divorces will be much less dramatic. The problem is, an undramatic divorce does not make the attorneys money!

Since judges were attorneys before they became judges, there is often a cozy relationship between judges and attorneys. In simple terms, when you argue - attorneys win. A contentious divorce costs more than non-contentious ones. A good way to increase the fighting is usually through emotional manipulation and false allegations. These are immoral and illegal but accepted in our legal system.

Opposing attorneys use every tool in their toolbox trying to get you to snap. Often one side will make false allegations or will stretch the truth quite far while at the same time, they are presenting their client as perfect. In the real world, no one is perfect.

It's also important to note that the way the courts, legal system as well as a lot of local law enforcement see emotional blow-ups between divorcing couples can be unfair against men. While I am in no way justifying or condoning abuse of any kind, I have to mention that you (men) screaming and yelling in your ex's face (if female) will probably be taken much more seriously by the legal system than when she does it to you. I have heard a story of a female ex breaking into her soon-to-be ex-husband's home (she had moved out and removed herself from the lease). She proceeded to trash the place by pouring the contents of his trash can out all over the home and broke a few things. The man called the cops, who refused to come out but agreed to call the woman. She yelled at and swore at the responding officer who called her to just tell her not to do that again. NOTHING happened to her. In fact, the officer called the soon-to-be ex-husband shortly after and just told him, "Well, that didn't go well...". Now, if the situation were reversed, it probably would've ended in jail time for the man (breaking and entering as well as other charges) and a Restraining/Protection Order against him. The point here is not to state that all legal or local law enforcement are sexist against men but that there is a discrepancy in how a man's emotional "blow-up" is interpreted versus a woman's. I urge you to prepare yourself emotionally for provocations of any kind.

Regardless of what gets thrown at you, be as calm as possible. It may be one of the hardest things you have to do during this divorce, but staying calm is important. You may face false accusations, being screamed at, and worse. But staying calm is winning the battle. If need be, pretend like a camera is recording everything you say and do to and around the ex. Try your best to be the calm adult in the midst of crazy!

You may get some filings in your court case and read them and think that "This is a bunch of garbage." And the truth is, it probably is. You have to recognize what is manipulative and what is of sub-stance in these court proceedings. This can be extremely difficult to do when you're in a delicate emotional state, such as when you're going through a divorce. If you were not going through a divorce, you may read this same legal proceeding and shrug it off as crazy.

Your job is to give your attorney all the information he or she needs to dispute the claim or claims that the other party is making against you. That information can include evidence such as documents, photographs or by providing witnesses. Many times the outrageous claims don't go very far in court, but they're not designed to go far in court. They are designed to emotionally manipulate you so that you will snap! They are hoping for an emotional outburst that they can then use against you. This is classic family law court, and unfortunately, this kind of behavior is tolerated by the judges and almost never penalized. The more that the other party has to lose, the greater these manipulations will become. Often it will start small and slow at first, and several months down the line, they will grow more bold. It's not uncommon to see high-conflict cases have inci-dents of domestic violence. To be clear, I'm not suggesting that all domestic violence that happens during court proceedings is a result of the legal system. I am saying that it can be an extra factor here.

When parties are separating and emotions are high, this makes it ripe for bad things to happen.

The best thing that you can do is learn to recognize when either the opposing attorney or your ex is trying to manipulate a situation in order to get a better position for themselves. Be self-aware that your emotions are high and you may easily overreact to even small things. It's good to have a friend or therapist that you can talk to in these situations prior to responding. If you have the resources available, it's always a good idea to let your attorney respond professionally in a majority of these situations.

The opposing party may try to claim through their attorney and legal proceedings that you are abusive to the children, that you are or were abusive to her, and that you're doing things that you don't actually do (like excessive alcohol consumption or drugs). Remember, both parties' lives are under a microscope here, and having one beer on a Saturday night can be turned into you being a raging drunk! Unfortunately, the laws in place to keep attorneys from making outlandish claims are rarely enforced. Every court in the nation has a perjury law (a law against lying), but in family law, these are not enforced and litigants are certainly not penalized for lying. Anybody can say anything, and it's up to the other party to defend against those claims.

One thing that attorneys should teach you when you become their client is how to control yourself emotionally in situations where you are emotionally delicate. Often attorneys will just take the facts from you and come up with a defense. Very few attorneys will console you and let you know that this is just another manipulation tactic. If you're able to do a little work and realize that you are in an emotionally sensitive place and that many of these claims are outrageous and will not go very far - you'll be miles ahead. The best antidote for the poison of false allegations, exaggerations and other emotionally manipulative techniques is to be able to see them for what they are and be able to accurately assess what risk they really have.

If you have an attorney, the best thing you can do is ask questions when these court filing comes in. Your attorney will be able to tell you if a specific claim has any credibility and how detrimental it is to you. If a claim can easily be shown as false, then it has little impact and is something that just needs to be addressed by the attorneys.

One technique that I think is helpful when responding during divorce is the 24-hour rule. When you receive any communication (text or email or even face-to-face verbal communication) from your ex, give yourself time to pause and respond the next day. This can be frustrating to the opposing party, who is looking for an immediate answer, often with an emotional manipulation to their benefit. There are very few decisions that need to be made on the spot, so unless it's an emergency, use your best judgment and remember that generally, responses can be given a day later. It's important to give yourself time to process, to adjust emotionally and to calm down.

One technique you can use is to tell your ex something along the lines of "I'll consider that" or "Thanks for letting me know. I will respond to you tomorrow". Having these boundaries is critical for you to maintain a sense of sanity during this process. It's much easier to give a response 24 hours later which is non-emotional, than giving an emotional one on the spot. Expect your ex to push back and need an answer right then. Unless your child needs life-saving surgery, you probably can wait 24 hours to respond to them!

Using this 24-hour technique, it's important to remember to respond. It's easy to forget, especially when you are busy. Not responding will generally cause you issues as well. Find a system that works for you. This could be a note on a calendar or a Post-it note. Come up with some system that you can use to reliably remind yourself to respond the next day. A helpful technique is to set aside a specific time each day to respond to your ex. Sitting down at nine or ten in the morning or maybe at seven at night after dinner is a good way to put yourself in the mindset of communicating with her consistently without it emotionally taking up your time during the day. Co-parenting apps are a wonderful tool for this because some of them send a "read message" when you have first read a communication sent from the ex. In that case, the ex will know you received the message and then you can respond within your preferred healthy boundaries (24-hr rule).

It's worth noting that it's better to not say anything or communicate at all than to give a highly charged emotional response. Emotional responses are ripe for the opposing attorney to pick out small details to gain an advantage.

Remember, when communicating with your ex, that less is more. Don't send two or three paragraphs of emotional word vomit when a simple "Thank you for letting me know" will do. The less you react to emotional manipulation, the better off you are.

When you are doing a good job of not playing into the emotional manipulation, the opposing parties will often "crank up" the heat on emotional manipulation. If you're able to recognize the small provocations now, know that when this heat is turned up, they will look even more ridiculous!

When going through a divorce, you also need to be cooperative. You must walk a fine line between not being emotionally manipulated and not looking like you are being uncooperative. This is a common claim that is used in family court every day. The argument is that one party is uncooperative and therefore, the other party should have the majority of time with the children and make all the decisions! Part of your emotional control arsenal needs to be that you are setting good boundaries and not reacting but that you are also communicating and working to the best of your abilities with the other party.

If you feel like you're losing control, or the situation has escalated where you are being emotional in front of your ex (or in communications to your ex), an important technique is to hit the pause button. Simply stop, pause and walk away or remove yourself from the situation entirely (even if it's just for a few minutes). The important thing is to take some time to reflect on how you got to the point of where you are and what you can do differently to ensure that the situation does not escalate again. This can be something as simple as asking your attorney to respond to communications for a period of time or recognizing poor boundaries and having better ones the next time. Remember, now that you are divorcing, you do not OWE your ex an immediate response unless it is a true emergency. You are ALLOWED to take time to think things through.

It's important to recognize that this is a process and that nobody gets it straight out of the gate. Recognize that emotional control (especially during the divorce process) is something that you will improve on as you gain more experience. If something doesn't go the way you thought it should pause and think about what happened. Then think about what you can do better the next time. It can even be helpful to write this whole process down on a sheet of paper and take notes. The important thing is that you reflect on how you got into the situation and how the outcome could have been different if you had reacted differently.

It's also important to remember that nobody's perfect and that this process of improving your emotional control may take a long time to develop. Make sure you're not down on yourself or overly critical to the point where you feel like you "can't do anything right." In a lot of ways, you have to be empathetic toward yourself and recognize the good things you did while also recognizing the bad (but not dwelling on them). You can only improve if you are honest with yourself and have the desire to do better the next time. Learning to control yourself emotionally and communicate with emotionally manipulative people (or their attorney) is not an easy process. It's something that takes time and energy, and it's something you must be very purposeful about.

With practice, keeping emotional control will become easy because you'll have done it over and over. What should become easier quickly is identifying the emotional manipulation for what it is. If you are having trouble with emotional control during your divorce, your first change should be to lean on a therapist. Let them guide you through the process. Emotions are a complex thing. A word of caution, if you are leaning on your friends to be your therapist - leaning on your friends too much during a divorce can burn them out and you run the risk of not having these friends after your divorce!

In summary, recognize manipulation, understand its impact, and learn what works for you to be cooperative with your ex while also maintaining your boundaries.

Chapter Thirty-Two

Legal Terms and Definitions

T ypes of Law

Chances are you are not very familiar with the different kinds of law. You would think that law would be a fairly simple thing! You simply write some rules, and everyone has to follow them. Not so fast!

Remember, lawyers have made small fortunes out of manipulating the rules. When you go to family court, lawyers are especially good at making good people look bad and bad people look good. They are very talented at taking the intent of the law and twisting it for their own purposes.

It helps to have a basic understanding of the different types of law. The different types of law are:

- Statutory law (laws that come about as passing of statuettes by regulators)

- Common law (a law that is established on the basis of previous law cases)

- Regulatory law (a law that is creative by executive action)

How will this affect your case when you go to court for family law? Chances are, the judge in your case will take a look at statutory and common law and come up with a ruling that he or she believes abides by both. It is not uncommon for statutory and common law to be in conflict with each other. In this case, it is up to the judge to decide which one is most applicable.

In the case where you do not agree with the judge's decision, you may file an appeal (in most cases). When you appeal the judge's decision, a higher court, typically an appellate court, will decide whether or not the judge made the right decision based on the circumstances and facts. Remember, the appellate court will also consider both statutory and common law, and they will also try to decide what the right decision is based on the facts in the case.

From an outsider looking in, this can be all very confusing. If you're not a lawyer and not looking at law cases every single day, it is almost impossible for you to know all of the laws (statutory and regulatory) and all of the court cases. It is very easy to look at some of the statutory laws and believe that you will get a certain outcome based on what is written in the statutory laws. It is very common in family law for judges to not follow statutory law to the letter. This is one of the things that makes family law so frustrating. You really never know what the outcome is going to be.

Common law is interesting because it is the law that is established on the basis of previous cases. Essentially under common law, judges and lawyers use previous cases to expound upon the statutory law. This means that a way that a judge ruled previously can be used as a persuading factor to roll in the same way in a current open case.

These can be harder to research because previous case law can go back for many years. Unless you are well established within the industry and have studied these cases, it is going to be hard for you, as an outsider, to know which are the right cases to compare your specific case to.

All this means that the law is very hard to follow. It's not as simple as looking at the laws themselves and seeing what it says. The outcome of your case could be affected by what the statute says, what decisions have been made in previous cases, and also in some part, based on what the judge wants to do.

Legal Terms and Definitions

It's important to note in this section that I'm giving a general overview of the terms and definitions you'll see in your divorce. Some of the names or terms may change slightly based on where you live. Some of these terms and definitions may not be called exactly what they are in this book. They may be changed slightly or may have different names altogether. But there will likely be the equivalent of something in your local court. If you want more information, some good sources of online legal definitions are the United States Courts website (https://www.uscourts.gov/glossary), the American Bar Association site (https://www.americanbar.org/groups/legal_services/flh-home/flh-glossary/) or Law.com (https://dictionary.law.com/).

It's also important to note that many of these things are tools within the legal system. Some of these terms below are documents which are used to solicit a specific action from a person or the court. It's important to know that oftentimes just because a tool is used, that does not mean that the party that is using that tool wants that outcome. Confused? You should be.

For instance, the mother may file for sole custody. At the end of the day, and in her heart, she doesn't really want sole custody. But she is willing to use her lawyer and the legal tool to inflict pain on you (the other party). Remember, custody is a thing you're in for the long haul, and do not worry about each battle. Just because something is filed doesn't mean that's what the other will get.

Divorce – From Law.com, "the termination of a marriage by legal action, requiring a petition or complaint for divorce (or dissolution in some states, including California) by one party. Some states still require at least a minimal showing of fault, but no-fault divorce is now the rule in which "incompatibility" is sufficient to grant a divorce. The substantive issues in divorces are a division of property, child custody and support, alimony (spousal support), child visitation and attorney's fees. Only state courts have jurisdiction over divorces, so the petitioning or complaining party can only file in the state in which he/she is and has been a resident for a period of time (as little as six weeks in Nevada). In most states, the period from original filing for divorce, serving the petition on the other party and final judgment (or decree) takes several months to allow for a chance to reconcile."

Attorney vs. Lawyer – In the legal world, words have very specific meanings. One of those is the difference between lawyer and attorney. This sums it up nicely "Attorneys, lawyers, and councils have all been educated and trained in law. Attorneys must pass the bar exams and practice law in court. Lawyers may or may not have taken the bar exam and may or may not practice law. Counsels provide legal advice and often work for an organization or corporation. The terms are often used interchangeably in everyday speech, despite the differences in meaning." (Attorney vs. lawyer, 2023)

Jurisdiction – You may have heard of the word "jurisdiction" before. For example, to a police officer, it essentially means where they are allowed to exercise their police officer powers. To a judge, it means that they have the right to hear and make decisions in a case.

Jurisdiction is typically based on where something specific happened (like where someone filed for divorce) or where the parties live. Depending on the legal action, jurisdiction can also be considered in different ways. Typically, if you're going to sue somebody for just about anything, you have to file the lawsuit where that party lives or does business (if suing a professional for work-related matters). This prevents someone from being served a lawsuit in an inconvenient forum. Essentially because an inconvenient forum would not allow that party to have a fair say in the matter and jurisdiction ensures that the burden is put on the person filing the lawsuit.

Jurisdiction can be an important part of a legal case because it can mean the difference between whether or not a judge has the power to make a decision or if they have to pass the case to a different court. In the case of family courts, most states hold family court at the state level but the state is divided by counties into districts. This means that you will go into a court in the district that you live in or sometimes in an adjoining district.

This can be much more confusing when the parties do not live in the same state. Generally, where the action was initiated is the state that will have jurisdiction. In an effort to make these things easier, the federal government has adopted a thing called the UCCJA (Uniform Child Custody Jurisdiction Act). The UCCJA helps determine which state has jurisdiction and when jurisdiction can be moved from one state to another. For example, if all parties live in the same state, then the jurisdiction can be moved to that state. If one party still lives in a different state from the other, then the UCCJA will be the tiebreaker to determine which state can have jurisdiction. This is important to know where to file court motions. If you file a court motion in the wrong state, you won't get anywhere and your motion will be denied.

I will note that moving jurisdiction from one state to the other (even if all the parties live in the same state that you're moving it to) can be very difficult. It's important to note that custody and child support can be moved together but oftentimes they are done as separate actions. When you're looking for a lawyer to do this, it's important that you ask very specific questions to ensure that they are familiar with this process.

Based on your specific situation, jurisdiction can be a very complicated thing. Like most things, it seems like it would be a very simple concept but sometimes it is not and this is where having a good lawyer is very helpful. If you don't have the ability to have a lawyer, the next best thing will be to find some way to get some legal advice in your local area from someone who is familiar with the local laws. You can check with local social agencies or local colleges that teach law to see if any provide pro-bono work that you would be eligible for.

Defendant or Respondent – From Law.com, "the party sued in a civil lawsuit or the party charged with a crime in a criminal prosecution. In some types of cases (such as divorce), a defendant may be called a respondent."

Plaintiff - From Law.com, "the party who initiates a lawsuit by filing a complaint with the clerk of the court against the defendant(s) demanding damages, performance and/or court determination of rights."

Motion – From Law.com "a formal request made to a judge for an order or judgment. Motions are made in court all the time for many purposes: to continue (postpone) a trial to a later date, to get a modification of an order, for temporary child support, for a judgment, for dismissal of the opposing party's case, for a rehearing, for sanctions (payment of the moving party's costs or attorney's fees), or for dozens of other purposes. Most motions require a written petition, a written brief of legal reasons for granting the motion (often called "points and authorities"), written notice to the attorney for the opposing party and a hearing before a judge. However, during a trial or a hearing, an oral motion may be permitted."

Ex Parte – From Law.com "(ex par-tay, but popularly, ex-party) adj. Latin meaning "for one party," referring to motions, hearings or orders granted on the request of and for the benefit of one party only. This is an exception to the basic rule of court procedure that both parties must be present at any argument before a judge and to the otherwise strict rule that an attorney may not notify a judge without previously notifying the opposition. Ex-parte matters are usually temporary orders (like a restraining order or temporary custody) pending a formal hearing or an emergency request for a continuance. Most jurisdictions require at least a diligent attempt to contact the other party's lawyer of the time and place of any ex parte hearing."

Hearing – From Law.com, "any proceeding before a judge or other magistrate (such as a hearing officer or court commissioner) without a jury in which evidence and/or argument is presented to determine some issue of fact or both issues of fact and law. While technically, a trial with a judge sitting without a jury fits the definition, a hearing usually refers to brief sessions involving a specific question at some time prior to the trial itself or such specialized proceedings as administrative hearings. In criminal law, a "preliminary hearing" is held before a judge to determine whether the prosecutor has presented sufficient evidence that the accused has committed a crime to hold him/her for trial."

Trial – From Law.com, "the examination of facts and law presided over by a judge (or other magistrate, such as a commissioner or judge pro tem) with authority to hear the matter (jurisdiction)." There are different kinds of trials and unlike in the movies, most family law trials do not have jurors who decide the case. That decision is usually just the judge.

Child Custody – From Law.com, "a court's determination of which parent, relative or other adult should have physical and/or legal control and responsibility for a minor (child) under 18. Child custody can be decided by a local court in a divorce or if a child, relative, close friend or state agency questions whether one or both parents is unfit, absent, dead, in prison or dangerous to the child's well-being. In such cases custody can be awarded to a grandparent or other relative, a foster parent or an orphanage or other organization or institution. While a divorce is pending the court may grant temporary custody to one of the parents, require conferences or investigation (in some states, if the parents cannot agree, custody is automatically referred to a mediator, commissioner or social worker) before making a final ruling. There is a difference between physical custody, which designates where the child will actually live, and legal custody, which gives the custodial person(s) the right to make decisions for the child's welfare. If the parents agree, the court can award joint custody, physical and/or legal. Joint legal custody is becoming increasingly common. The basic consideration on custody matters is supposed to be the best interests of the child or children. In most cases the non-custodial parent is given visitation rights, which may include weekends, parts of vacations and other occasions. The court can always change custody if circumstances warrant."

Joint Custody - From Law.com, "In divorce actions, a decision by the court (often upon agreement of the parents) that the parents will share custody of a child. There are two types of custody, physical and legal. Joint physical custody (instead of one parent having custody with the other having visitation) does not mean exact division of time with each parent but can be based on reasonable time with each parent either specifically spelled out (certain days, weeks, holidays, alternative periods) or based on stated guidelines and shared payment of costs of raising the child. Joint legal custody means that both parents can make decisions for the child, including medical treatment, but where possible, they should consult the other. Upon the death or disability of either parent, legal custody will go to the remaining parent and will give the active parent the sole ability to act as the parent for the child without further order of the court. The primary effect of this is a psychological benefit for the parent and the child so that a child can be told that both parents cared for the child, even though the child had to live most of the time with one of them."

Custodial parent – The custodial parent is the child's primary caregiver (*Custodial Parents & Noncustodial Parents—Custody X Change, 2022*). Sometimes seen in legal documents shortened as CP.

Non-custodial parent - The noncustodial parent generally spends less time with the child and is responsible for making child support payments (*Custodial Parents & Noncustodial Parents—Custody X Change, 2022*). Even in situations where the children spend equal time with both parents, one parent will be designated as the noncustodial parent. This is generally the parent that pays child support. Sometimes seen in legal documents shortened as NCP.

Visitation Rights - Designated time for the noncustodial parent to spend with the children.

Child Support - From Law.com, "court-ordered funds to be paid by one parent to the custodial parent of a minor child after divorce (dissolution) or separation. Usually the dollar amounts are based on the income of both parents, the number of children, the expenses of the custodial parent, and any special needs of the child. In many states or locales, the amount is determined by a chart which factors in all these figures. It may also include health plan coverage, school tuition or other expenses and may be reduced during periods of extended visitation such as summer vacations. Child support generally continues until the child reaches 18 years, graduates from high school, is emancipated (no longer lives with either parent),

or, in some cases, for an extended period such as college atten-
dance. The amount and continuation of support may be changed
by the court upon application of either party depending on a proven
change of circumstance of the parents or child. Child support should
not be confused with alimony (spousal support) which is for the
ex-spouse's support. Child support is not deductible from gross
income for tax purposes (but may allow a dependent exemption)
nor is it taxed as income, unlike alimony, which is deductible by the
payer and taxed as the adult recipient's income."

Spousal Support – From Law.com, "payment for support of an
ex-spouse (or a spouse while a divorce is pending) ordered by the
court. More commonly called alimony, spousal support is the term
used in California and a few other states as part of new non-con-
frontational language (such as "dissolution" instead of "divorce")
now used since divorce is "no-fault" in all states but two."

Alimony – From Law.com, "support paid by one ex-spouse to the
other as ordered by a court in a divorce (dissolution) case. Alimony
is also called "spousal support" in California and some other states.
Usually it is paid by the male to his ex, but in some cases a wealthy
woman may have to pay her husband, or, in same-sex relationships
the "breadwinner" may pay to support his/her stay-at-home former
partner. Many counties and states have adopted formulas for alimony based on the income of each party. Payment of alimony is usually
limited in time based on the number of years of marriage. Lengthy
marriages may result in a lifetime of payments. A substantial change
in circumstance, such as illness, retirement, or loss of income, can
be grounds for the court to grant a modification or termination of
the payment. Failure to pay ordered alimony can result in contempt
of court citations and even jail time. The level of alimony can be
determined by written agreement and submitted to the court for
a stipulated order. Income tax-wise, alimony is deductible as an

expense for the payer and charged as income to the recipient. Child support is not alimony."

Deposition - A deposition is where an attorney will quote "depose" someone so that they can answer a series of questions about the issue. Not all divorces require depositions but just so you are aware- it is kind of like an interview, usually taken under oath and usually recorded via video or audio. Most of the time, there is a court reporter (transcriber or stenographer) present who is typing everything that is being said. Oftentimes attorneys will depose someone when they are not sure what that person is going to say on the stand. Attorneys may also depose someone they think will be difficult to deal with or may not be truthful. It can be handy for lawyers during the trial or hearing to reference the deposition and say, "Well, you said such and such on this statement and today you're saying something different." Remember that attorneys often try to discredit people in the courtroom because then that makes what they're saying invalid. If an attorney can make you look like you are lying, you will lose trust with the judge or jury.

Sometimes depositions are held simply because your attorney or the opposing attorney may believe that an opposing party will not give up information easily. A deposition is a way to put somebody in a face-to-face situation where it will be much harder for them to conceal information. If you have to be deposed, dress as if you are appearing in court. Neutral colors such as blues, grays and browns tend to make people appear more honest to strangers. Red and black are often thought of as dominating and aggressive. Make sure you are freshly showered and well-groomed. It is very normal to be nervous before giving a deposition. Practice good self-care prior to your deposition. Be sure you have eaten and be sure to stay hydrated.

Subpoena - This is a court order. Subpoenas can require a person to come to court, go to a deposition, or give documents or evidence to someone (usually an opposing lawyer). It's common for these to be used to obtain things like bank records and employment information (including pay, retirement accounts, etc.). Generally, they are only used if one party has refused to provide the information to the opposing party upon request, but it's common in a high-conflict divorce for these to be overused as a way to create conflict. Subpoenas can be used with therapy records as well. If you are in a high-conflict situation and your custody of your kids is in jeopardy, get your kids into an agreed-upon therapist ASAP. If at any time your ex tries to paint you falsely as an abusive father, subpoenaing your child's therapist might be your saving grace of what keeps you in your child's life.

Hearing- A hearing is by far the most common thing to happen in a family law courtroom. Throughout your divorce process, it's likely that there will be a multitude of hearings unless you and your soon-to-be ex can maintain stability and stay out of the courtroom. Hearings are often held for a variety of issues, including child support, child custody, child welfare, and other miscellaneous issues.

The thing you must understand about hearings is that it is essentially based on emotion. While your attorney may present some evidence to the judge, hearings are not held to the same standard that evidentiary hearings or trials are held to. In other words, typically in a hearing the person with the best argument or the one that feels like the biggest victim will win.

It's important to note that just because something makes sense and is logical to you doesn't necessarily mean that you're going to win a hearing in Family Court. In fact, it's very common to lose very logical arguments and hearings for various reasons.

When you go to the courtroom and sit in a hearing, it is common to have many other parties with their own issues in there as well. Your issues will be heard in front of the judge, the attorneys, and whoever else is randomly in the courtroom. You have to remember that lawyers are often in the courtroom several times a week. For instance, in the jurisdiction that I am in, the court holds four sessions a week. Two on Tuesday and two on Thursday. It may be helpful for you to find out what your local court schedule is because that will help you know when is a good time to contact your lawyer and when you can expect them to be busy in court.

Remember, if you go to a hearing and don't get what you want, this is about the long haul. This is about winning the war and not the battle. It's also important to note that sometimes winning in Family Court means not losing as much as the other side or not losing as much as you could. Redefining your expectations will help you determine what is a true loss when someone loses in Family Court. A true loss would be losing all custody of your kids and all visitation rights. I hope this never happens to you, but if it does, get yourself into therapy and work on what you need to in order to get them back. The thing about Family Court is it is not final until all the kids are 18 (sometimes older if enrolled in school). Either party can take the other back to court at any time to renegotiate the terms.

Pretrial Conference Order (PTCO) - If you're going to trial, a Pretrial Conference Order will be prepared for both parties who will list their exhibits that will be shown during the trial and also the witnesses that will show up. Generally, it will also outline the issues between the two parties. A Pretrial Conference Order should also outline what relief is stated by the court or what decision the trial is supposed to make. You can think of a pretrial conference order (PTCO) as sort of a planning guide for the attorneys on both sides. Basically, you don't want to be surprised by anything in the trial, and the ethics rules require that the attorneys disclose what will be used during the trial so that they can both prepare.

It's also good to note that the PTCO can be amended (generally) up until the trial. Many jurisdictions will have restrictions on how many days the PTCO has to be completed before the trial, however, it is common for the judges to ignore these time limits. It's also not uncommon to add witnesses at the last minute and change things right up until the trial date. Unfortunately, that's not how the system is supposed to work but it IS how it works in some places.

Guardian Ad Litem (GAL) - This is someone that the court assigns to the case who is supposed to act in the best interest of the minor children. Generally, they are intended to be a neutral party that will make a recommendation to the court.

Mediator - Someone who works with both parties to try and come to a resolution to issues outside of court. Usually, a Mediator is an employee of the court system or county. They're supposed to be completely neutral to both parties and work in the best interest of all (especially the children).

Journal Entry - This is an official record made in the court. Generally, journal entries become public record.

Evidentiary Trial or Trial - This is a trial that is based on evidence. This is more formal than a hearing and has certain rules and procedures in place. Generally, this is when witnesses are called and evidence is presented in court.

Restraining or Protection Order - From Law.com, "a temporary order of a court to keep conditions as they are (like not taking a child out of the county or not selling marital property) until there can be a hearing in which both parties are present. More properly, it is called a temporary restraining order (shortened to TRO)."

UCCJEA - If your case involves two states, then you may need to be aware of UCCJEA (Uniform Child-Custody Jurisdiction and Enforcement Act). This is for cases when:

- You live in a different state than the divorce was filed.

- Your ex, children and you live in more than one state.

- You've divorced in one state and someone (ex, kids or you) has moved out of the original state.

The UCCJEA provides a way for states to deal with these situations with some order. Since two states are involved, and every state has its own laws - then which state's laws apply? The UCCJEA sets ground rules and give some guidance to interstate cases.

It's likely your lawyer may not be up to speed on UCCJEA information. Unless they specialize in these cases, most family law attorneys get comfortable in their local bubble. They are likely really familiar with the laws and local court rules in your county. Some attorneys may be familiar with the same in the county over, but typically attorneys tend to be very localized.

If you do have an interstate case, I would recommend that you do your research. The UCCJEA was "approved in 1997 by the National Conference of Commissioners on Uniform State Laws (NCCUSL) to replace its 1968 Uniform Child Custody Jurisdiction Act (the UCCJA)". This uniform state law replaced the earlier UCCJA. It's not a custody statute and it doesn't tell the states what the standards are. Further, the states must adopt the UCCJEA, of which 49 have been (as of the writing of this book). Sorry Massachusetts and Puerto Rico, you are out of luck!

The DOJ bulletin (Hoff, 2001) states:

"The UCCJEA governs State courts' jurisdiction to make and modify "child-custody determinations," a term that expressly includes custody and visitation orders.

The Act requires state courts to enforce valid child custody and visitation determinations made by sister state courts. It also establishes innovative interstate enforcement procedures.

The UCCJEA is intended as an improvement over the UCCJA. It clarifies UCCJA provisions that have received conflicting interpretations in courts across the country, codifies practices that have effectively reduced interstate conflict, conforms jurisdictional standards to those of the Federal Parental Kidnapping Prevention Act (the PKPA) to ensure interstate enforceability of orders, and adds protections for victims of domestic violence who move out of state for safe haven."

If your case involves people in more than one state, then it's likely the UCCJEA can help simplify some of the fighting between the states. The UCCJEA will likely NOT help reduce any conflict with your ex. It's important to note that the states must adopt the UCCJEA, and while a lot have - not all states have. Since this can change, it's important that you look up the current status of the UCCJEA adoption in the states that your case is involved in.

There are many more terms that you may hear through your divorce process. If you are unsure what something is, then I recommend first trying to do a web search. If you still do not understand, ask your attorney to explain it to you.

Chapter Thirty-Three

Legal Process

T he family court system is largely a state-based system, with most states having courts in each county. This means that while there will be some things that are consistent across the state, each court is likely run differently and will have different local rules. What this means for the citizens of this area is that they can get dramatically different results in different courts! Your lawyer may tell you what they think the judge will say based on their past experience, but it's only a guess.

There are some federal laws that apply that focus on what happens between states and for child support. These are the UCCJEA, the Federal Parental Kidnapping Prevention Act and Title IV-D of the 1974 Social Security Act.

- Uniform Child-Custody Jurisdiction and Enforcement Act (UCCJEA) - is intended to "deter interstate parental kidnapping and promote uniform jurisdiction and enforcement provisions in interstate child custody and visitation cases" (Hoff, 2001).

- Federal Parental Kidnapping Prevention Act (the PKPA) - establishes a home state, deters parental child abduction, and prevents inter-jurisdictional conflicts. Congress also made international parental kidnapping a federal crime.

- Title IV-D of the Social Security Act in 1974 (also established the Office of Child Support Enforcement) - Requires the states to publish their child support formula and review it every few years. It also establishes how much money the state will get from federal funds based on how much child support is awarded, how much is collected and other factors.

The Divorce Process

In the next sections, I'll describe the divorce process in general terms. A divorce can be a complex legal proceeding, so I'm just hitting the highlights here. Not all states may follow this same process, and some states may have extra steps or even do these in a different order. It's important that you check with a local legal professional if you have questions about what the process is in your state.

Filing the Divorce

The first step of the process is someone needs to file for a divorce. In many cases, this is done without the awareness of the other party. The attorney will file the motion with the court and typically ask for a temporary order "Ex Parte." This simply means that the request is for the judge to make a decision without the other party having any input and without their knowledge. Many times, the party filing the motion will ask for temporary orders giving that party the majority of time with the kids, they will ask to stay in the marital residence and they will ask for an amount of spousal and child support. Many times, these are signed by the judge without question. This is where the conflict starts! The person filing the motion is called the plaintiff.

Getting Served

The next step of the process is the defendant (person who did not file the motion) will get served. Usually, this is a formal process where a designated person (police officer, sheriff, or another official) will serve the party with the papers. This part of the process is as simple as the person delivering the papers identifying the person and handing them the papers. Once the initial motion is served, future motions in the same case can usually just be sent to the other person via US Mail. Many times, lawyers will email a copy and send a hard copy in the mail.

At this stage, if you are served and you do not have an attorney, this is the time to find a lawyer and give them the papers that you were served.

Hearing

Sometimes the next step is to have a hearing about some part of the divorce. This usually happens when the defendant's attorney comes on board and the defendant doesn't agree with something in the temporary orders. This could be about relocating out of the house, the time with the kids, or the amount of alimony or child support.

Discovery

In this stage, the parties request documents and evidence from each other. Expect to have to come up with a lot of documentation for your attorney. You'll give everything that the discovery asks for and give that to your attorney. They will send that information over to the opposing attorney.

Back and Forth

At this stage, the attorneys will go back and forth and try and reach a deal between both parties. This will include a parenting plan, alimony and child support and division of the property. The parties may meet all together (both parties and both attorneys) to try and reach a settlement. It's not uncommon for a lot of this back-and-forth to happen via email. This stage can include hearings about issues that come up that need to be resolved before the trial.

If the parties cannot settle before the trial date, then the parties go to a trial and the judge will decide for them.

Sometimes the judge will order or the parties will agree to participate in case management or mediation. This is a process that happens outside of court to help the parties settle the dispute. With mediation, the parties will work with a mediator, and that person will try and settle the disputes. With case management, a designated case manager works with both parties to get "their side", and then the case manager will make a recommendation to the court. The judge can then decide if they want to follow the recommendation. This is a highly simplified explanation, so if you are going to go through mediation or case management, ask your attorney what the process looks like.

Trial

Before the trial, there will be a hearing with both attorneys called a pre-trail conference order (PTCO) or similar. This is a meeting to ensure that both parties are ready for the trial, and they have met the rules to give each other the evidence they will use during the trial.

Post-Trial

After the trial, one of the attorneys will write up what the judge decided and both parties, both attorneys and the judge will sign it. That paper will be filed in the court records, and this becomes the final say about all matters discussed in the paper. If the parties want to challenge the outcome, they can file and appeal. Some states make it hard to appeal by having a short time that an appeal can be filed or other barriers.

What if you settle?

If you decide to settle and do not need to go to trial, then one attorney will write up the settlement and after the parties and lawyers sign, the judge will sign it. The paper will be filed in the court records, and this becomes the final say about all matters discussed in the paper.

What happens if you need to go back to court after the initial case is "settled"?

Rules vary by state and court but parties can take the other person "back to court" on just about any topic. When this happens, the process "resets," and the parties go through each step all over again. Some courts require a "significant" change to go back to court; others do not.

For some topics there is a time limit before the parties can go back to court unless something "significant" changes. One example is child support. In some states, parties can only go back to court every three years unless something changes (someone loses a job, someone makes a lot more money, one of the children passes away or turns 18).

Post-It Note Example

A court is a difficult place to settle disputes. A mediator once showed me and my ex a Post-it note. He said that the Post-it note represented both our lives together. He then folded the Post-it note in half and told us that this is how much our lawyers get to see of our lives. He then folded it in half again and again and showed us the very small piece of paper. He said this is what the judge gets to see, and this is what he or she has to make their decisions based on. He went on to comment that it's a very small slice of life to judge your future on.

In other words, you should avoid court at all costs if you can. However, sometimes you don't have a choice.

Crazy Motions

Part of understanding the court process is realizing how imperative it is to not take motions and filings by the attorneys too seriously. Anyone can say anything. The court process will prove if it's true or not. A motion in family court is seen as a weapon of intimidation to be used by an opposing party. They will often say things that are either completely untrue or they will make allegations that stretch the truth so far it's not recognizable. You must learn to ignore what the motions are accusing you of and focus on what the other party wants. Often you will learn what your ex is mad about in the motion! If you are being dealt several of these, they can become quite humorous after a while.

It's also important to know that parties will file motions for things that they don't really want. A motion will be used as a weapon and what the person filed for is not really what they want. I've seen this before with custody changes where one person wants to get back at the other. At the end of the day, they end up dropping their motion because they don't really want to take the children away from the other parent. The real intent of the motion is to inflict stress and pain on the opposing party. The unfortunate thing is that since the lawyers profit from this fighting, the judges don't discourage it.

Make no mistake about it, the more that a pair of attorneys can get someone to fight, the more they each stand to make! This is not to say that all attorneys are purely profit driven, however, this seems to be prevalent.

Chapter Thirty-Four

Custody

Custody Schedules

C When choosing a custody schedule, you may think you only have one or two options. Your lawyer or the court may give you a "standard" parenting schedule. A lot of people just pick that because they just don't know there are other options. In reality, there are many options and you just need to pick the one that works best for you, your kids and your ex.

The danger of many "standard" parenting schedules is that they relegate one parent to a very part-time visitor. This often means every other weekend - so 4 days a month plus maybe a weeknight. If you count the weeknights as a half day, that's still only 6 days a month on average. Compare this to the 24 or 25 days the other parent gets and it's easy to see that this does not give the non-custodial parent much time to do anything with the kids, including bonding.

The best custody schedule for fit, willing, and able parents is one where the kids spend approximately equal time with both parents (called shared parenting). This gives each parent time to bond with the children. It has other benefits, too, like the kids seeing that there is more than one way to live life. It also makes them less likely to see one parent as a visitor or as less than the other parent. Obviously, not every divorce will lend itself to the kids spending equal time with both parents, but if you can do that, it will be better for the kids in the long term.

It's also better for the parents in both short and long term. An equal parenting time arrangement gives both parents the same time opportunity to date, travel, work on their careers or even go back to school. When one parent has the kids all the time, there really isn't any time for that parent to do anything else. Sharing the time (and responsibilities) gives equal opportunity to both parents.

When looking at custody schedules, it's important to take into account everyone's needs and the reality of logistics. Things like what the kids' school, sports and activity schedules are will play a factor. So remember, you don't have to accept the "standard" schedule. It's also good to remember that you need to pick the schedule that works for the time being. As the kids age or as they get into different sports and activities, you may want to adjust or go to a different schedule altogether. That is really up to you and your ex.

When choosing your custody schedule, you have a lot of options. The key is to pick one that works the best for everyone involved. It should defiantly meet the needs of the kids first and then be as convenient as possible for the adults. Kids will have different needs at different ages. For example, if you have an infant - you may need to exchange more often (every other day). You will also want to consider daycare and school schedules. There are also activity schedules. The key here is how are you and your ex going to work together to maximize the time that the kids will have with both parents. Next, I will cover some different schedules and the pros and cons of each.

Week-on/week-off

The week-on/week-off schedule is a common one. It makes it easy to plan when you will and will not have the kids. It's also easy for the kids to know when they are with which parent.

With this schedule, you exchange once per week. For example, you could exchange Sunday evenings at 5 pm. The kids would then be with one parent from 5 pm Sunday to the following Sunday at 5 pm. Pick a designated place to exchange, and this one is pretty easy. You can put a meeting notice on the calendar for your "kid week" and have it repeat every other week and now you can see which weeks you do and don't have the kids when planning.

One con for this schedule is that a full 7 days can be a long time for the kids to go without seeing the other parent. A way to fix that would be to add an exchange midweek. If the parent that doesn't have the kids that week gets them Wednesday night (by picking them up from school and getting them to school the next day), then the kids get some face-to-face time with the other parent and the parent whose week it is gets a night off to rest or maybe even go on a date.

Adding the mid-week exchange is a great example of taking a schedule and modifying it slightly to work better for both families. Don't be afraid to think a bit outside the box to make it work for everyone.

<u>Every-other-day</u>

The every-other-day schedule is typically used when the kids are young. This ensures the kids don't get too much time away from either parent. If a mom is breastfeeding, this can be a good schedule because it allows the child to feed naturally with mom, and then mom can pump on her "off" days and give the frozen milk to dad regularly. The every-other-day schedule does take more coordination. Unless agreeing on something different on the weekends, the every-other-day will rotate who has what weekend days. With 7 days, one parent will end up with a Friday and a Sunday or just one day on the weekend - a Saturday. This can be good for parents that want to do something with the kids every weekend.

Every two days

Similar to the every-other-day is the every two days. This ensures that you will get two weekend days every now and then. This also gives both parents fairly regular breaks. With this one, you have the kids for two days and then two days off. Pretty simple.

3-4-4-3

There are some more creative schedules, but these can be hard to track in your calendar when you do and don't have the kids. The 3-4-4-3 schedule has the kids with one parent for 3 days then the other for 4 days. The first parent then gets them for 4 days and the second parent gets them for 3. This schedule splits the time during the weekend and during the week so that neither parent is doing all the weekday things (like school) and not enjoying the weekend time.

There are other schedules like the 2-2-5-5 and the 2-2-3. The number of ways that you can get creative with the schedules is almost endless. The important thing to know is that there are different options, and you should pick one that works the best for everyone.

When choosing schedules, it's important to keep in mind how that schedule will play out with not only your kids and you but also any other significant others now in the picture. You and/or your ex may have someone else in the picture and they may have kids. It's important to reduce conflict to try and find something that fits the best for everyone.

It's also good to remember that the schedule may need to change depending on the kids' needs. As the kids age, you may need to adjust the schedule. Their school schedule or activities may make your current schedule hard. It's important to be flexible if your ex asks you to change the schedule and they should do the same for you (should is the key word; you can't expect them to). If something isn't working out, set some time aside to talk about it, or better yet, send a message to them where you can discuss in writing.

Custody Exchanges

So far, we've talked a lot about the custody schedules and not much about the actual exchanges. Here are some tips to make those exchanges go smoothly.

Where to exchange

When it comes to exchanging the kids, you have several options. One popular option is to pick the kids up from the other parent's house. With this option, it gives the parent picking up the kids the maximum chance to make sure the kids have everything. There are some downsides to this if the parents live far away or if the parents are in conflict.

Another option is to meet at a public place somewhere in the middle. This could be a mall parking lot or some other retail store parking lot. Picking a place "right off the highway" can make sure exchanges happen with a minimum of extra driving.

During the exchange

When you are exchanging, it's important to be courteous and friendly, but be sure that you don't cross boundaries and definitely do not let your ex cross boundaries. Say please and thank you, and generally be a bit more formal than you are with your friends. If you go to their house and they invite you in, don't roam around. Stay in the entryway and let them bring everything to you unless they specifically ask you to do something else. If you are exchanging in a parking lot, don't reach into their car unless they ask you to get something. Stand by your car and let them bring things to you. This goes for both low and high-conflict situations. Custody exchanges can create conflict, and you want to make sure there is the smallest chance possible for that.

Exchanges in High Conflict Cases

If you and your ex are in conflict, then there are some things that you will want to consider. First is that you should reduce the number of times that you exchange the kids in person. She can drop the kids at school and you can pick them up (or vice versa). This is just one way of exchanging without both parties being there.

This method of using the school as the intermediary does have some disadvantages in that you have to leave everything the kids need for the other house at school. The amount of stuff that needs to go back and forth at exchanges can be minimized by buying duplicates, but some things like favorite stuffed animals or security blankets can't be duplicated.

If you have to exchange in person with a high-conflict ex, then another good option is to exchange in the parking lot of the local police station. This seems a bit extreme, but chances are the police station will have security cameras (and many now also record audio). Being close to the police station will also ensure that people think twice about doing something crazy or causing a scene. If something happens, you're already at the police station and just need to walk into the lobby. If your ex has falsely accused you of things, then I would definitely recommend it. Your kids may ask why you have to go to the police station to exchange. You shouldn't tell them it's because you and your ex are in high conflict (they will probably already know). It is ok to tell them something like "It's what we agreed on" or "Because it's convenient for everyone."

Living Arrangements

There are a few different living arrangements that you can consider. Depending on your situation, you will need to decide what works best for you. Some of these are better for the kids than others, so evaluate each one. The best situation maximizes the time with each parent.

Two equal residences - the kids have equal living accommodations at each residence. This situation allows the kids to develop meaningful relationships with both parents and for them to have their own space at each place. With a set schedule, kids adapt really well to this as long as they know when and who they are going to be with. Some parents move so they are close to each other. This helps with kid exchanges, but it can be nerve-wracking to have your ex as a neighbor, especially when you both start dating.

Kids live in one residence, and parents rotate each week - This is sometimes called nesting and can work in some situations. Sometimes this is a short-term solution and sometimes, it's a permanent one. This has its advantages in that the kids never have to change their settings and they have the same clothes and toys all the time. This can also have disadvantages. It can cause conflict over how the house is run or kept up. It can also be hard for the parents to see things from the other parent. It may also have some issues when each parent starts dating.

Kids live with one parent part of the year and another for the rest of the year – This can be an option when the parents do not live near each other. They may spend the school year with one parent and the summer with another. This option will be like the first in that the kids will need two of everything - one at each house.

Changes to the Family Law

Society changes much faster than the law. Years ago, the family unit looked different than it does today. In the 1950s, the dad was the breadwinner and the mom stayed home. Today that is often not the case. Both parents work and the kids are left with relatives or daycare until the parents are done with work. Some family court laws are still rooted in the family system that existed in the '50s, '60s and '70s when typically only one parent worked.

The laws, however, may not reflect this change. Many states still give one parent the majority of the time while relegating the other parent to be a visitor. It's important that if you want to be an active parent in your kids' lives that your kids get to spend time with you.

What is sometimes even slower to change than custody rulings is child support. It is not uncommon for someone to have 50-50 custody of their children and still pay child support as if they were a part-time parent! It's important for you to know what to expect in your state and your specific county. Courts can vary from county to county within the same state. Your attorney will know best what to expect in the particular circumstance in your case.

Once your case is over, if you feel passionate about changing the laws in your state, you can help change them! There are now several different organizations that are working to help improve family law. The change is slow and generally opposed by the bar associations (attorney groups). The bar associations try to protect their interest (which is keeping the status quo since it works in their favor to have rules and laws that give them the most power while also creating conflict).

<u>Case Management</u>

Sometimes parents have such a hard time agreeing to what the custody of the kids will be and what the living arrangements will be that the judge will order the case into a dispute resolution process called "Limited Case Management" or "Case Management." It may be called by other names. The basic idea of LCM (Limited Case Management) or case management is that instead of having the court take the time to look at all of the details of your case, you have somebody else do that and make a recommendation to the court.

Case Managers are typically psychologists or lawyers appointed by the court to be a neutral third party. Their job is to review the evidence, interview the parties and other interested persons and make a recommendation to the court. Oftentimes the court respects the individuals that make these recommendations because they are first appointed by the court. In other words, if a Case Manager or Limited Case Manager makes a recommendation to the court, it is highly likely that the court will go with that recommendation.

Limited Case Management (LCM) and Case Management are two different animals. LCM makes a one-time recommendation to the court. This process can take as little as a few weeks. During the process, the Case Manager can request additional evidence or things such as psychological exams. They will often interview professionals that are involved with the children, such as therapists and doctors. They will also interview family and friends. A "professional" in this case means someone who is licensed in one of the medical fields, such as a therapist or doctor.

Case Management, however, is a very different thing from Limited Case Management. Case Management is usually recommended to parties that have no way of solving the problems on their own. What that does is effectively "kick them out" of the court. While you can still end up back in court during Case Management, the entire process is designed in order to keep you out of court. The way the Case Management process does this is by appointing someone who is a neutral third party who will make all decisions in the case. This has been described as the "black hole" of family law. In these instances, you are entrusting one individual to make all the decisions for your family. In the event that there is a disagreement, you must pay this person to listen to the evidence and testimonies from both sides and make a determination as to what will happen. Once they make a decision, you have very little power to challenge it.

When dealing with either Limited Case Management or Case Management, the biggest mistake that I personally made was telling the Limited Case Manager what my problem was and *what I wanted the solution to be*. It is imperative when dealing with these persons to tell them what your problem is and what *you would like the desired outcome to be.* Try, at all costs, to avoid giving them a predefined solution. With that said, the Limited Case Manager or Case Manager really needs to know what your issues are. They also need to know what you have done to try and work with the other parent and solve these issues on your own. It's important for them to know where the breakdown was in solving these issues. They also need to know what you want the final outcome to be, BUT they do not need to know how to get there! If you think about it, this is really their job...to find a solution. DO NOT TELL THEM HOW TO DO THEIR JOB. If you are going to Limited Case Management or Case Management with a *solution*, then you are basically cutting them out of the equation. Nobody really likes to be told how to do their job.

When dealing with LCM or Case Management, remember to first tell them: what your issues are. Second, tell them how you tried to solve that on your own with the other party. And third, tell them what you would like the desired outcome to be.

Generally, if you end up with one of these processes- your biggest goal will be to reduce conflict. Most people just want to go about living their lives, being happy, and not have to worry about Case Management and all of these things that drag you down on a daily basis. So it's fair to tell your Case Manager that you want the conflict to end.

All in all, Case Management or Limited Case Management is designed to reduce the burden on the court. In most cases, it will help you resolve conflict quicker, faster and cheaper by reducing the amount of times that you end up in the courtroom. The Limited Case Manager in my case stated that "most times parties are mostly in agreement, although they don't understand that they are". He said sometimes all he needs to do is show them that they really both want the same thing and help them come up with a solution that will work for both parties on the items that they disagree with.

Don't make the mistake of going through Limited Case Management representing yourself pro se. Where an attorney will really help you out is by helping you navigate the local system. Even within the same states, courts often vary in how they handle different issues. An experienced attorney will be able to tell you how the court normally rules on specific items. Even if you don't have the ability to have an attorney, I would highly recommend that you seek out somebody who's been through the process that can tell you what things the court (the specific court that you are going to be in) cares about.

<u>Maximum Distance Clause</u>

As I close out this chapter, I want to add one thing: When you are negotiating your custody schedule, it's important that you get in the legal paperwork a clause that specifies the maximum distance the parents can live from each other. Co-parenting will work best when both parents have regular time with the children, and for that to happen, both parents need to live reasonably close to each other.

You will need to decide what works for you, but in reality, you should live as close to each other as possible. This will make picking up "forgotten" things at the other house easier. It will also make it easier to attend school events or to pick the kids up at the last minute if the other parent can't (and vice versa). In addition, when your kids become teenagers and start driving themselves to and from each parent's house, this has your newly licensed teenager driving shorter distances.

Not only is this a practical thing, it also gives you some protection. Specifying that both parents must live within 20, 30 or 40 miles of each other will make sure that one parent doesn't take the kids and move halfway across the country. If they do, it gives you good legal standing to keep the kids near where you live.

Establishing two solid homes near the kids will work best for the kids in the long term.

Chapter Thirty-Five

Child Support and Alimony

The Intent of Child Support

The intent of child support, in theory, is to make sure the children have approximately the same resources at each household after divorce. The problem is states are extremely poor at putting this into practice. There are a few reasons for this, with the first being how the states are incentivized by the federal government. Another problem is that child support formulas have become overly complex and can be manipulated depending on a number of different variables. Another issue is that there is often no accountability for the person receiving support. They have no obligation to actually show they are using the money on the kids. All of this creates conflict for the parties that are involved. One person stands to pay a lot of money, while the other stands to gain it.

Having fair and equitable child support has been a problem for many years in our country. The good news is there are constant efforts to reform family law all over the country. With states moving to pass shared parenting laws through the hard work of some dedicated parents and organizations, child support reform will happen.

Since dads overwhelmingly pay child support instead of receiving it, the rest of this chapter is written through that lens. The information is the same, though, if you are one of the few who is receiving child support.

Child Support Formulas

Every state has its own way of "calculating" how much one parent owes the other for child support. Most times, the formulas are so complex they require an expert to fill out. This is one way that the "legal" machine makes sure you have to use a lawyer! The formula is so complex and nuanced that you will have to pay a legal professional just to make heads or tails of it.

You may be able to find a child support calculator. Be wary of free ones, although they may be good. Most lawyers will use software that is specifically written for their state. That software has to be updated regularly because the states often change the rules by tweaking them. With all this, it's best to leave the child support calculation to someone else unless you plan on doing a lot of research.

In some states, they take the income of both parties and then try and determine how much one should pay the other so that the kids have the same standard of living at both houses. In reality, the formulas may be reasonable when the parties make about the same amount of money, but when their incomes are different (one high and one low), then they start to be a mess.

The states are required by the government to have a way to calculate the support. Part of that calculation is the cost of living in that state. There are also different economic models that fall into play here. Some models grossly overestimate the costs. These models also fail to take into account that things can cost the same regardless of income (the store doesn't charge you more for bread based on your income, for example).

If you spend any time studying the formulas, it will likely leave you mad. Often these formulas are put together by a child support committee which is usually made up of lawyers and judges. They will typically have someone paying child support and someone receiving child support. Still, often these voices do not have enough votes to overpower the lawyers and judges that have a financial interest in keeping people in conflict.

The state's formulas often take several factors into account. These factors include the amount of parenting time that each parent has. If you have equal time, some states have an adjustment. Some states will have a "cliff" so that the difference between 49% and 50% time can mean a lot of money! These "cliff" effects cause people to fight because often there is a lot of money at stake each month.

Other factors may include who buys the clothes and who pays for "direct expenses" like school fees, extracurricular activities, and school lunches. Some formulas will make the person receiving child support pay certain things, so make sure once the child support order is final that you understand what you should and should not pay.

Daycare and medical expenses may also be a factor. Overall, when you have someone calculate child support be prepared to be asked a lot of questions! You should also expect to provide a lot of docu-mentation here. Guessing at numbers can be very expensive when it comes to child support.

It's important to note that states may have different kinds of child support that can be ordered. The typical one is where one parent pays the other and that parent pays all the child's expenses. Some states also have "shared expenses" where both parents pay into a common account and the kids' expenses are paid from that account. In states that have multiple ways of dealing with child support, this often causes conflict as one person will want the way that is least expensive to them (or most beneficial), and the other person will want another way because it means they get the most money each month.

Spend the time to get it right the first time by getting to know your state's child support law. Your attorney will ask you a ton of questions, but once the divorce is final, it's up to you and your ex to make sure you know who pays for what. Asking your attorney every time is an expensive way to get your questions answered. Going back to court to settle child support disputes is even more expensive.

Each state is required by the federal government through Title IV-D to have published child support guidelines. A quick Internet search usually will find this. Just search your state name and "child support guidelines." I would recommend downloading this and reading it before you go over child support with your attorney. This will save you a lot of money if you don't have to spend time with your attorney to educate you. That said, remember that your attorney is a professional who deals with these things every day. The child support guidelines are a start, but your attorney will tell you in practice how the local judges interpret the guidelines. At the end of the day, these are usually only guidelines and the judge may order something completely different.

<u>Hidden Alimony?</u>

Many states have hidden alimony built into their child support formulas. This is the money that is in excess of the children's needs. This becomes epically apparent as the payee and payor's incomes are further apart. This problem is further complicated because the states don't require an accounting of what child support is spent on. The person receiving child support can spend it on whatever they want. It would be up to you to prove that they are not spending it on the kids through a challenge in family court, and unless you have solid evidence, most attorneys will tell you this is not a fight worth having. Even if you do prove that they are not using the support on the kids, many judges don't care.

While the subject of hidden alimony is infuriating, there is not much you can do about it. Short of changing your state's guidelines, more often than not in court, you will be branded as someone who "doesn't want to pay their fair share." That could cause the judge to order you to pay more than you currently owe!

The best advice I have is to listen to what your attorney says in cases like this. If they think you can get your obligation reduced and you have the money to fight it - then by all means, go to court. Otherwise, you are better off not fighting these things.

While the child support system needs reform in just about every state, cases where the divorce happened in one state and the child support is in another poses a unique problem. In these cases, UCCJEA says that only the originating state can give alimony. This is to prevent someone from paying alimony in two states. There is nothing, however, that prevents the current state from ordering high child support (aka hidden alimony). Since there is no accountability for the person receiving child support, they are free to use that money however they want to. States may find themselves in a legal bind, though, since child support is not taxable as federal income and alimony is. If the IRS catches onto this, the states could be accused of "hiding" taxable income from the federal government (defrauding the government through tax evasion).

Inter-State Cases

Interstate cases pose a unique problem since every state has its own flavor of child support. Sometimes parents are divorced in one state and then move to another. Or maybe one parent moves. Sometimes the kids spend time in two different states. In all these cases, the UCCJEA lays down the groundwork so that states do not conflict with each other.

The UCCJEA has specific ground rules for which state has jurisdiction and which state doesn't. It also lays out a timeline that requires finishing cases in a timely manner. Each state can choose to adopt a certain version of UCCJEA, so it may be good to look up each state and pull those specific versions of the UCCJEA that are involved.

It's important to note that lawyers don't typically deal with inter-state cases regularly, so you may need to bring this to their attention and ask them to do some research. In my past experience, one lawyer didn't know anything about the UCCJEA, and I had to find a different lawyer!

<u>What are expenses?</u>

Since each state has its own guidelines, each state will define what is and is not a child expense differently. A common term used is direct and indirect expenses. Direct expenses are things that directly relate to the kids. These are expenses that you would not have if you didn't have kids. Think school fees and daycare expenses. Then there is indirect. Those are expenses that you would have but are increased because of the kids. Think mortgages, food, utilities, and other basic living expenses.

Some states put a lot of weight on what the kid's expenses actually are. If this is the case in your state, then you should keep detailed records of what money you spend on your kids. Keep receipts whenever you can. It would not hurt to use a financial accounting system like QuickBooks, but anything is better than nothing. A simple spreadsheet will do. The point is to keep records and prove the money that you are spending on the kids.

Once the child support is determined, it will be important for you to understand what should be paid for by the person paying child support and the person receiving child support. The guidelines mentioned earlier should help, but you still may need to ask your attorney a quick question or two to make sure you are not double paying on something (paying the child support and paying an expense the other person should pay). This is really common, so be careful that you don't double pay on some expenses.

Sometimes it's easier to pay for something (especially if the amount is small) rather than fight it. You will want to be careful, though. Paying for something more than once may set a precedent that the other person will use against you in court. They could say you paid it once and that you need to keep paying it. There is no magic rule here. Just try to find the best combination of what you can financially afford with the least amount of conflict.

Tracking Expenses

Tracking expenses is important because you may have to show what you spent on the kids. Child support can be re-calculated every so often (usually 3 or 4 years) if one party or the other files. This means that when it comes time to re-calculate how much you owe (or are owed), you will need to know several things, like the income of both parties and what money needs to be spent for the child's needs.

If you are spending money on things that the person receiving child support is supposed to be paying for, you will need to show proof of this in court. This means having a good accounting of the finances and also showing receipts.

You can track expenses in several ways. The easiest and least expensive is a spreadsheet. QuickBooks or similar accounting software can also be used. If you use accounting software, you can keep electronic copies of receipts and in most places, an electronic copy of a receipt is all that is needed. These programs make it easy to take a picture of the receipt and attach it to the expense. You will want to check with your attorney to see if you need a paper copy of receipts for your local court to accept them as evidence.

The downside of using accounting software is that it takes time and it usually costs money. The upside is that it will present the most accurate financial picture possible and is less likely to be questioned in court.

When tracking expenses, you will want to put receipts into different categories. These will show the judge how much and how often you spend money on certain things. You will want to check your state's child support guidelines to see what categories are considered. Generally, you will want to track anything that is considered a "direct expense." Here are the categories that I use (pro-tip - in your accounting software, put these all under one main category as subaccounts so it will be easier to generate a report of just these expenses later on):

- Child Support

- Clothing

- Communications/Tech

- Dependent Life Insurance

- Dependent Daycare

- Extracurricular Activities

- Food

- Medical

- Miscellaneous

- Non-HSA Medical

- Non-School Education

- Personal Grooming

- School Related Expenses

- Special Clothing

- Spousal Support

- Toys

- Transportation

No matter how you track your expenses, I highly recommend doing so until all the kids are aged out of child support and you are no longer paying. The one thing manipulative people can't stand is the truth, and having this data will be a great ally for you! It's going to take extra time and effort to track these things, but it will be worth it.

As an example, your ex may claim that you're not providing clothes or that there is never any food at your house. A simple financial report can show how often and when you buy clothes and food. Of course, you actually need to be doing these things for the data to help you! It can also hurt you. Your attorney will decide if the information that you have is helpful or not in your specific case.

Paying Child Support

If you are ordered to pay child support, then it's important that you pay it regularly and on time. Not paying your child support isn't an option since most states take an aggressive stance on child support enforcement. Some states will even take away your driver's license and penalize you in other ways. Courts can find you in contempt of court and put you in jail for not paying! This leads to a vicious downward spiral since it's kind of hard to make money when you're in jail.

Your divorce decree will have a determination on custody and child support, which are two separate things. It's important that if you are paying child support that the other parent doesn't withhold time from you if they haven't received child support and vice versa. Child support and time with the children are two separate things. The amount of time that each parent spends with the kids will certainly calculate how much child support is paid, but once the amount is set, the other parent should not use this as a means to withhold the children.

Some parents have been known to do this even when the full child support amount is paid. There is some expense that they claim the payor needs to pay. In this case, document that they denied you time with the child and you will need to bring them to court. While the states do not spend time and money to chase down parents that deny the other parent time with the children, they will spend time and money to chase down those that do not pay child support!

When you actually pay child support, you can do it a few different ways. Some states have you pay the other party directly (write a check, never give cash!) without the state being involved. This is the least common because there is no tracking, and it becomes a he-said, she-said requiring many financial documents if it needs to go to court.

Some states require you to pay child support through a service or a state agency. This ensures that they can track the payments in case there is ever a question of the amount paid. This allows the state to take you to court easier if you are not making payments. Of course, the state also benefits by collecting a "fee" off each child support payment, which amounts to millions in revenue for the state.

Some states ensure you pay child support through the state agency or third party by saying that any money paid directly (not through the state) is a gift. If you "pay" child support directly, and the state later determines that you never "paid" your child support, you could owe back child support on money that you've already paid!

If you don't pay child support, the state can garnish your wages. That means that the state will take child support money before you get your paycheck. This usually happens when someone has been ordered to pay back child support or has shown that they are not reliable in making their child support payments.

In short, if you are ordered to pay child support, make sure that you understand how you are supposed to pay it for the state that you are in. Make sure you pay it on time every time. If you have a problem paying consistently and have a job that gives you a regular paycheck, you can request that the state pull your wages automatically as a volunteer garnishment. One benefit of this is that it will be automatic. The downside is that if there is an issue (like support is supposed to stop or they take too much money), it may be hard or impossible to recover funds.

<u>Ending Child Support</u>

Usually, child support ends when the kids turn 18. Of course, it can't be that easy. If you're getting divorced and you have older kids, then make sure in the paperwork that there is an agreed time when child support will stop. If you don't have that, then you will need to petition the court (i.e., file another motion) to end the child support. This petition can be accepted by your ex, you both sign it, and it gets filed with the court. They can also choose to fight it, causing you to have a hearing or trial. This is why I always recommend that you keep excellent financial records when you are paying child support!

Child support usually ends when the kids turn 18, but some states require you to carry it through the high school years. This means you may end up paying child support until the child graduates high school if they turn 18 before they graduate. Some cases have even come up requiring one parent to pay for children as adults going through college! Check the laws in your state for the specifics.

You will want to talk with your lawyer and make sure that you understand when support can end. Nothing says that once the kids turn 18, you need to be done supporting them financially. You may want to help them out once they turn 18 for one reason or another, but once they become an adult, you can usually support them directly without having to go through your ex.

It's also worth mentioning here that everyone will have a unique situation. If you have kids that are disabled or have special needs, then support may continue past 18.

Injustice in Child Support

I could write for pages and pages on the injustice in child support. In theory, child support is supposed to afford the children an equal financial opportunity in both houses. It makes sense that they wouldn't live like kings in one house and be in poverty in the other. The reality is child support in the United States (and most of the world) is poorly executed. It's made worse by the federal government giving the states an incentive to receive federal money through Title IV-D.

There are injustices in how much people are ordered to pay. There are injustices in how the money is collected, in the fees the state collects, and how the state will use child support to "pay itself" back from those that have received welfare. The list goes on and on.

Unfortunately, there isn't much that you can do to change any of that while you are getting divorced. While there has been a slow movement to reform child support, the reality is that the current system is not going to change drastically any time soon. The best you can do if you are ordered to pay child support is to grin and bear it the best you can. See a therapist if you need to. Whatever you do, don't take your frustration out on the other parent or the kids!

Can you go to jail?

In short, yes. You can go to jail for not paying your child support. If the judge finds you willfully neglected in paying child support (you had the money and just chose not to pay it), they can put you in jail for contempt of court. Remember, this is serious business. If you owe child support, you need to pay it.

Second Jobs and Child Support

Child support is usually calculated on the total of both the mother's and the father's income. This means that if you get a second job and increase your income, then you may owe more in child support! Most states also require you to report any changes in income to your ex and then it would be up to them to file a petition to have the child support adjusted. Some states require a 10% change in the payment amount to make sure that people are not filing changes over pennies.

If you do decide to work a second job, you will need to weigh the benefit of that additional income vs. what you may need to pay in additional support. Your lawyer will be able to help you with those what-if situations. It's always good to run some numbers first and make sure that the extra work and stress are worth the effort.

When the Ex Won't Pay for Something

When the ex won't pay for something, it can be infuriating. Here you are, having paid child support and they won't spend that money on what they are supposed to! The problem is that keeping your ex accountable is very, very expensive. Unless you have a provision in your court documents, you will need to file a contempt of court.

The best advice that I have for you is if they will not pay, and the kids need it, then pay for it and keep the records. Keep the receipt and make a note. If you ever go back to re-calculate child support, then you can use this evidence that this money is not being used for child support. Depending on the state and the judge, this may or may not matter.

The most important thing is that your kids have what they need. If the thing they won't pay for is something nice to have and not a need to have, maybe you let it go. You can still make a note of it in case you ever go back to court. The one thing you do not want to do is let your kids suffer unnecessarily. If they need something, get it for them. But if it's something they don't truly need, neither of you must buy them unnecessary things.

<u>Child Support Best Case Situations</u>

In the best case, child support is used for the benefit of the kids. One way that you can ensure this happens is to have clear and open communications with your ex. Of course, this requires your ex to work with you!

While the child support guidelines may tell you about what the child support is supposed to be used for, the guidelines leave a lot to be desired. Arguments will come up about paying for this or that. You will need to decide if it's worth arguing over or if it's easier to just pay. Remember, when child support is re-calculated, you can always bring evidence that your ex is requiring you to pay for things that should have been paid for with your child support payment.

<u>Alimony</u>

Alimony is meant to be money that is paid to the lower-earning spouse so they are not in poverty after divorce. This is a holdover from days when men worked and women didn't. These days it's become mostly irrelevant, but the laws are slow to change, so we still have it even when both people work.

The way states calculate alimony differs, so check the laws in your state. The amount of time that you will need to pay alimony varies too. Some states require you to pay it based on how long you were married; others require you to pay it until death.

Alimony is separate from anything to do with the kids. That's what child support is for. If you are divorced and have no kids, alimony would still be something you may need to pay. Alimony usually isn't something that can get recalculated, like child support. One important thing to note is that if you move from the original state where you get divorced, that new state cannot order alimony. The UCCJEA specifically states this.

Since each state calculates alimony differently, it's important that you research the laws in your state and ask your lawyer for the finer points of alimony in your state.

Chapter Thirty-Six

Property Division

One of the major parts of your divorce will be the property division. This will likely be frustrating and heartbreaking all at the same time. You'll need to stay strong, but you will get through this process.

In this process, you'll divide the assets (anything that has value) and liabilities (these are debts or any money you owe). If you owe money on something determines if it is an asset or a liability. In a perfect world, both spouses would equally split the assets and liabilities so that both come out with the same amount or values (net positive or net negative). We don't live in a perfect world, and often one person will benefit more than the other.

During the property division, you will need to make a decision on how much this money or stuff is really worth to you. There will be some things that you are tempted to fight for that will cost you more in attorney fees and your time than it's worth. If you spend one hour fighting for a $100 item, your attorney will be charging you much more than that in that one hour. You could have gone out and bought a brand-new one!

My best advice is to get in and get out with a minimal amount of fighting over property. I do not recommend letting your ex saddle you with all the debt while taking all the cash, either! Your best bet is to figure out what motivates your ex and use that as leverage. If she really wants a particular thing, let her have it, but make sure you use that as leverage to get something you want!

Most states will look at what the combined assets and liabilities are at the end of the marriage. Some states make it way more complicated. As of the writing of this book, nine states are "community property" states. These states want to keep a running tally of who-owes-who from the beginning of the marriage. These states are Arizona, California, Idaho, Louisiana, Nevada, New Mexico, Texas, Washington, and Wisconsin (Property Division by State, 2022).

If you are in a community property state, then your property division is much more complex. You could be on the hook for paying 1/2 the amount of payments to loans that you had prior to getting married. This could be a student loan you took out in college before you were married. The rules differ by state and often times there is an argument if the other spouse had a "benefit" from that debt or property. It's complicated and while the idea is that it's more fair, it usually just makes the property separation more expensive.

Property separation can also get complex when one spouse tries to hide assets from the other. Remember how I mentioned getting copies of all the financial records at the beginning of this book? This is where that paperwork comes in handy! It's not unusual for a spouse to try and hide property (a car, boat, business income/assets or even real estate) from the other in hopes that it will not be addressed in the divorce. I would not advise doing this as it can get you in trouble. On the other end, if your ex is hiding things, it's up to you to prove that she is. If one spouse is hiding property, then the judge may impose sanctions (or fines) and can even throw you or her in jail.

When doing the property division, it's essentially a giant balance sheet. You will gain in some things and you will owe money for others. At the end of the sheet, both spouses should have approximately the same value of assets or liabilities (depending on if you are net positive or in the hole).

Cars

If you have two cars, then you keep your car and she keeps hers. You'll want to look at the values of the cars (use Kelly Blue Book or similar) and subtract from the value what the remaining loan amounts are. This is the net value.

After the divorce, you will want your name off your ex's car loan (and vice versa). Usually, to get someone's name off a car note, they will need to re-finance the car. Some people are OK with keeping their name on an ex's car loan to keep things simple, but this probably isn't the best idea. In some states, divorce papers may be enough for the loan to take someone's name off the car note, but this is pretty rare. Your attorney will know what is allowed in your state. If re-financing a car is difficult, then your best bet may be to trade it in and get a new car with a new loan.

From a leverage standpoint, a car is usually a pretty easy thing to replace. If you are not too emotionally tied to a vehicle, this may be a good thing to give up if she is demanding it from you.

Other things you'll probably have to divide up include:

1. Marital home and other real estate.

2. Household Property (including furniture).

3. Recreation / Hobby (boats, guns, etc.).

4. Kids' Property.

5. Tools required for your job.

6. Family Heirlooms.

The rules for property division differ wildly from state to state. You'll need to get specific legal advice from your attorney on your situation. Remember to try and make non-emotional decisions and try and avoid getting sucked into a fight over something that is not worth fighting over. Get in, and get out! The majority of your material items can be replaced easier than going through the pain of trying to keep them in a divorce battle!

Chapter Thirty-Seven

The Magic Bullet (False Accusations and Protective Orders)

First, a disclaimer. It is essential that any form of abuse, including domestic violence or sexual abuse, be taken seriously. Survivors need to have safety and support so they can start the journey of healing. The law needs to deal with the abusers. This section is not to downplay actual abuse but to educate you on the dangers of false accusations that can happen during a divorce.

An all too common occurrence in family court cases is the issue of false accusations. The industries call this the "Magic Bullet." The bullet reference is because it's an attempt to kill one party. The magic is because the accusations come from nowhere, and often they are absurd! These accusations are often something that are very serious. If found guilty, the accused party would likely serve jail time!

Common accusations include abuse of some kind, usually sexual or physical abuse of a woman or children. Being accused of sexually abusing your kids is a serious accusation that could cause you to lose custody of your kids forever! What happens to someone who falsely accuses you of something so heinous? Usually nothing and that is one of the systemic problems with the family court system. With no accountability and no penalty for falsely accusing someone, this is often a last resort by someone who feels like they are "losing" the family court battle.

What happens when these accusations are made? The answer is-it depends. Often these accusations will be made and the person making the claims will seek a protection order. While the names vary across the country, they will be called something like a PFA (Protection from Abuse) or a PFS (Protection from Stalking). A person can go request one of these generally by going in front of a judge ex parte (without you there or your knowledge). The judge will order the PFA or PFS and you will be served these papers, usually by law enforcement.

This is just where the nightmare starts. You get served the papers at work or somewhere else. Usually, you will be kicked out of your home if you are living with the other person. The police may go with you to your home and let you take some essential items (clothes, toiletries), and from that point, you will not be allowed back in. Now homeless, you'll need to find a place to sleep - either a hotel or a friend's house while this whole ordeal is going on.

A hearing will be set and the time/place will likely be on the papers you are served. At this point, you should give your attorney a copy of your papers and address any claims that the other party is making against you. In some places, if the claim is absurd, the attorney can have a meeting with the judge and get the order thrown out. In other locations, you will need to wait for the hearing until anything can be done. This can be 2, 3 or 4 weeks! It's important to remember to remain calm during this process. You will be under a microscope during this whole process.

In the meantime, you will need to follow what the order says. Generally, this will be no contact with the other party (or your kids). It may specify places you are not allowed to go (like the family home or the kids' school). The order may say you need to pay the bills at the residence you were kicked out of. If you were falsely accused, you can see how these accusations will have a huge impact on your life, even if only temporarily. If you're found guilty, these abuse orders can have longer-term effects like preventing you from owning a firearm or holding certain jobs.

Going through all this is truly a nightmare. If the accusations are false, you will need to work with your attorney to defend yourself. These accusations can be hard to prove (or disprove), so you will want to take your defense seriously. Put some time into gathering evidence and giving that to your attorney.

If these allegations are made and they seem out of character for you, chances are the accusing party will have a harder time convincing a judge that these things really happened. But don't take that to mean that it will be easy to prove your innocence. Often character witnesses will be brought in and evidence will be shown.

How likely is it that you will have false allegations made against you? Some data shows that 85% of protection orders are against men. Further, some estimate that of that 85 percent, 90 percent are products of tactical divorce considerations rather than actual protection from abuse (Cordell & Cordell, 2015). You're at a much greater risk to fall into this statistic if you are in a high-conflict divorce. It's in these high-conflict cases that the percentage of cases that involves some sort of protection order goes up dramatically.

If your case is high-conflict, you need to be on the lookout for baiting. If the opposing party feels like they are "losing," they may try and bait you into acting out of character. Be VERY careful of this. A common technique is to make an outrageous claim and then wait for you to react to it. That anger in the reaction will be used against you if only to reinforce their bogus claim. The thought process is, "See, they are abusive because they got upset when I accused them of something"! The best thing to do is not react to anything, no matter how outrageous.

What happens to those that make these claims falsely? The short answer is nothing, which is one of the things that makes our family court system so broken. They can make all these claims, you will defend yourself and there will be absolutely no consequences for the person that made the claim. They will not go to jail (even if you went to jail over their accusations). They will not have to pay you back any money (even though they cost you money to live somewhere else and pay for a house you're not living in). They won't even be told they need to apologize.

One thing you could do once the allegations are found false is sue the accusing party in civil court. This will likely be expensive and there is no guarantee that you will gain anything.

The ramifications of a false allegation will haunt you for a long time to come. Causing you psychological trauma, it can take lots of therapy to properly deal with it! You will need to deal with it, otherwise you may experience symptoms such as anxiety, PTSD and other disorders. The other party may use these problems against you in future court battles, so it's important that you deal with your trauma and don't let it cause you problems in the future. In short, find a good therapist and see that person regularly until you've properly dealt with that trauma.

How do you protect against a false allegation?

The best way to protect against a false allegation is to be very careful how you act around and with your ex during and after the divorce process. The biggest tip I can give you is to remember that your ex is now someone who you don't have a personal relationship with but rather a business relationship with. Treat your actions and interactions with the other person the same way you would as a colleague or co-worker. You're friendly and courteous, but not the same kind of friendly as someone who is your best friend.

If you are at high risk for a false accusation, then make sure your communications are written where possible (email or text message). Have as few in-person or over-the-phone interactions as possible. Make sure you take your emotions out of your communications. Remember, it's just the facts. You don't need to give your opinion or what you think to the other person.

Can you make false accusations against the other party?

While you can do whatever you want, you shouldn't do this. The biggest reason is that it's morally not right to lie, but there are other reasons. One of those reasons is that you may not be successful in getting a PFA/PFS because of your gender. Courts will generally believe anything a woman tells them but not believe what a man says. This double standard is heinous, but it exists.

What if I have a legitimate reason to get a PFA/PFS?

If you need to get a PFA/PFS (and you should if you have a legitimate reason), then be prepared to have evidence to show the judge. You will also need to show a clear need and evidence of that need. Work with your attorney to make sure they believe you have a good need and the evidence to support that before going in front of a judge. Courts generally believe that men do not need protection, so make sure your needs are clear when you ask for one.

Chapter Thirty-Eight

Going to Court

D<u>ressing for Court</u>

When you actually attend court, you will see that people dress in all different types of ways for their court appearance. Some people dress extremely professionally and look just like the lawyers that are standing next to them. Others will be dressed like they just came from the gym (in very casual clothes, i.e., sweatpants, athletic shorts, tank tops). And, of course, there are always a few entertaining people that look like they're ready to hit the club. How you dress when you attend court will be up to you. The way you dress will be noticed by the judges and lawyers presiding over you. That impression can either be good or bad.

A building I used to work at had a cafeteria. There was a guy named Louis that owned and ran the cafeteria operation. One day, I went down to the cafeteria to get some breakfast and was charged one price. The next day I went down to get breakfast again, and I was charged a lesser price. I asked Louis why it was cheaper today than it was yesterday (as I had ordered the same thing) and he told me that he charged me based on the shirt I was wearing. If you're wearing a button-down shirt, he charged more!

The way you dress influences the impression that you give to other people. Just like my short example, Louis had assumed since I was wearing a button-down shirt, that I made more money. Of course, the secret I learned here would be to wear my polo shirt to that cafeteria if I wanted to save money! I'm not saying this practice is fair or even legal, but it does illustrate how people are influenced by how you dress.

You may deduct that dressing "to the nines" in a very nice suit and good dress shoes is probably the way to go in court. You may think if you look as professional as you can, you will garner the most respect from the court staff, lawyers and the judge. However, I don't recommend this in most cases. And here's why:

If you dress too fancy, then you will not get any sympathy from the judge. Let's face it, being a judge *is* a human endeavor. Judges are asked to determine cases based on case merit, the evidence in the case, and the arguments from the lawyers. However, judges are human. And while they are not supposed to be influenced by external factors like how you dress, my experience is that it plays at least a small part in their decision.

If you're going into court and your claim is that you do not have money to pay the other party, it doesn't make much sense to come dressed in a $2000 suit. While you may own that suit and it's been hanging in your closet for years, it may be more prudent to dress in something that is less expensive.

The same goes for the other end of the spectrum. You come to court looking like you just left the gym in sweatpants and a sweatshirt; chances are you may not be taken very seriously based on your appearance.

So the trick when trying to decide what to wear to court is... balance. Since this book is mainly focused on dads, my fashion suggestions will be aimed at males. However, if you're a female reading the book, the same advice holds true. Just adapt the fashion suggestions to the female wardrobe.

For formal attire, I would recommend a modest suit and button-down shirt. A tie is optional here depending on how professional you want to look. You should ask your attorney what they recommend. Try to pick out neutral colors (gray, dark blue, tan, beige or brown) and definitely avoid any bright colors. Red can be seen as an angry or dominating color. This is not the time to wear a bright red tie! Too much black can be seen as expensive and also dominating. Make sure that your shirt (and tie) coordinate and that your color choices are appropriate. In most men's fashion styles, either brown or black shoes are the most common and they go with nearly everything. Make sure that your shoes and your belt match in color. If you're wearing a tie, the tie should be extended down to the top of your pants.

The advice that I'm giving here is generalized. Different courts may have different expectations. You should always listen to the advice of your attorney (who is in court several times a week). Your attorney will know exactly what the judges are looking for and it is always best to follow their advice. They have the inside scoop on your specific local court. With that said, you should choose your dress based on who you really are. I would not recommend going out and spending thousands of dollars on attire to wear to court.

I will caution you, however, about dressing too casually. Dressing too casually may give the judge the wrong impression. Even if you typically dress very casually, this can have a negative effect on somebody who is judging you based on your appearance alone. Throw in some allegations by the other party or some damaging evidence, and your defensive argument in the judge's eyes will quickly erode. In the event of deciding whether to dress more formally or more casually, it is best to err on the side of caution and dress more formally.

How to act in Court

When you go to court, you're probably going to be nervous. A courtroom situation is not familiar to most of us unless you're a lawyer. You'll be in an unfamiliar place, and it's ok to recognize that you'll be nervous. Remember that court is a very formal place. In our everyday conversations, we tend to be informal. We use first names, we smile and we have casual body language. Court is completely opposite. Court is very formal. Names start with Mr., Mrs. and Ms. You don't speak unless spoken to. You only answer the questions that you are asked. In a way, it's weird to have someone (your attorney) talk for you.

Your attorney should give you some pointers on how to act in court. Before a hearing or a trial, they may spend some time going over the facts and quizzing you on certain things. Follow their lead.

You should also know that the other attorney is going to try and trip you up if they question you on the stand. Don't hate them for it, even though it's hard not to. They are going to say something that you will answer quickly, but later on you will think, "I should have answered that another way." For tough questions, it's ok to pause briefly to think about your answer. If the question seems unclear, it's OK to ask the attorney to repeat the question. Just try not to fall on this tactic more than once during a questioning session. In court, just remember to be courteous, answer truthfully and don't be a jerk. Remember that impressions matter. You don't want to come off as a jerk in court. The other attorney will definitely try and make you look like one but don't act that way or you will remove any doubt in the judge's mind that you aren't a jerk all the time and to everyone.

Ethics in Court

You have judges and lawyers who are extremely fair and ethical, and you will have some that are not fair and ethical at all. It will be up to you to determine which side of humanity each player sits. It's not uncommon for attorneys to stretch the truth or otherwise act unethically because they know that there will be no consequences. Attorneys who often act unethically are rarely held accountable. The time and effort it takes to discipline an attorney is enormous and often the states require overwhelming evidence in order to determine wrongdoing. Also, remember that lawyers often become judges. The office that disciplines lawyers at the state level is typically run by other lawyers. In other words, the system is inbred (for lack of a better term).

What's worse is the organization that lawyers belong to is called the Bar, or the Bar Association. These associations lobby for the state to make laws in the best interest of the lawyers. That often means that when laws come up that will reduce conflict between parties or otherwise make divorce easier, the Bar Association will spend money to fight it. This is one reason why it is very hard to change parenting laws. The lawyers profit from the conflict and therefore will fight to defend unfair laws.

Parlay - Pirates Code

"And secondly, you must be a pirate for the pirate's code to apply and you're not. And thirdly, the code is more what you'd call "guidelines" than actual rules." - Capt Barbosa, Disney Pirates of the Caribbean.

If you watch the adventures of Capt. Jack Sparrow in the iconic Pirates of the Caribbean movies, you may remember the above quote. Capt. Barbosa's reply to this statement?

"Welcome aboard the Black Pearl, Miss Turner."

Indeed, divorce is much like being on the famous "Black Pearl." It often feels like you're sailing along a ship with black sails and a cursed crew. You're not an attorney (pirate), so special rules do not apply to you.

You may wonder how the code fits into family court. There are a lot of similarities. Family court is much like the pirates' code. The rules are not hard and fast, and many times they are used as guidelines rather than strict rules. The laws and how things work are not always obvious. Common sense often seems to be left shore-side. Fear not; with some explanation, you can learn to navigate these treacherous waters!

When trying to understand the court, it's important for you to understand a little bit about yourself first. Are you the kind of person that is extremely logical? If so, you might find the court process maddening! If you're the type of person that deals a little bit better with abstract principles and ideas, then understanding the court in its process will likely be an easier task. Most of us sit somewhere in the middle between the logical and the abstract. If you're in the middle between logical and abstract thinking, then you'll find it confusing on many levels. Either way - you're not the only one. Just about everybody who is not a lawyer is confused and bewildered by the process until you've been through it a few times.

Now, let's talk about the laws. Recognize that even though there are laws, judges are not obligated to follow them. Judges use so-called "judicial discretion." This is the power of the judge to decide loosely based on the law. It's up to his or her discretion to interpret the intent of the law and ensure that the decision meets the general guidelines. The problem with judicial discretion is that it often causes judges to stray far from the intent of the law. The judges also get to decide which laws apply and which ones do not. This is one of the most maddening things about family court. It is also the thing that makes family court inconsistent from judge to judge. Judges can even be inconsistent from day to day. Some courts may have very consistent judges and the lawyers will be able to tell you how they will likely rule. In other courts, some judges will be completely inconsistent. This is where a good attorney that's experienced in your local area will come in handy.

But what happens when you get a judge's decision that you don't like or have severe issues with? Any judge has the risk of their decision being overturned by a higher court. You may have heard of the appeal process. This happens when someone doesn't like a judge's decision and believes they have evidence or some compelling reason to get a higher court to look at the case. In an appeal, this means that the case will be essentially retried or that the judges in the appeals court will rule on certain merits. They can also send the case back to the lower court for another trial. This typically happens when a procedure is not followed, or when there is something significantly flawed with the judge's decision in the lower court.

Chapter Thirty-Nine

Divorce Tech

O rganizational Tools
One of the weird things about being divorced is that your life can be "examined" as if under a microscope at almost any time. Your ex can make claims to get the upper hand in custody or child support. You'll need evidence to dismiss her claim. Technology has made it very easy to keep records and evidence. Tons of data is generated in our everyday life. Here are some tools that you may want to consider using.

Note-taking apps - Apps like Evernote and Bear Note. They are very useful because you can store all kinds of information in them. Web pages, PDF documents, images, and emails all can be stored in these accounts. The apps on tablets and phones make it very easy to get information into them. Some scanners even work seamlessly with this software, so you can scan something and it is stored in the app automatically. The info is stored on the cloud, so the loss of a computer or tablet doesn't matter. You can also organize the information by notebooks and by tags to make info easier to find.

File storage - Things like Dropbox and Google Drive. These cloud storage apps allow you to store any kind of file. They are stored both on your computer and in the cloud, so if your computer is destroyed or lost, you still have your files.

Document Scanner - One of the most useful pieces of tech in my divorce was the document scanner! I personally used a Fujitsu ScanSnap iX500. You'll be sharing thousands of pages of information with your lawyer and your ex, and the scanner makes it easy to get a piece of paper into a digital form. Smartphones have apps that scan but for multiple pages, a physical scanner is the way to go. Research the scanners before you buy because you will want one that is compatible with the software that you use. Most of these scanners will automatically upload your document to your note-taking app (like Evernote) or your cloud storage app (like Dropbox). This will save you a step from moving these documents manually. The bonus of something like Evernote is that for PDF documents, it will search the document for text which can make finding a document later on much easier.

Smartphone Camera - Never underestimate the power of a picture. Remember, a picture is worth a thousand words! Taking a simple picture can document a situation. Save that picture to your note-taking app and you are ready to go if the issue comes up in court. If you can, taking videos is even better.

Shared Calendars - Shared calendars such as Google Calendar can be helpful, but be careful about what you share. If you share your personal calendar, then your ex will know all your plans. The best bet is to make a new calendar just for the kids and share that with both parties. This will make sure that only the kid events are seen by either party. Most of the current parenting apps have a shared calendar. I would urge you to use one as it streamlines pretty much all the necessary communication needed in ideal and less-than-ideal co-parenting situations.

Parenting Apps- Technology has helped parenting, too. A co-parenting app can help you and your ex stay on track communication-wise. These apps will be the place where you send messages, have a shared calendar, and track expenses.

You can do the same thing using other methods (like a shared Google calendar and email), but the benefit of these apps is that you can provide your attorney and even the judge a login to this information. They can also be very helpful when going to court because they can be a treasure trove of evidence. Because the data in these apps can be used in court, people probably tend to be a bit more civil on them.

Remember that if you sign up for one of these, you'll be using it until both your kids are 18, and there is a cost associated. Another issue that may be a challenge is getting your ex to agree to use one. Sometimes the judge or your lawyer can write that a co-parenting app must be utilized. If you and/or your ex are high-conflict or there is a high probability of being in court often, I would highly recommend using one of the co-parenting apps.

Two popular parenting apps are Our Family Wizard and Fayr. I'll let you read the latest reviews to determine which one works best for you. Once you sign up for the app, your ex will need to do the same and the accounts will be linked together. Most apps also allow you to invite professionals to have access to your account. These are judges, lawyers, mediators, and therapists.

Once you start using the app, you will need to make sure that you use the app. Resist the urge to have conversations via text messages. Resist the urge to send emails. Don't be afraid to take a conversation from text or email and move it into the app. Just let the other person know by text or email that you will address the issue in the app. Having these communication boundaries is important to make sure that you have as much communication in the app as possible. This will be very useful if you ever go back to court.

<u>Financial Tools</u>

Unless you run a business, you're probably not used to keeping detailed financial records. While there is nothing that says you have to keep good financial records when you are divorced, it does help when you have to go to court for child support.

Accounting Software - Software like Quickbooks can help you easily track expenses and create reports. As talked about in the child support section, there are categories of expenses that your state will consider when ordering child support. Knowing how much you spend on each category can be helpful. Using accounting software to track your expenses is the best way, but it is also the most expensive and time-consuming.

Spreadsheet - You can also track expenses on spreadsheets. Just list the date, name of the place the money was spent, what it was for, the category of expense, and the amount. With this information, you will be able to show what you are spending money on. Most banks will let you download your data into a spreadsheet, so you can start with that data to save you some time.

Receipts - Make sure you keep receipts or copies of receipts for things that you spent money on. Most places accept a digital copy of a receipt so you can take a paper copy of the receipt and take a picture or scan it. This is where having a scanner is very handy! Also, most accounting software has an app that allows you to scan the receipt and create an expense quickly.

Communications Tools

These days there are a ton of ways to communicate through digital means. You have text messages, instant messengers, and email. Then there are video calls, phone calls, and old-fashioned face-to-face communications.

When you get divorced, you have to now always think about your liability. The way you act and the way that you communicate can all be used against you. All of these means of communication either automatically record what you are doing and saying, or they have very easy ways to record you. This means that you should pretend that any communications with your ex (or anyone else really) can be recorded and used against you in the future. The good news is the same rules apply to your ex. Anything they say or communicate can be used against them.

In general, it's best never to have any sort of emotional exchange with your ex. Keep it short and sweet, just to the point. Try and keep all your communications business-like. Don't let them suck you into an emotional conversation, especially if you are in person.

Below are a few notes about different types of communications:

Text Messages and Instant Messages - Everything you write in a text message is saved automatically. Screenshots are an easy way to show them in court. The one thing that really is bad about text messages is that it is easy to take something out of context. Try and keep texting short and sweet. Use these for coordinating logistics (kid exchanges, etc.).

Email - Every email is saved. Even if you delete it from your email, it will still be saved on the other person's email. Keep emails short and sweet. If you are using a co-parenting app, then try not to use emails at all. If you get an email from someone (like the school), don't forget to CC your co-parent when replying. It may also be helpful to talk with your co-parent before replying and making decisions about school or extracurricular activities. To cover yourself even further, you can save outsider emails and responses to a pdf file and include the attachment on a thread in your parenting app.

Phone - While it's harder to record phone conversations, it is still certainly possible. Sometimes phone calls are needed because the situation is urgent. Sometimes it's just easier than texting. If your ex is high-conflict, phone calls should be the last resort since anything you say or they say may be used against you. It's easy to twist words or take them out of context.

Video call (Zoom, MS Teams, etc.) - Video calls are just phone calls with the ability to see the other person. It's easy to record video calls, so remember that. You also need to remember that the other person can read your body language.

Face-to-face - There are some communications that are hard to have over any other means. You will have to decide how comfortable you are with having face-to-face communication with your ex. If you are both high-conflict with each other, then it's best not to have any face-to-face conversations at all. If you can work together well, it can save you a lot of time and will be easier. You do need to weigh the risk of the other person using your words against you or making false accusations (that you hit them or sexually assaulted them).

Recording (video or voice conversations) - Be sure that you are aware of the laws in your state if you intend to record the other person. In most places, if you are in public, it's fair game to record. Some states require that you tell the other person if you are recording a phone conversation. It's up to you to know the law.

Other Tech

Security Cameras - If you don't have them at your house, it would be a good idea to install them! Newer cameras are easy to install because they are wireless and even battery-operated. You simply hang them up and change the batteries every year or two. Then you set them up to record in the cloud and you are protected. It's good to have security cameras to show if someone breaks into your house, but it's also a good backup for you. This will record everything in case your ex tries to do something to your property. They will also record the kids coming and going from your home.

Vehicle Tracking - This can be done on a smartphone and even in some dash cams. Let's say your ex claims that you are never on time to exchange the kids and that she is lying. You could easily show data from your phone or tracker that you were indeed on time and where you were. This may be case specific, but the point is to leverage technology where you can.

Social Media

Social media is something that you need to be careful with when you get divorced. Any part or all of your social media history can be used in court, even if you have the privacy set to "friends only." The opposing side can (and usually will) subpoena the other person's social media accounts. Any posts that can be used against you. These can be used as a way to show your character, how you treat people and what you may be saying about your ex. It's best to keep your personal conflicts off social media and remember that anything you post on social media is "public," no matter how private you think it is. Don't post anything you wouldn't mind showing your family, friends, co-workers, and the rest of the world.

Political Memes - Political memes may sound funny when you post them, but they can easily be used to show a negative character. The best advice is not to post them at all.

Pictures of smoking, alcohol, or illegal substances/activities - If you are doing any of these things on your social media, there is a good likelihood that they will be used against you in court!

Inappropriate pictures of children - People often post pictures of their kids and do not think a thing about it. You do need to be careful of posting pictures of kids in bathing suits or in baths. There are folks looking for images like this, and these kinds of images can make you look like you have poor judgment.

Blocking your ex and their family members - If you are in a high-conflict situation, chances are your ex may use her friends to get information on you and one of those sources can be social media. You can easily block people on some platforms while others, you cannot. If you can block them and it makes sense, then you should. It's not uncommon for an ex to recruit someone to snoop on your social media accounts if they themselves do not have access.

Privacy - On some platforms your posts can be set to public, friends of friends, or friends only. I would recommend setting it to friends only. You can usually even have it go back and make all your previous posts have this same privacy setting.

Nothing is private - The best advice to think of when posting anything on social media is to assume you are posting that information on a corkboard that everyone in the world can see! Once you post something, it's public. While some of the social platforms give you some privacy controls, the reality is once you put something out in the world on social media, it's easy for someone to copy it and post it somewhere that you have no control over. You should take the same mindset when sending emails.

Delete, Delete, Delete - If you have things posted that, looking back, you would rather others not see, then you can always delete them! Some services make it easy to delete, while with others, you will need to do it manually. Some people regularly delete all their posts on Twitter that are older than a year or two. Many times tweets have not aged well and these have been used to characterize someone falsely in the present or even to show that they are a hypocrite. When in doubt, delete it!

Chapter Forty

Divorce Papers

Once you get divorced, you'll end up with a set of divorce papers (sometimes called a decree) that spell out what to do in certain situations. The papers will call out who pays for what, say what the custody schedule is, where to exchange the kids and how certain assets are split. These papers may be one document or several. I am grossly oversimplifying this description, but each state and local court has their own way of doing things, so it's best to ask your attorney what to expect.

In this section, I'll cover some things that are good to have in your divorce papers. If you want these in your papers, you need to ask your attorney about them. Your attorney will need to come up with the specific language. The suggestions here are not written in legal-ese and cannot be used as is. I'm simply introducing the idea. Chances are your attorney already has it written up from a previous client! The things in this chapter are suggestions and may or may not be helpful in your situation.

With the divorce papers, it's important to remember that the papers are what you go to if you and your ex disagree on something. If you want to do something different, then it's ok to do that as long as you both agree. If you both decide you want to change the pickup/drop time or location (as long as you **both** agree), then go for it! It's when you both don't agree that you need to fall back on the papers and follow the written order. There are some limits here, so check with your attorney if you are unsure. For example, changes to alimony, property division and child support payments will likely need a paper filed with the court to change.

This is not an exhaustive list either. There are many different situations and scenarios, so I've covered some things that I've seen as helpful. It's a good idea to have a discussion with your attorney to see what they like to include. If they've been at family law for any amount of time, chances are they have a list of their "favorites" that they like to include.

In the sections below, there will be some sections that are standard to that document. For example, a parenting plan generally always has where and when to exchange the children.

Parenting Plan

A parenting plan is simply a document that explicitly calls out things about parenting the children after divorce. This will include when and where to exchange the kids. This can get detailed or it can be high-level.

It will typically also include a holiday schedule with mom having certain holidays on the even year and dad having the remainder of the holidays on the even year. Typically the holidays would "flip" for the odd year. For example, if mom has the kids for the 4th of July on the even years, then typically dad will have the kids on the 4th for the odd years. How the holidays are split is up to the parties involved. There are many creative ways to split who has the kids on which holiday and how many holidays you list in the parenting plan.

There are some "extras" that you can put into the parenting plan. These things may be helpful if you are still in a high-conflict situation or if you have someone that likes to push boundaries often.

Special rules around holidays (like travel) - You may ask for special rules around the holidays. This is helpful if one parent or the other needs to travel to see their family. It could be that for some holidays, the actual day is split. For example, one parent could have the kids for Christmas morning until noon, and then they go to the other parent's house. The next year you flip so the person that had them after lunch on Christmas gets them for Christmas Morning.

Specify when and how often the other party can call - Some parents feel like they need to have constant contact with their children. This is usually a bigger concern when the kids are young and before they start using smartphones. You may want to specify how often (every night or just every other night?) and what time the other party can call.

Anti-harassment clause - This is useful if you are in high-conflict. It can be standard in some parenting plans. It can protect you from being accused of harassment when you are simply trying to co-parent.

Must live within a certain distance clause - Sometimes after the divorce, a parent will want to move into the next county or even the next state. This can put a burden on the other parent to meet halfway and it can make co-parenting difficult. It's a good idea to have this clause to specify what will happen if a parent moves away and what the expectations of the other parent are.

Travel clauses - Travel clauses can be helpful if you need extra time to travel with the kids, which would interrupt the normal parenting schedule. It's also good to have these to keep the other parent from abusing travel as an excuse to have the kids when they are not supposed to. A good travel clause will say how time would be made up if one parent misses out on time with the children. It should also define who pays for travel expenses like passports.

Parenting Apps - It's a very good idea to use a parenting app to co-parent. These apps will help you send messages back and forth and also track expenses and things like doctor's appointments. Our

Family Wizard and Fayr are just two examples of parenting apps. The parenting plan should specify if you have to use one, which one, and who pays for the subscription.

Child Support

You will have papers that spell out any child support obligation. Sometimes these legal bits are included in the parenting plan. The child support clauses will spell out who pays who, how they are paid, and when. They should also state who pays for what expenses (like school fees and school lunches).

In some states, they use the terms direct and indirect expenses. Direct expenses are expenses that you have because of the kids, and if the kids were not born, you would not have these expenses. School lunches, school fees, and extracurricular activity fees are good examples of direct expenses. Indirect expenses are expenses that you would have even if the kids were not born, but these expenses are usually more because of the kids. Indirect expenses include living expenses such as rent or a mortgage and utilities for that living place.

The papers should also call out who buys the children's clothes. Sometimes the formula has each parent buying clothes for the kids at their respective house and sometimes one parent needs to provide all the clothes for the kids.

In general, it's best to have details in your child support orders because when things are not detailed it can lead to arguments and conflict later on down the road. For example, if you get divorced when the kids are young, who is going to pay for their cell phone bill when they are teenagers? Does someone need to contribute to a college fund?

Another long-term consideration is what happens when the kids turn 18 and become adults. The support obligation should stop, but there have been cases where a parent has argued that it needs to go longer. Thinking about putting some of these long-term clauses in can really save you later.

One clause that my attorney put in our child support order was a clause for split expenses where the other parent needs to reimburse a parent who spent money on something. An example of this is medical expenses where one parent pays a co-pay, doctor bill or prescription and the other parent needs to reimburse the spending parent some amount. The clause stated that the other parent had 30 days to reimburse the expense or they owed the spending parent the full amount of the expense. This clause gives the parent that needs to pay the reimbursement a reason to pay the expense in a timely manner.

Another consideration for reimbursable expenses is to have some language about what specifically is reimbursed. As an example, if clothes or shoes are an item that you are splitting costs on, one parent could buy designer clothes at high prices and expect a reimbursement while the other parent wants to buy more moderately priced items. A clause stating the purchasing parent must get some sort of approval or agreement on purchase cost (or even purchasing in the first place) can help avoid conflict down the road.

<u>Property Division</u>

Your divorce papers will also include language about dividing your property including cash, debts, real estate, cars, boats, your household stuff, and anything else that you hold together or separately during the marriage.

These clauses will spell out who gets what and sometimes are needed to make the financial transitions after the divorce is final. One example would be splitting a 401K retirement fund.

Since property division is very unique to each state and each situation will be different, it's hard to give you many guidelines here. My best advice is to listen to your attorney. If you have a particularly complicated situation, you may need to bring on a financial attorney or accountant to supplement your main attorney. In these complex situations, it's generally a good idea to get an independent evaluation of the worth of assets or liabilities to keep one party from claiming things are more or less than they really are.

Part 4 - Victory

Chapter Forty-One

Moving On

Healing: Leaving the past in the past.

Moving on is hard to do. The first step is sometimes the hardest part, but once you get going, it gets easier. That's not to say you won't have challenges along the way because you will. Once you get moving on your journey to healing and making a better life, you need to keep at it. At some point, you'll look back, see how far you came and wonder why you didn't start earlier!

Once you've accepted that you can't change the past, you can learn from it. This is an important step. It's important because you don't want to repeat the past, so you MUST learn from it so that in the future you can avoid whatever mistakes you made. Learning from the past is not easy and usually it takes a lot of self-reflection and some professional help from a therapist. If you want to truly heal, this is going to be an important part of moving forward. Find a therapist, and get to work!

Part of accepting the past is forgiving those who may have hurt you. Forgiving is not easy, and there are a ton of books and articles on that subject, so I'll let you do your own research. Remember though, that forgiving is not the same as forgetting. You should never forget, but you should forgive! This means that you may need certain boundaries with those that hurt you in the past. How rigid those boundaries are may depend on what kind of a person they are and how much they could hurt you in the future.

Remember that in order to start this journey of leaving the past in the past, you have to have the desire to move on. This may sound silly because you may be telling yourself that you want to move on, and though that may be true, you have to want to move on AND also be ready to put the work into moving on. That work includes learning, emotional work, and some critical evaluation of your current and past life choices.

Remember that moving on and healing will take some time. You can't move on in a week or a month. You may try and convince yourself that you can, but in reality, to fully move on after a long-term relationship can take a year or even a few years. You can speed this process up by educating yourself on where things went wrong in the past and how you could have done better.

While you likely will have others to forgive throughout this healing, remember to forgive yourself as well. You practically have to forgive yourself first before you can forgive others. You have to do this so that you can have compassion for others. It's nearly impossible to have compassion for others if you don't have compassion for yourself. You have to love yourself and it's important you don't expect superhuman things out of yourself.

Through all this, you have to remember that your kids are a part of the equation as well. They are a *big* part of the equation. Regardless of their age, they are human beings who mourn losses and unexpected changes, too. You also have to remember that your kids may be slower or faster than you to move on. Not everyone is going to heal and move on at the same speed! Just remember that it can be frustrating at times, but if you are aware that they may not be in the same place as you, then it should be a lot easier. It's important that you recognize that your kids may need more time than you need to emotionally be in a good place with a divorce that they did not choose. It's also important that you understand that the kids may be OK with the divorce, even if one of their parents is having a hard time with it. Sometimes kids recognize things in their parent's relationship long before adults accept the realities of a less-than-ideal marriage.

Reframing

You can't change the past, but you can change how you think about it. You're not rewriting history. You're simply recognizing what happened and deciding that you're not going to let that past narrative become your future narrative. There are lots of articles and books on this, but the best way to learn to reframe your past experiences is with a good therapist.

Embracing Trauma

Going through a divorce is a traumatic experience. There is no question about it. Even the lowest conflict divorces are traumatic. You are splitting your life up, having to adjust to seeing your kids less and dealing with all the financial stress that comes from divorce. It's traumatic.

With anything as traumatic as a divorce, you will need some time and help to get through it. That's where it can be helpful to embrace your trauma so that you will be able to move through it and eventually come out the other side stronger.

That said, you will have a hard time embracing your trauma if you are still experiencing it. You need to be past your trauma and probably six months (or more) past the trauma happening before you really start the process of moving forward. So, if your divorce is still ongoing, you can read on, but I hope you come back and re-read this section when it's been about six months after the divorce.

One thing to remember about the trauma of your divorce is that you can't change the past, but you can learn from it. The "Adversity Hypothesis" says that through the experience of the trauma, it can lead to *"growth, strength, joy, and self-improvement"* (Afianian, 2019). Some believe that only through the experience of trauma and adversity can you get to extraordinary achievement. Think of it this way; your divorce could be the experience you needed to open up your greatest achievement!

It may be helpful to know when you read articles about trauma, the professionals will classify trauma in different ways. There are generally two categories of trauma, often called "large T" and "little T."

Large T trauma is "distinguished as an extraordinary and significant event that leaves the individual feeling powerless and possessing little control in their environment" (Barbash, 2017). Examples of large T trauma can be sexual abuse, war, terrorist attack or even a vehicle accident. Large T trauma is defined in the DSM-V manual as PTSD.

Little T trauma "are events that exceed our capacity to cope and cause a disruption in emotional functioning" (Barbash, 2017). These are not necessarily life-threatening, but the individual can feel helpless. Some examples of Little T trauma include divorce, legal trouble, financial problems, interpersonal conflict, and a variety of other situations. It's worth noting that a single Little T trauma may not be a big deal, but prolonged exposure or multiple situations can add up. Little T trauma doesn't even have to happen all at once, it can accumulate over a lifetime.

Whether your trauma is from a large T event or smaller little T event(s), the way you can start to move past them is through good therapy. I've discussed in other parts of the book how to find a therapist so I won't cover that here, but you can refer back to earlier in the book if you need advice on how to find a therapist now.

Please don't expect miracles when you first go into therapy. Changes take time, and it's likely that you will go to your first few therapy sessions thinking it's not doing much. What you're initially doing in therapy is validating the things that happened to you and your feelings about those things. You're also teaching yourself how to think differently. All of this takes time. If you have the right therapist, then you will start to notice a difference. Just keep at it, and try to be consistent with your therapy sessions.

Your trauma may have been recent, or it may have occurred in your childhood or anywhere in between. A good therapist will help you recognize and validate your traumas. Therapy will help you process your feelings and move on in healthy ways. If your trauma comes from your childhood, then your therapist may use the ACE assessment scale *(Adverse Childhood Experiences (ACEs), 2022)*. ACE stands for Adverse Childhood Experiences, and it's a scale to help determine the amount of trauma that someone may have experienced (or is experiencing) during their childhood. The results will give your therapist a good idea of where to start with therapy.

Recognizing and validating your trauma will help you move on from it. If you try to move on without dealing with your trauma, it will hold you back. The best thing you can do is to do the work to move through your trauma so you can have a better life in the future.

Some tips for moving on:

Focus on the kids

Sometimes when you're in the darkest depths of the divorce, it can be helpful to focus on the kids. Focusing on having a good relationship with your children (now and in the future) and being the best dad you can be while keeping them physically and emotionally healthy can be your lighthouse in the midst of this storm. Those priorities can be the light that guides you in these dark, treacherous waters. No matter all the ill feelings you have against your ex, if you do what's best for the kids at that moment, then you are doing the right thing. Eventually, you will get far enough away from the divorce that it will not be so consuming.

Take every situation as it comes and ask yourself, "What is best for my kids?". If you let the answer of what is best for your kids guide your decisions, you will make fewer decisions that are self/ego focused and more that are holistically focused on your kids.

It's only stuff:

When going through a divorce, it's likely that you'll lose lots of your "stuff" and money. While as frustrating as that is, remember that you can't use any of your materialistic things when you die. I know that sounds stupid and cliché, but it's the hard truth. I suggest you learn to let go of being angry about losing the materialistic things because once you grow after the divorce, you'll be able to get new things of whatever you lost. One way to look at this is to pretend you just walked away from everything that you own (materialistically) and then had to start fresh.

Self-care

Of all the things we learn in school, they spend little to no time teaching about self-care. The trouble is that self-care is important to keep you going. Managing your mind and body is like taking care of a car. If you never change the oil, never put gas in and never charge your battery, then you're not going to go very far! You need fuel and battery power to even start! Similarly, changing the oil is important for long-term maintenance. You can go a little while without changing the oil, but it's eventually going to catch up with you.

Self-care is similar to the analogy of keeping your vehicle running. There are things you need to do often and others that are helpful more periodically. Now that you are towards the end of this book, if you feel your self-care is lacking, I urge you to revisit the chapter on self-care. Sometimes a new routine is precisely what we need to keep our fuel levels high and everything running smoothly.

You also have to evaluate the people around you and how your routines and self-care may affect them. If your house is always a mess and dirty, your kids may not like that. It'll probably also be harder to find a date (just FYI). So take a moment to look around and ask yourself, "Do I need to spend some time organizing and cleaning up?". There's no one right answer here. Everybody's a little bit different. You need to find what works for you, your lifestyle and those around you.

After you have cleaned and organized at home, it's a good idea to also do the same at work. Look around your desk or workspace and ask yourself, "Is it as tidy and organized as it could be?". Are you comfortable with the way it is? At work, you should have a little more scrutiny because others are going to judge you simply because they are in your space. You can decide if you want to let somebody into your private spaces at home, but you have fewer choices with your workspace. Remember that keeping a tidy workspace can affect raises and promotions, although your boss may never cite this as a reason. At work, you're actually in competition with everybody else, so every little bit helps.

Last, if you have a vehicle, clean it inside and out. Get the oil changed if needed and fill up your gas tank if you can afford it.

Remember there are short and long-term self-care items and that self-care isn't something that you can just do when you feel like it or when you get into a crisis. Self-care is something that needs to be conscious in your routine every single day, with some added long-term self-care every now and then for those long-term benefits. You need to decide what self-care things are important to you, and then you need to make sure you take the time to do them!

As guys, we don't tend to put a lot of thought into things like self-care. We're macho men, right? We don't need to take all this frilly stuff. It's important that you take care of yourself so that you can take care of others. Remember that self-care is kind of like being on an airliner. They tell you that in the event of an emergency, to put your own oxygen mask on before helping others. You won't do anybody else any good if you are slumped over in your chair because you put an oxygen mask on others before you put it on yourself!

Self-care has a lot of benefits. When you take care of yourself on a regular basis, you'll be less stressed and more aware of when you have choices that you can make about your life. Without self-care, you can feel like you are just barreling through life and life is controlling you. Without self-care, you are not in control of your life.

Routine

Routine is a lot like self-care in that it's easy to think that it is not very important. The reality is that routine eliminates your body's need to make decisions, thereby freeing your brain up for other things. Without routine, our lives are chaotic and our brains have to work overtime.

You should make a new routine for things like getting ready in the morning or getting ready for bed at night. You should also have routines for starting and ending your workday.

Chances are you'll already have some routines, but it will be helpful for you to write them down and identify where you may have areas that you want to add some routine to. If you have trouble remembering or following routines, then it can be helpful to put a little cheat sheet wherever you typically do those routines (like for instance, in the bathroom).

You want to make your routines so that you can accomplish them. If your routines are too complex or have too many items in them, chances are you'll get discouraged and won't do them. You'll find that once you train your brain and body to do these things on a regular basis (ideally daily), you'll stop thinking about them and they will just happen. You'll start to notice after a while that you can do these routine things without thinking about them. You'll know you've established routines when you find yourself drifting off to think about other things as you mindlessly brush your teeth or comb your hair. Because now your brain has freed up valuable decision-making energy for other things.

Just like anything else, too much routine can be bad for you. Remember, the key to most things in life is finding a good balance. If your entire day revolves around strict routines, chances are it will feel unfulfilling and you will be bored. Don't strive to make every part of your day routine, but you should strive to make the parts that you need to do every day (like hygiene) or things that you must do once a week (like taking out the garbage bins or mowing the lawn) routine.

Routine can include self-care items like brushing your teeth, but it can also include social ones as well. For example, when you arrive at work and get settled in, you may want to make a routine of saying hi to certain people. One example of a routine that I do as a manager is I will walk around and say "Hi" to all of the employees on my team. Some other social routines that you may want to incorporate would be calling or texting friends or family weekly or monthly. Social routines don't have to be daily.

Routines and habits help you. It is now believed that it takes around 30 times (or days) of doing something for it to become a habit. If breaking a bad habit is something that you are working on (i.e., quitting smoking), it may take twice as long.

Don't forget that you can change your routine if it's not working for you. It may be helpful to periodically sit and think if your routines are working for you. What could be better? Are you doing things that don't really have any value? It's okay to evaluate and adjust as necessary. You won't always get things right on the first try, and that's okay. The important thing here is to evaluate your routines now and then and make adjustments as necessary. Are you always rushing to work? Set your alarm to get up earlier. Can't find your car keys? Designate a spot for them that you always put them at the end of the day.

Visualize the New You:

When moving on from a big event in your life (especially something as dramatic as a divorce), it can be helpful to visualize what the future is going to look like. This can be helpful for getting you moving in the right direction. Visualizing can help you identify what you want your goals to be. Visualization is pretty simple. First, find a relaxing place to sit. Next, close your eyes and think about some things that you'd like to do in the future. It can be helpful to write these things down so you remember. You can add to this list as you go. You may have to do this number of times, especially as your situation changes because visualizing the new you is not going to happen all at once or even overnight. This will be something you need to do periodically. As you do it over time, you may find that your vision of the "new you" changes. And that's completely okay.

You can let yourself go wild here. Visualizing is like brainstorming and there is no wrong answer. Once you write these things down, you may want to evaluate how realistic some of them are. Humans can accomplish amazing feats, so don't set the bar too low. However, you do want to make sure you don't set the bar too impossible, either. People can do amazing things when they put their minds to it, set some goals and work hard.

So… what does the new you look like? Does it include being single forever or finding a new mate? Does it involve living where you're living now or maybe somewhere else? What kind of a life do you want to have? What about the kids, money, places to go visit? What does the ideal you look like? What goals do you want to accomplish? What things do you want to avoid? Write these things down and put them somewhere where you can go back to them in six months or a year and see how you're doing. This periodic goal checking can be very handy when deciding if your goal has changed or evaluating how you are on the journey to getting to those goals.

This is one area where thinking about this and then going to see a therapist can be very helpful. Therapists can help you walk through this "new you" and even help you get started on the journey to get there. Don't be afraid to ask for a little help because none of us really get there alone.

<u>Finding Happiness</u>

There have been plenty of books written on how to be happy or finding happiness. My personal belief is that you have to decide to be happy. This means: deciding that you're not going to live in misery and that you're going to be content with what you have <u>for the moment</u>. If you don't like how your life is at the moment, then you should have some goals and be working in some capacity toward fulfilling those goals.

I personally think those that are always chasing happiness will do just that, and they will never really be happy. But those that decide that they are happy will be happy. I know it sounds stupid, but once you try it, I think you'll find that it works in precisely that manner. If you decide to be happy, you will be happy. For example, your small apartment is a mess. It needs to be cleaned, you're broke and you miss the home you had when you were married. On a positive note, you have a roof over your head. Dirty toilets to clean mean that you have running water and a bathroom. If you choose to be grateful, you might be surprised to find happiness within it.

I know some may say, "Someone that's depressed can't just de-cide not to be depressed." And that is true. The fact is depression is a medical condition that can require professional help. However, somebody who is depressed can overcome their disease (usually with the help of a professional therapist) and become happy. While this book can't diagnose you with clinical depression or give you a step-by-step guide on how to be happy, my point is just to make you aware that you do have a choice when it comes to being happy or sad, and I wanted to give you the knowledge that you have that option.

Chapter Forty-Two

Goals

Setting Goals

Sometimes after a big life event like a divorce, the last thing that you want to do is think about "goals". It's easy enough to sit there, wallow in your sorrow and feel like a victim. Eventually, you will need to pick yourself up, put one foot in front of the other and move on. The sooner you do that, the better.

You don't have to set goals right away, but you can, and you probably should. Planning some goals for post-divorce is helpful while going through your divorce, even if you can't get started on them until the divorce is finished.

Don't beat yourself up though, if you find this difficult. In the chapter on "Self-Care," I talked a bit about setting some goals for yourself. I think it's helpful for us to revisit that now:

- What are the differences between goals and dreams? Goals are simply dreams that you accomplish! Therefore, the best way to accomplish your goals is to dream a bit.

- Think to yourself, "What do I want my life to be like? What do I want to do? What places do I want to see? What things do I want to accomplish?".

- What kind of dad do you want to be to your kids? What do

you enjoy doing for fun with them?

- What brings you happiness? What are you passionate about?

This brainstorming is an important part of dreaming. No idea is a bad one at this point. It may help to write down your ideas, set them aside, and come back to them later. When you're doing this exercise, be sure to think of some short-term goals and some long-term ones as well!

When I got divorced, I lived in a duplex. The living was reasonably priced, but I knew I wanted to move into a single-family home. It took me more than five years, but I finally accomplished it! Another long-term goal for me was to publish this book. Each person will have their own short and long-term goals, so be sure to brainstorm enough so that you have a collection of both short-term and long-term ideas.

Once you've got your brainstorming done, sort these goals into short-term and long-term categories. What short-term means for you is something you will need to decide, but I recommend somewhere between 1-3 years. Long-term can be 3-5 years or even 5-10 years. You may be at a place in your life where short-term is today and long-term means this week, and that's ok, too. Just pick what is right for you.

It may be helpful to put each goal on an index card or in a spreadsheet. It's OK to be indecisive about whether something is short or long-term. Just move it from one pile to the other. Once you have your piles, then I would recommend that you let them sit for a week. Take some time to think about the things that you wrote down and see which ones you think about the most.

After a week or so, rank each thing in each pile from 1 to how many things you have. Rank the thing you want to do the most "1" and the next "2" and so on. It's OK if you rank these a few times before finally coming up with your final list. Once you've ranked both your short-term and long-term items, then let them sit again for a week. Again take some time to think about each of these things and what you want to do the most.

Finally, come back and evaluate both your short-term pile and the long-term one. How does it feel? Do you have the things in the right order? Are things in the right pile? Next, evaluate each item for how achievable each thing is. Think about the resources that you have (time and money). Will doing these things negatively impact your life (like your ability to do these things around your job)?

Rank each item with a 1, a 5, or a 9 for how hard they will be to accomplish with your resources. Ones are achievable with your resources (time and money). Fives are achievable but with some work (maybe saving money or vacation time), and nines are going to be difficult. Once you've ranked all your piles, then you should be getting a clear picture of the things that you should work on first. Those that have the lowest number from this resource ranking are things you should work on first. Work on the goals that have the lower standard numbers for both rankings. Don't discount the other items, but this process will help you make some headway on your goals. When it comes to goals, it's important that you have some early successes because this will give you even more drive to work on those harder goals that may take more dedication, time or money.

Once you accomplish some of the easier goals, it's time to start working on the harder ones! Success will create success. It's ok to feel like you're stuck in the mud at first. Eventually, things will catch and you will start moving forward.

<u>Bucket List</u>

The term bucket list blatantly means "things you want to do be-fore you kick the bucket." In talking about short-term and long-term goals, the bucket list category is worth mentioning. Bucket lists are those things that would be amazing to do, and you may want to plan for them as a long-term goal. You may not ever accomplish your bucket list items, but if you do, it would be amazing!

For me, my bucket list items include some travel to exotic places. My life will be just fine without accomplishing these things, but if I do end up going- it would be amazing! Use your bucket list to dream!

<u>Accomplishing Goals</u>

Once you have some goals, you should pick two to three of each from the short-term and long-term lists. Print them out on a piece of paper and post them in your home and at work (if you can). It's important that you see these daily. It's a good reminder of what you are driving to, and it will help motivate you. I personally like writing my goals on a whiteboard or even on the bathroom mirror!

If you can, on a daily basis look at this list and write down one or two things that you're going to do to work on that goal. This will help you keep on track to accomplishing them. There are many self-help books on setting and achieving goals, but be sure to pick a method that works for you and stick with it.

Be sure to celebrate when you accomplish your goals. Celebrate often. It's a pleasant reminder that you are moving forward and accomplishing things. Celebrate partial milestones too. There is no shame in celebrating when you're a quarter or halfway to a goal!

<u>Sustain the Gain</u>

Once you accomplish a goal, you may need to maintain it. For instance, if you buy a house or a new car, you need to make the payments! You may think it goes without saying, but you need to make sure that with whatever wins you do get, you do what you

need to do to sustain them! Some goals will be a "one and done."
Others will need maintenance. Just be sure that you evaluate what
you need to do to make sure you don't go backward after having a
win.

Chapter Forty-Three

Finances

Set a Budget

A big part of moving on for you will be to take control of your finances. If you're going through a divorce, this may seem tough or impossible, as your divorce may control your finances. Once the divorce is complete, take some time to evaluate your current financial situation and where you want to improve it. Once you know how much you'll be paying for child support and what your other expenses are, you will be in a good position to put pen to paper (or numbers to spreadsheet) to figure out where you stand financially. Setting a budget is definitely not the most exciting thing in the world, and it is easy to put it off for a long time. My recommendation is to not put it off and to set your budget as soon as you can.

Ideally, you should have your initial budget set while you're going through your divorce. Although, with the emotional toll that the divorce takes on you, it may be hard to sit down and actually do this kind of thinking. While you're going through the divorce, do your best to spend as little money as possible and to live well within (or below) your means.

Previously, I touched on some tips for setting a budget, but I think it's important to revisit your finances now that you are here. As a friendly reminder, you do need to set your budget for your basic needs such as housing, food, utilities, child support, kids' expenses, and so on. Setting a budget isn't rocket science. You simply need to make sure that you earn more money than you spend.

Things like utilities and rent are due monthly. You also have to remember that not all months have the same number of weeks in them. Some months have four, and other months have five weeks of expenses in them. For example, if you're calculating your expenses for food, some months you will need more budget than others depending on how many weeks are in that month.

I recommend using a spreadsheet if you have access to a computer. Find a template online that you like and fill it in. Sitting down and figuring out the budget is one thing. Staying *within budget* is something else.

<u>What can you afford?</u>

When you get divorced, you may have this feeling like you want to go crazy and spend money on those things that your ex would never let you spend money on. While this may make you temporarily feel good, it may put you in a bad position long-term as far as finances go. It's important to sit down and make some decisions about what you can and cannot afford based on numbers and dollars.

Chances are, when you are married there are things that you could afford that you can no longer afford (now that you are divorced or divorcing)—getting divorced places a financial strain on you that you did not have when you were married. The numbers tell us that most men end up paying child support, and if you're in this same boat, chances are it will have a large financial impact on your budget. You are now having to pay for your own residence plus the children's expenses or child support. This means you'll have fewer financial resources and you'll have to make some decisions about what gets left out of the budget so that you have enough money to be financially stable.

Common things to look for to slim your budget out are your vehicle (can you drive a less expensive vehicle?), your standard of living for housing (could you live in a less expensive house or apartment?), and your expectations about entertainment (vacations and eating out our typical non-essential expenses).

Remember that when cutting things out of your budget, they don't have to be forever. Maybe you'll get a promotion at work and have more budget available later. Then you can start to add back some of these things that you had before your divorce.

Divorce typically creates financial damage for both parties. It may be a reality that you end up going bankrupt. If this is the case, remember that while you will have bad credit right after the bankruptcy, it will give you a chance to rebuild your credit. Eventually, enough time will pass after the bankruptcy, and you will emerge with less debt and in a better financial position.

Planning for Disaster

One thing that you need to do after your divorce that you may not have done before your divorce is to make some financial plans for when things are not so good. This disaster planning will come in handy whenever you're hit up with expenses that you are not expecting. This could be expenses for car repairs, house repairs, or even future lawyer bills. Having some money saved aside will ease stress and allow you to pass through these difficulties much more easily. When coming up with your budget, you want to put some money aside for savings for just this purpose. Make sure that you are saving money for these emergency expenses on a regular basis.

One of the easiest ways to save money is by leveraging the automatic direct deposit that many employers offer. Many employers allow you to direct deposit your check into more than one account. For instance, she could have 50 or 100 dollars deposited into your savings account and the remaining balance into your checking account where you would pay bills from. However you do it, it's important that you do it on a consistent basis. If you tell yourself that you'll get around to transferring money into a savings account, chances are it will never happen or not happen very frequently.

It's a lot easier to have an expense come up and know that you have the money in savings to pay for it rather than having to go through the stress of scrambling to figure out where you're going to get the money to pay for this unplanned expense.

As you get more financially stable, you might add some more money to the rainy day fund. Experts will say different things, but having a few months to 1/2 a year of living expenses in a savings account will give you a significant cushion in case anything significant happens (like losing your job or having to go back to court and pay for lawyers). It may seem daunting or unrealistic to be able to save up this amount of money, but with the right planning and living within your means, you'll be able to save more money than you thought you could. Think of it this way; you could skip a fast food meal once a week and eat canned soup and salad. That's ten dollars each week that you could have automatically transferred to your savings account. If you did that for a whole year, you would have saved $520 dollars!

Retirement

When you go through a divorce, most likely your retirement savings will be affected. It's not uncommon to have to give half of your retirement to your ex. If this is the case, then you will need to start re-saving for retirement. Unless you increase how much you save for retirement, you will have to work longer before you can retire. It's a good idea to visit a financial counselor to determine how much money you can afford to contribute to retirement and they can calculate based on this figure when you'll be able to retire.

Many companies have employee benefits programs that will match how much money you put into retirement up to a certain percentage. If your company does this, then take advantage of it because it's basically free money! If you don't have much extra cash, you can contribute what you can afford, but try your best to put in at least the minimum amount that your company will match you. If your company will match up to 3%, then put in 3% if you can afford it. Contribute more if you can afford it. With many of these programs, if you only put in 2%, then the "company matching" will also only put in 2%. Losing out on 1% of money does not sound like a lot, but when you compound its effects over 20 years, it can be a significant amount of money.

If your financial situation improves after you've been divorced for some time, you may want to look at your retirement funding on a *yearly* basis. Take a look at what you are currently contributing and what you can afford to contribute. You want to have a solid retirement so you're not depending on things like Social Security when you actually do have to retire.

If your current job does not offer any sort of retirement savings benefit, explore what other companies are offering so that you can get the maximum benefit.

<u>Investing</u>

It's a good idea after becoming divorced to become financially smart. You will have the same amount of money, but you will have expenses such as child support that you did not have before.

One way that you can grow your financial future is to put off buying things in the now and instead invest that money. Unlike in times past, you do not need a significant amount of money to start investing. A couple of hundred dollars is all that is needed. Traditional opportunities for investing include the stock market and mutual funds. Depending on where you live and your financial ability, you may have some other unique opportunities.

With all investment opportunities, you want to weigh the risk versus the opportunity. If you have a commitment of child support, you will want to have extra caution when investing. You want to make sure that you don't overextend yourself. Being financially conservative will be helpful here. Make sure that when you're investing, you do not depend on the money in the investment for anything in your daily life. You don't want to end up in a situation where you've invested some money and lost it, and now you can't pay rent or child support.

Investing is a lot easier these days than it used to be. Investing can be as easy as online banking for some people, and a good way to watch your stocks grow and fall if you check your balances daily. Beware, gambling addicts! If gambling is something you have struggled with in the past or currently do, be cautious of being consumed by investing.

Chapter Forty-Four

Dating

The Dating World

There is a reason the chapter on dating is at the end of the book. You may want to jump right back into dating. It may tempt you to put dating in front of some other things, but dating should really come after two things. One - you have had some time to work on yourself emotionally, and two – you have become financially stable. So many men jump right back into the dating world with predictable results. For those of you that jump in head first, I hope it works out! If you find dating is significantly less satisfying than you thought it would be, take some time to reflect on why.

Knowing that you are ready to date will be different for everyone. First, you must have your house in order (figuratively and literally). Get all the legal proceedings behind you. Live on your own for a bit. Have your house the way you want it. Get into a good groove with your kids and let them have you all to themselves for a bit as you evolve into a single dad.

You have to be emotionally ready to date again. Not only that, but you have to be ready to trust a woman again. This is no small task, and it takes time. If you don't do this work, you'll likely drag your past relationship into the new one, and this is a sure bet way to fail! This is why I advocate through this book to find a good therapist. Going through a divorce is a traumatic experience, and you will need help navigating through it. A good therapist will help you navigate your specific situation.

Trust me, find a therapist and stick with it. If you don't like the first therapist that you go to, don't be afraid to try a different one. Once you find someone you are comfortable working with, don't hop to a different therapist. Do the hard work. Dig your heels in. It will be emotional, and it will be tough but do the work. You will be glad you did.

Dating Apps

Dating in the world these days is much different than it was when I was growing up. Back in the day, you had to approach a woman. You had to find a way to strike up a conversation and hope that she wanted to talk to you. With dating apps, you can do the same thing without even getting dressed. You can swipe from your living room on your couch. You can have 20 conversations at the same time!

This new dating scene has its ups and downs. On the upside, you have a bigger selection of women to date. But so do the women. Suddenly, your competition has grown significantly. Now you have to be that much better than the next guy. Physical attraction, financial stability, and emotional stability are all things you now need to bring to the A-game level. Women are picking the best of the best because they can. And why wouldn't they?

Another upside is that it's easier to meet someone who doesn't live near you. You can look in the next town over or even the next state over! This opens up many possibilities.

One huge downside is catfishing. This is where someone (girl or guy) posts pictures that don't look like they do currently. These could be pictures of them several years ago or even a few months ago. Sometimes it's just a lot of makeup and a flattering camera angle. Sometimes people post pictures on their profile that are not even them! You show up to the date and wonder where the person from the picture is! This is a huge red flag! If someone doesn't look like their picture, what else are they lying about? For me, this is a hard pass, and it should be for you, too. Also, it goes without saying - don't ever be a catfish. Catfishing is not just pictures. Someone could lie or exaggerate their accomplishments or their position in life.

On dating profile pictures, there are some things that you can look for as red flags. If someone has a lot of pictures with friends and you're having a hard time figuring out who the dating profile is for, you should skip this profile. Another thing to look for is the person posting pictures of random places or objects and not of them – they clearly have something to hide. Watch out for the person with the photos that just have a close-up of their face or part of a face, they could be very insecure or hiding something.

You also need to beware of scammers on these dating sites. Common scams include foreigners pretending to be a woman. If their English is "off," chances are that person is not who you think it is. Be careful of someone who lives far away or someone who seems too good to be true. They will talk to you for a long time and then try and scam you some way (often after you've sent photos that would embarrass you). Be very careful of these scammers, and spoiler alert – usually, they are not even women!

Scammers are usually pretty easy to spot. Things to look for are very professional pictures, bad English, and asking to send money. There are a million and one scams out there. Just remember that if it's too good to be true, it probably is. If you're a 5 or 6 and she's a 9 or 10, she may not be real.

Once you've got past the catfish and the scammers, now you have to watch out for the online strippers and prostitutes. Yes, the oldest profession has made its way online! You want to make sure you don't engage with these folks for several reasons. Many gals will lead guys on only to ask them to "subscribe" to one service or another. Others still will solicit you for straight-up prostitution. Since this is illegal in most places, you want to steer clear. Online prostitution is especially dangerous because you have no way of knowing if the person (or persons) on the other end of your messages is law enforcement. There is no faster way to lose your kids in a custody battle than to be dealing with a charge of soliciting prostitutes!

With the catfishes, prostitutes, cops, and scammers, it's worth mentioning to never give out too much information on these apps. Use them to see if you want to go on a date and set up a time to meet in a public place. I would caution you to communicate through the app only until you've met and decided you want to do date number 2. If something goes wrong, you can unmatch them and not have to worry about a stalker. Don't give out your address or your phone number before you've met in person. Be cautious with full names and addresses! Certainly, don't give out any sensitive information. Remember, you never know who really is on the other end of those messages!

Besides all the downsides of dating apps, people do have success with them. It's that sliver of hope that keeps these apps in business. If you think you're ready to brave the crazy waters of dating apps, here is a rundown of some common apps. These are what is available at the time of publication, and there certainly are others out there. This is not a complete list, and it's not an endorsement for any of these apps in any way.

Tinder - Generally, if you are younger, you will probably have better luck than if you are older. Tinder is known as a "hook-up" app for when you're looking for a quick fling rather than a serious relationship. It works by making a profile and you start swiping. Left to "reject," right to "like." When they "swipe right" on your profile, then you match! This app seems to have a lot of scammers and bots, so proceed with caution.

Bumble - With Bumble, men and women make a profile with pictures and swipe left or right. When they both swipe, they "match." What makes Bumble unique is that the female has to make the first move after two people match. This changes the dynamic a bit and if you are talking with a gal, then you know she is interested in you because she had to swipe and start the conversation. This app seems to be mostly bot and scammer free, although your experience may vary. This site seems to have a lot of genuine, real people if you want to date long-term.

Ok Cupid - On this site, you make a profile and can like other profiles. When both people "like," you match. This seems to have many scammers, women selling subscriptions and prostitutes.

Hinge - This site's marketing is that it is a dating site that is meant to be deleted - meaning you will find someone and no longer need the site. On this site, you make a profile and "like" others' pictures or answers to questions. They will see your "likes" and can start the conversation. The same goes for you. If someone "likes" something on your profile, you can start chatting with them. This is one of the better "free" sites if you are serious about dating. This site occasionally has scammers.

Plenty of Fish (Also called POF) - On this site, you make a profile, and people can "like" your profile. You can "like" others, too. This site lets you send messages without them having to do anything (such as "like" your profile). This site can be hit or miss depending on where you live. This site sometimes has "local events," which is by far still the best way to meet people.

Facebook - Facebook has gotten into the dating game! The way that it works is like some of the other sites (where you make a profile and "like" others' profiles). When you "like" someone, they see it and can start the conversation. The reverse is true, they can "like" your profile, and you can start chatting with them. Facebook has one additional feature that is unconventional. It's called "secret crush," and you can list people you have a crush on. If they list you as a crush too, then the app will let you know who that is and will let you chat with each other.

At the publication of this book, there have been many more dating apps created for people of specific age groups, religious preferences, and special interests. These can be worth trying out depending on if you're looking for someone that has the same specific interest as you. Some examples are dating sites that are specific to Christians (Christian Mingle). Another example would be sites specific to farmers.

No matter which dating app you go with, they each have their ups and downs. A word of caution here - in an effort to find a mate, you may find yourself downloading several of these apps and using more than one. While it may feel like you're making progress, this may not be the most healthy thing for you. Watch out for how much time you spend being sucked into these apps. If you find yourself without any time, you may want to think about how much time these dating apps are taking away from you.

The Dating App Game of Ten Thousand Rejections

It doesn't matter which dating app you use, but you should devise a quick way to screen people out. For that reason, it's very important you find out how to "reject" people on your dating app. This may seem counterintuitive, but with all the choices on these apps, you need a way to weed out the ones that are just OK and only talk to the ones that are really good.

You should have two or three "go-to" questions that you can ask potential mates to see if you are a match personality-wise and situation-wise. You can also ask about where they are in life and where they want to go. One question that I like to ask is if they prefer comedy or horror movies. This will tell you which they prefer and you can see if they match what you like.

Things that you will definitely want to ask before the meeting:

1) How long have you been single? - This tells you that, yes, they are single and gives you some context of how long they have had to heal or if they are just jumping into another relationship.

2) Do you have kids? How many? How old are they? Do you want more? These questions will be important as it lets you know what their life is like when kids are involved.

On the dating apps, I would recommend that you have enough conversation to establish that there is interest, then move to an in-person meeting. Don't get emotionally attached to someone over texting for months on end without meeting them in person.

First Dates and On

If you've been out of the dating game for a while, then you may not be surprised to learn that things have changed. Dating has also gotten complicated. Long gone are the days where society had an expectation of what men are supposed to do when dating. The old book would say to open doors, pay the check for dinner and never talk about sex, religion or politics on the first date.

Here's a rundown of what I think you should do on a first date. This is by no means an exhaustive list. It also may not be culturally appropriate in some places. So, take it for what it is and modify it for your unique situation.

I like to go on a coffee date or meet for a drink on the first date. This is a low-pressure way to simply meet the other person and see if there are any sparks. If there are not, it's a lot quicker to finish a coffee than it is to eat a whole meal. Oh, and remember the catfishes? If someone is a catfish, you can bail a lot earlier and without having to spend a lot of money or wasting a lot of time!

When you go on a date, you will probably be nervous but remember you are there to enjoy this time, too! First dates are about seeing if there is an interest in pursuing the relationship further, so remember to *be yourself*. No matter how cliché that sounds. One of the worst things you can do is not be yourself early in the relationship. This will set you up for failure in the future. You have to be genuine from the start!

On a date, expectations can vary wildly from one person to the next. Some people will want to know your whole story, while others are just looking to see what kind of a person you are. The best advice I can give you is to open yourself up some, but don't tell them every detail. I recommend staying away from sex, politics, and religion. If you have a second or third date, you can get into those things later on.

Avoid talking about your ex in any negative manner. At this point, they don't need details. You could say something like, "She's a good mom, but we just were not happy together." A generic "it's complicated" is a good response if that seems to be more truthful to your reality. If the relationship continues, you can be vulnerable at the right time and let her in on all the details (if she even wants to know).

Who pays on a first date is something that is a hotly debated topic in today's feminism-centric culture. Some say that whoever asks pays. Some say the man always pays. Some say each pays (also sometimes called "going dutch"). It makes it very confusing because everyone has their own expectations! Every situation is different, so there is no one size fits all. What I like to do is get my card out to pay for both, and if she says that she will pay for her, then let her and don't argue. This is again where a coffee date or drinks is better than a meal. The financial cost here is lower, and it makes this conversation less of a big deal. I've been told that women sometimes feel "obligated" to have relations with you if you pay.

This is just one of many toxic things that you have to watch out for in today's dating scene.

One thing to watch out for is if someone is nervous. Chances are, you will both be nervous, and that means you may both do things that you otherwise would not do like being extra clumsy, stumbling over your words, and even forgetting things. This is totally normal, and maybe don't hold this against them! If you are extra nervous, you may even want to tell them that you are. Saying something like "I'm really nervous" should give you some leeway from judgment by them. They may even tell you that they are nervous, too!

Feminism has made dating, well, complicated. Some women prefer the old-school chivalry with men opening doors and pulling back chairs at the dinner table. Feminists often hate these things and see them as aggression against women. It makes it very hard to figure out what you are supposed to do manner-wise on a date. The best thing you can do is be you. Act how you think you should. The right woman will love you for who you are and the manners you already have.

A word of note about extreme feminists is in order: If someone makes you uncomfortable because of who you are, then it's probably time to cut the date short and go home. It's not likely you will have any sort of meaningful relationship if someone has a hatred for your gender. A lot of self-proclaimed "feminists" are actually misandrists. Feminism is defined as "the advocacy of women's rights on the basis of the equality of the sexes." *(Oxford Languages, 2022 Oxford University Press).* Misandrists, on the other hand, are defined as "a person who dislikes, despises, or is strongly prejudiced against men." *(Oxford Languages, 2022, Oxford University Press).*

One thing that's especially important to look for on a first date (or any date) is the body language that the other person is giving off. You can tell when someone is closed and reserved; they will have crossed arms and short answers. That's probably a sign the date isn't going well, and it may be a good time to cut things short. If there is flirting going on, and she is open and expressive, then she's interested. It's easy to read someone's body language once you look for it. It will tell you a lot.

You may hear people say that they "didn't see the red flags," and that happens a lot to both men and women. One red flag that gets missed is do their actions match their words...? Have they done what they said? Or do they say one thing and do another? This red flag is easy to spot if you use this simple test: Do their actions match their words?

Some people will be really into you for one reason or another. It may be that they are attracted to you and that you like the same things and have the same goals and dreams in life. Sometimes though, someone is looking to improve their situation or get out of a bad situation. Be cautious of the women who are extra into you when they may have other motives.

One thing that is relatively common on first dates now is for a woman to bring a "wingman." This person, typically another woman, is someone brought along for safety. They will usually sit several tables away, but sometimes closer so you don't even know that they are there. It's not a bad idea for a woman to be considerate of her safety, even though I think it reflects poorly on our society that they feel they need to do this. If someone sitting a table or two away seems to be listening in on your conversation, it's probably because they are the wingman.

When you meet someone for the first time, do it in a public place. You never know if you meet someone in private what may happen or what they may accuse you of (even if you did nothing). In addition, tell a trusted friend or colleague where and when you are going and with who. In the chance that you disappear, the police will at least have some information to go on.

Now that the date is over, you've got to decide if you want to see this person again. It's perfectly OK to reject them, just do it respectfully. Simply send them a thank you and that you didn't feel any spark, but you wish them well. Make sure you do this in a timely manner, too. Don't ghost, it's rude.

If things went well and you do want a second date, then ask them soon after the date. I would try and do it after you get home. Send them a text and ask for that second date. If the sparks were really flying, you could do it in person at the end of the date but waiting to text them gives them time to think instead of being put on the spot.

Relationships, Cell Phones, and Social Media

Social media has made relationships more difficult. Social media brings a new dynamic to relationships because it's one more thing that will steal your time. On top of that, it provides a platform to have multiple sources of relationship conflict.

"Likes," "comments," and "sharing" posts may all be sources of conflict between you and your new partner. In a healthy relationship, neither person will be overly jealous of your existing social network. You may cause conflict if your new partner sees a person whom you "like," "comment," or "share" a post as a potential threat to your relationship.

Social media also sucks up a significant amount of your time, even though you may not realize it. If you're on Apple or Android, you can get reports of how much time you spend on different kinds of apps on your phone. You may be surprised to find out exactly how much time you're spending mindlessly playing with your phone. I'm not advocating getting a non-smartphone. However, you do need to be aware of what is a reasonable amount of time to be on your phone versus spending time with your partner or your family. Every situation and everyone is different, so you will need to use judgment on what is best for you.

The best thing you can do is to have conversations with your partner to see what their feelings are on the subject. It may be that they are the ones spending too much time on their phone, or you both may be. It's best to have on-purpose conversations to see how you're both feeling and how much time you think is appropriate.

Time spent isn't the only factor here. It may be the times throughout the day that you're using your phone that may feel inappropriate to the other person. For instance, checking your phone during dinner or while out with friends may cause the other person to feel left out. These habits can be hard to break, especially if you have been single for some time and gotten used to not having to worry about someone else. Be cognizant of the effects that using your smartphone has on the people around you. Having conversations with them is the only way you'll find out how they really feel and what the facts truly are.

If you find you or your new partner have issues with each other's phone usage, appropriate times, or outside online relationships (i.e., "likes," "comments," or "shares"), you can make progress in changing those habits. Cell phones and social media are extremely addictive. They are designed that way to make the most money possible for phone designers and social media companies. Changing habits is not an easy thing, and it will require time, dedication, and understanding from your partner.

Chapter Forty-Five

Blended Families

D ating and blending families together is really, really difficult. Blending families is probably one of the hardest things you'll do after divorce (if you choose to). Don't get me wrong, it can be a very rewarding experience for all involved, but it does take more time and effort to do it correctly. Not only do you have two different sets of families with different upbringings coming together, but you also have to worry about blending different sets of schedules, all while trying to maintain some sanity between the adults.

When you date after a divorce and you have kids, you have to think about what your kids' life is going to be like if you have a long-term relationship with the person that you're dating. If they truly are your forever person, then you'll need to consider what life will be like once you get married and live together.

Here are some guidelines and things to think about:

- How long have you two been dating? I highly recommend not introducing the kid(s) until the two of you have been exclusive for at least six months to a year.

- What age(s) are all the involved children? Younger kids tend to accept a new partner/step-parent easier than tweens, teens or adult children.

- Was this new partner involved with you before the divorce?

If so, this person may be harder for children of any age to accept. Definitely best to still wait six months to a year before introducing the kids.

- Is your ex high-conflict? Even the *perfect* step-parent will have to endure things from a high-conflict ex. It is not uncommon for high-conflict exes to devote their lives to destroying any relationship their children have with you and/or whatever partner you choose to integrate into the kids' lives.

- How do you and your new partner feel about parenting and disciplining the children? Do your parenting styles match, or are they in conflict?

- New partners should be called by their first names or an agreed-upon nickname. It is never OK to demand your kids call a step-parent/spouse/partner, Mom or Dad or any of the like. To do so can be considered parental alienation. If your kids want to call them mom/dad, that's OK but don't demand it.

<u>When to introduce the kids</u>

As I mentioned before, you don't want to introduce the kids right away to your new relationship. Relationships can come and go, so you want to make sure that you only introduce your kids to the ones that you know are going to last. I recommend you are steadily dating somebody for at least six months and maybe up to a year. This will help protect your kids from making emotional bonds with too many different people in their life. If kids meet new potential partners too often, it can be traumatic for them.

When you introduce the kids, you want to make sure you deliberately plan something out. Make it as easy as you can on both sets of kids and both parents. Don't try to plan anything too elaborate or complex. A meeting at the park or at a restaurant is probably good for the first meeting. Keep the first meeting simple and without expectations.

Once you have the first meeting with both sets of kids, you can explain to them that you are now dating the other adult, and you can explain to the kids what they can expect from this new relationship. It's important that you're upfront and honest with your kids to the point that's age-appropriate. Make sure you answer all of their questions (if you can) and let them know when things are uncertain (like perhaps when you're moving in together).

Kids are curious by nature, and they will probably have lots of questions, so be patient with them and be prepared to answer the questions you expect (and expect some that you don't). Keep in mind that any information you share will more than likely be shared with your co-parent as well. Do not put your kids in a loyalty bind and expect or hope for them to not share this information with your ex. It's also a really good idea to let your co-parent know that you are introducing your kids to your new partner and their kids.

After the first meeting, you'll want to start doing activities with both sets of kids. Younger kids learn through play. Depending on the ages of the kids, you'll want to do activities that they enjoy and that are age appropriate. If you have a wide range of ages, you may need to do different activities that will be enjoyed by different ages. Maybe you bring the younger kids to the zoo and take the older kids go-karting. Things like amusement parks, fairs, or bowling can be fun for all ages. You know your kids best, so talk with your partner and see what both sets of kids would enjoy doing together.

As the kids spend more and more time with each other, they will probably try to feel each other out from a dominance perspective. Don't be surprised if one or two of your kids try to be the dominant kid in the group. This is just normal group social dynamics, but be sure to make sure that none of the kids feel threatened or bullied.

It's extremely important that you encourage respect between all the children. There should be no name-calling, and if there is you will want to put a stop to it immediately. Remind your kids that they need to treat others like they would want to be treated. This is something that you and your partner must be in lockstep on and in total agreement.

So you've decided to blend. Now what?

This topic (in itself) is probably worth an entire book. If you are blending two families together, it's worth it for you to do some research and read about good techniques and what to watch out for.

Not only do you have to blend two different sets of schedules together, but you also have to deal with everyone's emotions. Chances are, every person in the blended family (from adults to children) will be at different stages of dealing with the divorce(s) that they were involved with.

Sometimes families have a hard time bonding in the beginning, and after some time, they come together. Other times, families blend well in the beginning and then travel through rough waters. No matter what the blended family experience is like in the beginning, it will take work and effort to maintain both the adult relationship and the children's relationships to the new adults in their lives and with their existing biological parents.

The Key to Successfully Blending a Family is your Ex

Your kid(s)' other parent, your ex, is the true key to whether or not you will be able to have a blended family. Children who are *given permission* from their other parent to love and accept new people, usually do so. Especially if this person comes into their lives at a young age (say under the age of 5) and treats them well. This permission needs to come in the form of your ex's actions and words.

Blending families with older kids/tweens/teenagers or adult children is another challenge. However, the ex's input is still very much important to being able to blend. If your ex, at the very least, insists that the kids respect your new partner as an adult authority figure in their lives, then you've got a good basis for blending.

<u>Blending Families with a High-Conflict Ex</u>

Attempting to blend a family with a high-conflict ex is a constant battle for the kids' hearts and minds. In a high-conflict ex's mind, the new spouse has no right to "parent" the children at all. A new spouse or step-parent trying to take on any parenting roles in a high-conflict situation will likely be met with disdain (outward or hidden from you). It is likely that even if the kids don't have a problem with the new spouse themselves, your high-conflict ex may create problems and emotionally manipulate the kids into seeing only the negative in your new partner's actions.

You want your new partner to be all in with your kids and ideally, they will want to be as well. Many well-meaning stepparents in high-conflict situations find themselves having to "disengage" to reduce conflict for everyone. Many stepmoms in high-conflict situations will tell a new step-parent to take a "not my monkeys, not my zoo" approach to keep the waters calm. This may not be what either of you wants for your blended family, but it may be necessary if your ex is high-conflict.

On the flip side of this, "not my monkeys, not my zoo" also pertains to any messes the kids make, laundry, making of their meals, and other things. All parenting duties should rely solely on the biological parent except in rare cases (special occasions, emergencies, work meetings, or appointments). In a high-conflict situation, your new spouse can support you, but you still have to be the primary parent in all things related to the kids with your high-conflict ex. This is also really good advice, even if your ex isn't high-conflict.

Strong boundaries will also be needed here as far as your high-conflict ex communicating with your new spouse. Polite greetings and emergency-only communications are good boundaries. Often, high-conflict exes will initially start trying to communicate with the new partner more than they do you. While at first it can seem that your high-conflict ex is taking a liking to your new spouse, there is usually a more sinister agenda here. With that in mind, it's important for you and your ex to do all of the communicating and for your new spouse and your high-conflict ex to communicate only when necessary. It is definitely OK for them to have each other's numbers. If a high-conflict ex starts reaching out to your new spouse instead of you, it's important for your partner to maintain strong boundaries and defer all communication back to you. Strong boundaries from the beginning will protect your new spouse from your ex's wrath and help reduce conflict and alleviate stress within your new partnership.

Basic Guidelines for Blending Families

Let's assume that you're dating someone who has children, and you're looking at possibly blending your families together. There are several things you need to consider, including:

- Where to live.

- Which children will get their own bedrooms, and which will have to share.

- Who is going to have to make compromises, and are the compromises relatively equal between the two different families that are coming together?

There's a lot to think about!

One of the best things that you can do before even thinking about blending a family is to really, truly date the person that you are considering blending families with. This isn't like when you were younger and had no responsibilities because now you have children and adult responsibilities to consider!

You have to really make sure that this person fits your needs as a partner and they are in a position to be a good partner as well. This means they should not be bringing excessive debt to the table (and the same goes for you), they should have emotionally worked through their divorce, and they should be ready to put in the work that it's going to take to blend your families together.

Before blending a family, you should have long talks about different topics on blending your families. This is serious stuff and deserves more than just a quick chat about what you think about this or that. Really get into the meat about who's going to live where and what compromises are going to be made for each family.

When I say really date someone, I mean take some time to have some quality time between each of you. This is the person that you're asking to be your partner, and any small problems you see without children in the equation will be amplified when children are in the equation. Do your research and ensure you have enough experience with that person that you feel like you truly know who they are and where they are coming from.

Here are some things you can do together to see how they are in some stressful situations:

- Go on some trips together. You should go on several vacations together (just the two of you). Later on, it may be helpful to go on vacation with all the kids as well because that gives everyone a taste of "living" together in neutral territory.

- It's helpful to work through some sort of challenges together (like try putting some IKEA furniture together). That way, you can see how each of you acts and reacts under stress and pressure.

- Maybe get lost together a time or two! How do you each handle the stress of being lost?

- Date long enough that you've each had to deal with each other having a seasonal cold or flu.

How you both act and react during stressful situations will tell you a lot about who somebody really is and if you work well together. If you're going to blend the family together successfully, you are going to have to work very well together.

This is not to say that you're going to find a perfect partner. We need to find someone who is "perfect enough." Even better, "perfect for you." You may have some things from your divorce that are boundaries that you are not willing to move or change, and that is okay. Do your best to find a partner who is willing to work with you and to make compromises when necessary.

<u>When Things are not Going Great</u>

There may be times when it feels like blending the families is not going very well. The best thing you can do in a situation like this is to listen to your kids. Try to tune into both their verbal and nonverbal cues (their body language). Kids will generally be pretty honest about these things, and all you have to do is listen to them. They may not always know the answer to how to make things better, but really that's your job as adults. You will definitely go through some rough spots, and that's completely fine. Sometimes you may not know where to get help or where to get advice for this sort of thing. There are plenty of books and articles. You can also ask friends or family who have blended families before, or you can seek the help of therapists who specialize in family therapy if the situation is especially complicated.

Blending your families can be a very rewarding experience as you move on with life from your old one and make fresh memories with your new partner. The road won't always be easy, but with determination and dedication, it can be very rewarding.

Your kids vs. her kids

You may need to help your kids through the motions of having new kids around. It's likely that your kids will start to feel each other out. They may try and figure out who is the alpha child and who can be pushed around. It's going to be important that you and your partner watch how the children treat each other and give them general corrections when needed. Make sure that they respect each other, and you want to watch out that a click dynamic does not form between the two families. The two sets of kids should not be pitted against one another. When you see things like this happening, simply correct your kids and watch for it to happen again.

Introducing your children in a deliberate manner will go a long way. Your kids may have questions along the way, and it's okay to answer them as long as your answers are age-appropriate. They may be wondering what the new family situation may be like. It's pretty common for kids to ask what bedrooms they will have or what house they will live in. It's okay to tell your kids you don't know yet if you haven't made any solid plans for the future.

I also recommend that you have an open conversation with your kids and ask them what they think. After an outing with the other family, you should ask the kids how it went, what they liked and what they didn't like. Do this when you are not around your new partner or her kids. You may be surprised at how open your kids are! You may find out things happened when you were not around.

Encourage your partner to do the same with their kids and compare notes when the kids aren't around.

It's important that when you're blending families, neither set of kids feels like they are second-best or left out. It's easy for one set of kids to take the lead and for the other set to take a backseat. It's going to be really important that you ensure this does not happen. Balancing both sets of kids is going to be a challenge, and it is something that is going to need constant attention. You will want to make sure that things are fair between both sets of kids from the big things to the little things (i.e., getting each kid their favorite ice cream on a shopping trip all the way to equally helping each kid with their first car or college tuition).

For instance, it is easy for one child or one set of kids to demand that they always get their way. As a parent, it can be easy to just give in so that everyone stops complaining. This is probably the worst thing that you can do, but it is also the easiest. It's a lot harder to talk with each child about compromise and getting three or four kids to all agree on something. It's important that you put this effort in. As they grow up, if one set of kids thinks that they are less favored than the other, this will cause issues between both sets of kids. Making sure no one gets left behind is hard but not impossible. You just need to make sure you pay attention to the small things as they are happening. Good communication with your partner will help with this.

One of the most common complaints from children of a blended family is that one set of kids gets treated better than the other. It is up to you and your new partner to focus on keeping things as fair as possible between the kids. It's easy to see how spending more money on one kid at Christmas time versus the other, or how one kid getting help with a car and the other not will instantly result in some resentment among the kids regardless of who spends the most time with you.

It's important you talk with your partner about everything regarding the kids. You will want to talk about how they were interacting with each other and about any conflict you may have observed. Talk about the things you want to do with the kids together and some things that you may want to do with each set separately. Talk about what went well and what didn't go so well. Blending families is certainly an evolving process, so you will need to observe what happens that is good and what you need to improve on.

It's also important not to leave the kids out of these discussions. It's okay to ask the kids what they thought was fun or went right or what things may need to be different in the future. Blending a family is all about taking two different sets of people and having them work together. You can't fully make both families work together without input from the kids. Make sure you do a lot of listening. You may need to prompt them by asking questions or better yet, have a once-a-month family meeting. A family meeting can be where you all order takeout, air your grievances and just check in with each other as a family. It is very easy for kids to NOT talk about whatever problems they may be having in the blended family with you and worse yet, be going home to a high-conflict ex and blow any minor issues way out of proportion.

If your kids have concerns or they voice their opinion that something didn't go well, make sure that you don't toss it by the wayside. Take it as serious feedback. Listening to your kids' concerns and validating them will go a long way in helping to move forward with the blended family (or helping you to see potential problems that may not be hitting your radar).

One thing that you'll want to have a good discussion with your partner about is disciplining the children. Some families allow the stepparent to discipline the stepchildren, while other families decide that only the biological parent should discipline the biological children. However you decide this is up to you, your ex/co-parents and your new partner. This is definitely something that you and your partner will want to agree on strongly.

One of the things about a blended family is that there will be compromises, and probably lots of them. Compromises will happen in all different areas from things that you do, and how your living space is arranged to kids' schedules and activities. Compromise is the only way that blending a family works. In fact, it's one of the main ingredients. That's not to say that everybody has to lose out on what they want. Compromise is all about finding the best solution that works best for everyone. It is certainly difficult to do, but with time and communication, you will figure out what works best for everyone involved.

One thing that may help in blending your family is to set up a set of ground rules that both sets of kids will follow. It's important not to have different rules for the different sides. Keep the rules simple and easy to follow. Things like bedtime and when they can play are things you will want to have some rules or at least loose guidelines for. With technology and most kids having cell phones, one rule you may want to have is no cell phones at the dinner table or when eating. This should be an example of an easy-to-follow rule that you can apply across both sets of kids. Another example as the kids get older would be a curfew. Some states and/or counties have curfew laws for children under the age of 18, which makes this a little easier on parents. It's important you and your new spouse agree on the curfew for your oldest child, as it sets a precedent for the younger kids to follow as they grow up.

What the rules are and how strict you are with them will depend on your individual family. Again, this is something you will want to have deep conversations with your partner about. You should each work together to come up with the rules together and be invested in enforcing those rules across both sets of kids.

There is definitely a lot to consider when blending families. It takes a lot of time, effort, and intentional work but it can be very rewarding! Remember that it's not all butterflies and unicorns and that you will have challenges. As long as you and your new partner are willing to put the work in, you can get through the messy middle!

Chapter Forty-Six

You've Survived!

Congratulations! You made it to the end of the book, and if you've read this far, that means that you are a dedicated father who wants the best for his children and for his future. For that, I commend you a thousand times over!

Going through a divorce is traumatizing at best. Between the emotional changes, financial challenges, and dealing with the legal system- it is NOT easy. Don't expect yourself to be healed or over the divorce quickly.

Divorces take years to recover from. In my situation, I think I was five or six years past the divorce before I felt like I was making a turn on the road to recovery. It's okay to feel like you're stuck and not making progress. You will have periods where you don't make any progress! You will also go through times when you make a great amount of progress. The fact that you finished reading this book is a huge step in your journey to recovery.

It's been said that it takes a village to raise a child, and I believe that is true. Now that you're divorced, you need to cultivate your own village and support system to help you raise your children. These support systems are not built overnight, so be patient. Your support system may change as the children mature and grow older.

No matter what stage you are in on the road to recovery from your divorce, you should take a minute to think about where you are and where you want to go. Follow the advice in the section on goals to get you started.

I wrote this book with the intent of giving you an introduction to all of the different subjects that are likely to come up in your divorce and after. I certainly have not covered every single topic! Because there are so many topics, I was not able to cover any topic in too much detail. If you have topics that you are curious about or want to know more about, you can do your own research. You can use an Internet search engine to find articles or books that are relevant to the things that you have questions about.

Just like finding your village to help raise your children, you need to find your own support system. Everyone's support system will be different but this can be family, friends, and even a therapist. Identify who those people are that you will go to when you need help or advice on different topics, from being a father to dealing with your emotions throughout this process.

I highly recommend that you find a good therapist you like and who you are comfortable with helping you through this entire process. When you go to therapy, you will have some sessions that feel like they are breakthroughs, while others you won't feel like you get anything out of. The trick with therapy is to keep with it for a period that is long enough to help you see the changes in your life.

In therapy, you want to go over topics like how you are feeling currently and getting over the emotional distress of the divorce itself. Also, do the work to find out what really caused your marriage to fail. You can't hardly move on to a new relationship until you understand what was wrong with the old one. And no matter how bad your ex was, there are still things you did that contributed to the divorce. A good therapist will help you talk through all these different issues in a manner that is healthy for you.

Besides therapy, it may be helpful to find a support group of similar people in your situation. This can be a group at a church or a men's group. Sometimes the best support that you can have is knowing someone else has gone through a similar situation and getting their input on how they navigated through that tough time. While there are significantly fewer social resources for men than there are for women, they do exist. Check your local organizations, such as churches and social groups, to see what is available in your community.

Just remember through this entire process that you are in a period of transition. Nothing is static when you're going through a divorce, and it takes time to recover both emotionally and financially from this process. One big part of this transition will be to have reasonable expectations of yourself. As men, we can be extremely goal oriented. This means putting a timeline on when something will happen or when you will accomplish something by. However, when you're recovering from a divorce, sometimes it's hard to put a timeline on certain things. Just be kind to yourself and make sure you give yourself plenty of room for those ups and downs that are sure to happen.

I wish you the best on your journey! This is a transition phase for you. What comes in the future is up to you and what you do from here on out. While it may not feel like you're in control of your life right now, <u>things will get better if you keep moving in the right direction</u>. It's up to you to make choices and decisions that will steer you in a better direction after your divorce.

If you found this book helpful, please recommend it to a friend! Knowledge is power (in life, but especially in divorce), and this book was my way to be able to spread that knowledge to more people. If you really enjoyed the book, please head over and review it on

Amazon and other places online. It really helps me to get this book noticed by people who need it.

The very first step to being a good dad (post-divorce or in general) is deciding you are going to be one. Reading this book and hoping to glean some knowledge from it was your second step. We all make mistakes along the way. We are human. What makes you a good dad is recognizing those mistakes, learning from them, and sharing your triumphs (or even failures) with other dads in your situation.

You only get one chance to raise your kids. It's cliché, but they do grow up fast! Make the best of the time that you do have with them, and be the best father that you can be. They will thank you for it later!

Knowledge is Power

During my journey, I did a lot of reading and watching videos. I wanted to learn about the different topics in this book. I found out that some sources are better than others. I wanted to leave you with some of my favorite sources. While I may not have directly quoted them in this book, they had an influence.

Rich Cooper – From his YouTube channel, Rich describes himself as "a best-selling author, podcaster, car guy, investor, HNW coach & entrepreneur. I unplug you from the matrix of comforting lies, with clear, concise, cold, hard and uncomfortable truths." While his main YouTube channel doesn't seem to be named as someone who gives a lot of dating and relationship advice, you may find it helpful. His book will definitely have you thinking about things like choosing a mate and dating in general.

- YouTube Channel - https://www.youtube.com/@EntrepreneursInCars

- YouTube Channel - https://www.youtube.com/@TheUnpluggedAlpha

- Book "The Unplugged Alpha" - https://www.amazon.com/Unplugged-Alpha-Bullsh-Guide-Winning

- Facebook - https://www.facebook.com/EntrepreneursInC

ars

Doctor Ramani – Dr. Ramani has some great videos on how to deal with a narcissist and, more importantly, how to heal from one. She also has a podcast and an online course.

- YouTube Channel - https://www.youtube.com/@DoctorRamani

- Facebook - https://www.facebook.com/doctorramani

Dr. Tara J Palmatier – Dr. Palmatier is active on Facebook with the "Shrink for Men" Facebook page. She also has a book out that will help you if you are trying to move forward from a personality-disordered person.

- Facebook https://www.facebook.com/Shrink4Men

- Book "Say Goodbye to Crazy: How to Get Rid of His Crazy Ex and Restore Sanity to Your Life"

National Parents Organization (NPO) – NPO is a national non-profit dedicated to improving divorce laws nationwide. They have been instrumental in passing shared parenting legislation in several states. Their mission is "To improve the lives of children & strengthen society by protecting every child's right to the love & care of both parents after separation or divorce."

- YouTube - https://www.youtube.com/@NationalParentsOrg

- Web - https://www.sharedparenting.org/

- Facebook - https://www.facebook.com/nationalparentsorganization

References

I've listed the references here in alphabetical order of the last name of the author.

4 Types of Boundaries in Relationships After Separation. (2021). Retrieved October 18, 2022, from https://www.onwardapp.com/blog/4-types-of-boundaries-in-relationships-after-separation

Adverse Childhood Experiences (ACEs). (2022, June 6). https://www.cdc.gov/violenceprevention/aces/index.html

American Psychiatric Association (Ed.). (2022). Diagnostic and statistical manual of mental disorders: DSM-5-TR (Fifth edition, text revision). American Psychiatric Association Publishing.

AACAP. (2020). Screen Time and Children. Retrieved October 18, 2022, from https://www.aacap.org/AACAP/Families_and_Youth/Facts_for_Families/FFF-Guide/Children-And-Watching-TV-054.aspx

Afianian, A. (2019, February 16). Why You Must Embrace Trauma. The Startup. https://medium.com/swlh/here-why-you-must-embrace-trauma-a062f1986acc

Attorney vs lawyer. Online Studies of Legal Masters Program. (2023, January 10). Retrieved February 14, 2023, from https://onlinemasteroflegalstudies.com/career-guides/become-a-lawyer/attorney-vs-lawyer/#:~:text=Attorneys%2C%20lawyers%2C%20and%20counsels%20have,or%20may%20not%20practice%20law.

Barbash, E. (2017, March 13). Different Types of Trauma: Small "t" versus Large 'T' | Psychology Today. https://www.psychologytoday.com/us/blog/trauma-and-hope/201703/different-types-trauma-small-t-versus-large-t

Bruce, D. F. & PhD. (2022). Exercise and Depression. WebMD. Retrieved October 17, 2022, from https://www.webmd.com/depression/guide/exercise-depression

Cain, A. C. (2006). Parent Suicide: Pathways of Effects into the Third Generation. Psychiatry: Interpersonal and Biological Processes, 69, 204–227. https://doi.org/10.1521/psyc.2006.69.3.204

CDC. (2022, June 2). Move More; Sit Less. Centers for Disease Control and Prevention. https://www.cdc.gov/physicalactivity/basics/adults/index.htm

Compton, W. M., Conway, K. P., Stinson, F. S., Colliver, J. D., & Grant, B. F. (2005).

CDC Products—Data Briefs—Number 309—June 2018. (2019, June 7). https://www.cdc.gov/nchs/products/databriefs/db309.htm

Child Crisis AZ (2017, June 5). 5 Important Ways Fathers Impact Child Development. Child Crisis. https://childcrisisaz.org/5-major-ways-fathers-impact-child-development/

Community property. (2022). LII / Legal Information Institute. Retrieved October 19, 2022, from https://www.law.cornell.edu/wex/community_property

Cordell & Cordell (2015, March 26). The Nuclear Weapon Of Divorce: Orders Of Protection. Dads Divorce. https://dadsdivorce.com/articles/the-nuclear-weapon-of-divorce-orders-of-protection/

Custodial Parents & Noncustodial Parents—Custody X Change. (2022). Retrieved October 20, 2022, from https://www.custodyxchange.com/topics/custody/special-circumstances/custodial-noncustodial-parent.php

Definition of DISCIPLINE. (2022). Retrieved October 18, 2022, from https://www.merriam-webster.com/dictionary/discipline

Depression. (2022). Https://Www.Apa.Org. Retrieved October 17, 2022, from https://www.apa.org/topics/depression

Dewar, G. (2019, June 2). Why kids need daylight to thrive and learn: The benefits of bright light. PARENTING SCIENCE. https://parentingscience.com/kids-need-daylight/

Douglas LaBier, PhD. (2015, August 28). Women Initiate Divorce Much More Than Men, Here's Why. Psychology Today. https://www.psychologytoday.com/blog/the-new-resilience/201508/women-initiate-divorce-much-more-men-heres-why

Dwyer, J. (2020). The challenge of managing conflict. Psychology Today. https://www.psychologytoday.com/us/blog/got-minute/202002/the-challenge-managing-conflict.

Grief. (2022). In Wikipedia. https://en.wikipedia.org/w/index.php?title=Grief&oldid=1111324388

Hoff, P. M. (2001). The Uniform Child-Custody Jurisdiction and Enforcement Act: (527312006-001) [Data set]. American Psychological Association. https://doi.org/10.1037/e527312006-001

O'Malley, Scranton, L. L. O. 201 F. A., & www.omalleylangan.com, P. 18503344-2667. (n.d.). Legal Dictionary—Law.com. Law.Com Legal Dictionary. Retrieved October 20, 2022, from https://dictionary.law.com/

People In Therapy Are Often In Therapy. (2019, August 1). https://themindsjournal.com/people-in-therapy-are-often-in-therapy/

Post-Traumatic Stress Disorder. (2022). National Institute of Mental Health (NIMH). Retrieved October 17, 2022, from https://www.nimh.nih.gov/health/topics/post-traumatic-stress-disorder-ptsd

Prevalence, correlates, and comorbidity of DSM-IV antisocial personality syndromes and alcohol and specific drug use disorders in the United States: Results from the national epidemiologic survey on alcohol and related conditions. The Journal of Clinical Psychiatry, 66(6), 677–685. https://doi.org/10.4088/jcp.v66n0602

Paruthi, S., Brooks, L. J., D'Ambrosio, C., Hall, W. A., Kotagal, S., Lloyd, R. M., Malow, B. A., Maski, K., Nichols, C., Quan, S. F., Rosen, C. L., Troester, M. M., & Wise, M. S. (2016). Recommended Amount of Sleep for Pediatric Populations: A Consensus Statement of the American Academy of Sleep Medicine. Journal of Clinical Sleep Medicine, 12(06), 785–786. https://doi.org/10.5664/jcsm.5866

Property Division by State. (2022). Www.Divorcenet.Com. Retrieved October 30, 2022, from https://www.divorcenet.com/states/nationwide/property_division_by_state

Stinson, F. S., Dawson, D. A., Goldstein, R. B., Chou, S. P., Huang, B., Smith, S. M., Ruan, W. J., Pulay, A. J., Saha, T. D., Pickering, R. P., & Grant, B. F. (2008). Prevalence, Correlates, Disability, and Comorbidity of DSM-IV Narcissistic Personality Disorder: Results from the Wave 2 National Epidemiologic Survey on Alcohol and Related Conditions. The Journal of Clinical Psychiatry, 69(7), 1033–1045.

The Extent of Fatherlessness. (n.d.). National Center for Fathering. Retrieved October 18, 2022, from https://fathers.com/statistics-and-research/the-extent-of-fatherlessness/

The Grief Recovery Method—Home. (2022). The Grief Recovery Method. Retrieved October 16, 2022, from https://www.griefrecoverymethod.com

The Importance of Fathers for Child Development | Psychology Today. (2021). Retrieved October 18, 2022, from https://www.psychologytoday.com/us/blog/parenting-and-culture/202106/the-importance-fathers-child-development

Trauma. (2022). Https://Www.Apa.Org. Retrieved October 16, 2022, from https://www.apa.org/topics/trauma

Torjesen, I. (2015). Children whose parents attempted suicide are at raised risk of similar behaviour, study finds. BMJ, 350, g7862. https://doi.org/10.1136/bmj.g7862

W. Bradford Wilcox & Nicholas H. Wolfinger. (2017, February 9). Hey Guys, Put a Ring on It. National Review. http://www.national review.com/article/444746/marriage-benefits-men-take-note

Wansink, B. (2007). Mindless Eating: Why We Eat More Than We Think (NO-VALUE edition). Bantam.

When Should My Kids Snack? (2019). Retrieved October 18, 2022, from https://www.eatright.org/food/nutrition/dietary-guide lines-and-myplate/when-should-my-kids-snack